CLIMBING
SLEMISH

An Ulster Memoir

Dennis Kennedy

Note for Librarians: A cataloguing record for this book is available from Library and Archives Canada at www.collectionscanada.ca/amicus/index-e.html
ISBN 1-4120-9943-9

PUBLISHING™

Offices in Canada, USA, Ireland and UK

Book sales for North America and international:
Trafford Publishing, 6E–2333 Government St.,
Victoria, BC V8T 4P4 CANADA
phone 250 383 6864 (toll-free 1 888 232 4444)
fax 250 383 6804; email to orders@trafford.com

Book sales in Europe:
Trafford Publishing (UK) Limited, 9 Park End Street, 2nd Floor
Oxford, UK OX1 1HH UNITED KINGDOM
phone 44 (0)1865 722 113 (local rate 0845 230 9601)
facsimile 44 (0)1865 722 868; info.uk@trafford.com

Order online at:
trafford.com/06-1700

10 9 8 7 6 5 4 3

AUTHOR'S NOTE

Climbing Slemish had its origins in conversations in the 1970s with Winnie Greer at her home in New York State about her childhood at the foot of Slemish in the first decade of the 20th century. In so far as detailed research and personal recollection permit, it is an accurate account of three Ulster families, interconnected by place, religion, marriage and circumstance, over most of a century. Only when no factual information has been available, have I used my imagination to fill the gaps. My thanks are due to those whose recollections have helped me reconstruct the past, and to my immediate family for their tolerance of my obsession with Slemish, and with family.

Dennis Kennedy

Belfast, 2006.

CLIMBING SLEMISH

The wind blew down off the frosty slopes of the mountain and cut through the small crowd gathered around the open grave. The minister was not one to take account of trifles like the weather, and, warmed by his own zeal, was hammering home the message of salvation, an exercise that could not be rushed. He had already called the same people to take account of their spiritual welfare less than an hour earlier in the funeral chapel at the hospital in Ballymena, but he saw no reason why they should not be reminded again.

Some had edged away to find shelter against the stone wall that ran around the graveyard. One man had strayed further than the others, and was peering closely at the inscriptions on the neighbouring graves. He had no desire to listen to the preacher; he could tell with depressing accuracy what was coming next, and he knew the end was not nigh – it was at least fifteen minutes away.

The names on the stones were all familiar; some of them he recognized, the McMasters and the Curries certainly, connections of his mother among whom he had spent many childhood holidays. He peered closely at one, reading the freshly inscribed name at the bottom of a long list on a piece of weathered granite. It was Mary McMaster, the elder of the two forbidding spinster sisters at the lower farm, who had died just a few years earlier, in her eighties. He had not seen her since the last time she had poured him a glass of her home-made ginger cordial in the Spartan kitchen of the lower farm, as he sat, scrubbed and clean, along with his mother and brother on one of their mandatory visits down the loanin. That was fifty years ago.

He glanced up the rows of names on the stone until one caught his attention. It read *In loving memory of Alexander, aged seven years,*

1

called by the Lord, 12th November 1910. Alexander, he thought – of course, it was Sandy. It was the little boy Winnie had told him about, sitting in her house in Poughkeepsie in New York State, and looking back over three-quarters of a century to her childhood at the foot of Slemish, and describing how she had heard the news of Sandy's death, squinting down through the knot hole in the landing corridor, the same knot hole he and his brother had used as children to keep an eye on the gossiping adults below.

Suddenly a century seemed a very short space of time. He glanced around the small graveyard, an undulating stonewalled enclosure in the middle of a field. It must have looked very much like this almost a hundred years ago when little Sandy had been buried on another winter-day. He peered up at Slemish, which would have looked exactly the same one hundred years ago, and he thought of Winnie, sitting in her house in America, with the painting of Slemish on the wall, and asking had he been to Slemish.

She loved talking about Slemish and about her friendship with his mother, and had greatly taken to him the first time he had visited her when he said he had climbed it seven or eight times, and thought it was a wonderful place. Every time he went to visit her in succeeding years her first question was always had he been to Slemish. He thought too of the first time his mother had taken his brother and himself to the top. He was barely nine years old but had been longing for ages to climb the mountain. It had been a lovely summer's day and he remembered vividly every detail, not least his mother's happiness. Since then he had had lots of other mountains to climb.

The minister issued his final warning to the assembled sinners, and the crowd broke up into conversational knots as they tramped down the muddy lane back to their cars. Before he joined one of the groups he glanced up at the mountain again and decided that it was high time he climbed it once more.

Maybe next summer.

1 THE STREET

The street was an odd name for it. Old people sometimes called it the loan, others just the yard, and visitors from the town, when they came, which was rarely, spoke of the farmyard. But to the McMasters who lived at Kellstown, and had done so since their grandfathers had crossed from Scotland some time in the 17th or 18th century, it was the street.

In so far as it had either beginning or end, it began at the top, where it curved down off the loanin that led on to the Wallace farm, past the planting, down past the dwelling house and the midden, to stop at the stable. The midden was straight across from the farmhouse door, and was fed a rich daily diet of kitchen waste, cow and horse dung and any other rubbish generated on the farm. It was a central feature of the street, and in warm weather an inescapable one. A turn off to the right between the house and the stable took you to the rick-yard and a startling view of Slemish – the massive presence dominating the farm and the people in it.

To the left of the midden, the street dropped down close to the burn, and became once more the loanin, leading down to the second McMaster homestead. Where the ways parted the spout formed the focal point for most of the daily activities of both the street and the household. At it a pipe from the burn brought water into a square pool formed by neat granite boulders, from where it spilled back down again to rejoin the burn. All water for the household, except drinking water which was carried in buckets from the spring on the hill above the farm, and all water for the animals was drawn from the spout.

It was at the spout that the young of the family – and young visitors – washed themselves, their clothes, and often the dishes from the table. Behind the spout a single plank bridge under the trees provided a short cut across to the main lane that continued down to Wallace's. That farm was part of Kellstown, and was now joined by marriage to the other two farms, one of the McMaster daughters having recently married the widower Jamie Wallace.

By the first decade of the 20th century, the street was lined on one side by the turf shed, which also housed the cart, and still had the wooden tether posts on its walls from the days when it had been a byre, by another shed for calves or pigs, by the threshing shed, with a thresher operated by power generated by a water-wheel in the burn that ran behind the buildings on that side of the street, and by the dairy – dark and damp, shaded by trees and close to the spout.

On the other side of the street, at the top, was the small boiler house, where potatoes were boiled daily in a large copper over a turf fire to provide feed for the calves, the pigs and the chickens. Next to it was the byre, with stalls for a dozen cows ranged either side of a central aisle, with croups to take the dung.

Above the byre was the loft, sometimes called the barn. It was approached by a flight of outside stone steps that formed a porch over the doorway to the byre. The heat of the cows below meant it was warm and dry, even in winter, and a suitable place for storing corn. The doors of the farm buildings were painted the traditional deep red.

Next was the dwelling house. It had recently acquired a second-storey and lost its thatch. Now the large kitchen, flanked by an 'upper room' on one side, and a parlour and a bedroom on the other, had above it three more bedrooms.

At the end of the street, set across it at right angles to the dwelling, were the stable and another cart shed. Pigeons roosted in the eaves, relentlessly pursued every time they took flight by a madly barking sheepdog called Bruce.

The street sounded funny to visitors for it was neither straight nor smooth. Its surface of rough stones was frequently covered in mud and cow-clap, the outflow from the croups in the byre trickled across it to the midden, and in wet weather it was best negotiated by stepping from stone to stone. But if visitors stayed long enough they would soon realise that it was very much a street – a place of business, where people moved between the boiler house and the calve shed, between the dairy and the spout, between the dwelling and every other part of the street. It was not a loanin, for a loanin took you from one place to another, nor was it regular enough, or sufficiently enclosed and defined to qualify as a yard. It was the street.

In early June 1911 the street was a scene of much activity. The new threshing machine, ordered from Millers' of Ballymena after long debate, was installed, and linked up to the drive from the water wheel that had worked the older more primitive mill. Neighbours came to help with the task, and to see the impressive machinery in action when they opened the sluice gates on the little dam on the hill.

The talk was of politics, and of the coming coronation in London.

George V was to be crowned King of Great Britain, Ireland and the British Dominions Beyond the Seas, and Emperor of India, and a committee had been set up to organise the Braid valley's celebration of the event. Not that the McMasters or their small farmer neighbours were on the committee, but they would play their part. The men were expected to help build the great bonfire on the top of Slemish that would be lit on Coronation night.

Robert Hugh McMaster had already promised the slipe and his mare to help drag the timber up the mountain. Others were looking forward to the sports to be held at Slemish - running, jumping, throwing the shot and whatever else could be safely arranged on the grassy humpback summit or the lower slopes.

It wasn't that the McMasters or their neighbours were ardent royalists. They were much too Presbyterian for that, and much too God-fearing and strict in their own behaviour, and the behaviour they expected from others, to have been uncritical admirers of Edward VIIth, with his much publicised love of horseracing and other pursuits. His son might be an improvement, but it was not in their nature or their religion to put their faith in princes.

The times, however, were special. At the end of 1910 the Liberals under Asquith had been returned to power at Westminster, but with a greatly reduced majority, and were now dependent on the large body of Irish Nationalist MPs to remain in government. Home Rule loomed over Ireland more menacingly than at any time since Gladstone had first proposed it in the previous century.

Across Ulster new Unionist Clubs were springing up, several in the Braid valley, and Irish Unionism was forging a sharper edge under its newly appointed leader, Edward Carson. None of those admiring Robert Hugh's threshing machine that day, or preparing the bonfire on Slemish, knew it, but a secret committee had already been formed to procure arms and begin work on the formation of an Ulster Army.

Had they known it, some at least of them would have been greatly troubled, for the McMasters and their closest friends were not just Presbyterians, they were born again Christians. Robert Hugh's father, Alexander, now dead, had had his life transformed in the '59 Revival which had swept the County Antrim countryside in 1859, a great wave of religious enthusiasm which saw grown men swooning and women giving prophetic utterance in halls, churches and tents throughout the county.

Alexander had neither swooned nor prophesied, but had been profoundly caught up in the enthusiasm for God and righteous living that raged like an epidemic from the original outpourings in the villages of Kells and Connor, ten miles south of Kellstown. He immediately renounced drinking, dancing, gambling, swearing and assorted other sins not mentionable at the time. He stopped playing cards, and never again kicked a football.

He resigned from the Teenies Orange Lodge which he had only recently been persuaded to join. He did all this in obedience to the Scriptural injunction to 'come ye out from among them and be ye separate'. His only associates from then on were those he met in Christian meetings or at his Presbyterian church. The custom of the countryside meant that he still worked together with his neighbours in saving the harvest, or on threshing days and at the market, but more and more he lived his life in a peculiar mixture of isolation from the world at large, but ever increasing intimacy with a small band of the elect, born-again Christians like himself.

This pattern was emphasised after his father's early death and his own marriage. He took over the farm and moved his new wife into the farmhouse. Mary Hall was a well-educated girl, from higher up the social scale than a small farmer from the foot of Slemish, and her family did not approve of the match. Nor did they approve of her newfound enthusiasm for religion. But that was the bond that brought her to Kellstown and tied her to Alexander. She too had been converted in the Revival, and yearned every bit as much as Alexander to renounce sin and live a pure life.

They said grace before every meal, and after the main evening meal Alexander would read a Psalm at the table and pray God's blessing on the family and the farm. Both, indeed, prospered, though the family proved more fertile than the hilly farmland. Within little more than a decade there were seven children – three boys and four girls – and the small cottage with its few acres down the loanin had been purchased as a second farm against the day when the sons would marry. There was even talk of adding a second storey to the farmhouse.

Before that could be done, Alexander died, just as the century itself was dying. He was, at 57, not young, but young enough to leave a fresh widow not yet ready to retire into a corner by the fire and let her sons take over. For more than a decade before that week of the coronation, Mary McMaster had ruled Kellstown. Much happened in the decade; the second story had been added, all three sons had married, and two of the daughters. Robert Hugh had brought his bride to live at Kellstown. Samuel Alexander had married and moved into the lower farm. Both marriages had already produced children, and the population of

Kellstown was growing.

Mary McMaster managed the farm and the family. She left most of the heavy work in the fields and with the cows to the men, and their wives, but took care of the money and of the decisions. Both farms were her property. She was a reader of books, and of the *Christian Advocate* and of *The Witness*, and also, though its spiritual value was not comparable, of the *Ballymena Observer*. She shared the daily round of cooking, baking, washing and fetching water, and looking after hens, calves and pigs, with her daughters until they married and left home, and thereafter with her daughter-in-law Jane, Robert Hugh's wife.

The house, like the farm, was efficiently run. After his father's death Robert Hugh became the sayer of grace and reader of Psalms at the kitchen table. Though the content changed not at all, the time spent on such family devotions became noticeably shorter. Robert Hugh was as strict a Presbyterian as his father had been, and his mother still was, but he had not ascended to the mountaintop of spiritual experience as they had done in the glorious year of '59. He refrained from alcohol and tobacco, did not play cards or go to dances, and took no part in politics, because he had been brought up to believe that this was the right and Christian way to live, not because his mind was so filled with zeal for God and his righteousness that there was neither room nor time for much else.

There was indeed, much else. There was the poor price potatoes were getting, and the fall in the market for calves. There was the new threshing machine. There was his sister Jeannie and her problem; there was his sister Mary and her drunken husband; there was his sister Lizzie and her forthcoming marriage. There was the political situation, for although he played no part in politics he was as concerned as the next farmer over the threat of Home Rule, and probably much more concerned over Rome Rule.

He knew all about the *Ne Temere* papal decree of 1908 and its threat to the Protestant faith in Ireland. He had read articles on it in *The Witness*, and he had followed the details of the McCann case just the previous year, when a Catholic father in Belfast, Alexander McCann, had left his Protestant wife under clerical persuasion, if not direction from Rome itself, citing the *Ne Temere* decree. He had taken the children of the marriage with him to be raised as Catholics 'in obedience to this cruel decree', as the papers put it, and the civil authorities had upheld the rights of the father to do so.

Robert Hugh was not a bigot; the few Catholics he had met, one or two small farmers and some farm labourers, he had found agreeable enough, though none was a neighbour. His contacts had been fleeting, usually buying or selling a calf at market, and he saw no difference between doing business with a Catholic and with a worldly Presbyterian. But he had no desire to live under Rome Rule; he had no doubts about the erroneous nature of Catholic theology and none at all about the profoundly undemocratic influence the Catholic Church exercised over society wherever it could. You just had to read the accounts of what was happening in Quebec, even if you had not grown up with *Foxe's Book of Martyrs.*

But most of all on his mind was his mother's health. She had been ill, on and off, since the spring of the year, but just this past two weeks had taken to her bed and was now under the doctor. It was serious, and the doctor had told him he might expect the worst, though it could be a matter of months rather than weeks.

Robert Hugh's concern was partly that of a son for a mother who had been father and mother to him for ten years, but he could not help also worrying about the future, and what would happen to the farm. Naturally, as the eldest son at home, and the one still working the farm, he expected to inherit it, with his older brother Samuel Alexander getting the lower, smaller holding on which he was now living. That would only be right.

But there was the third son, married too, and living in town, and there were his sisters. His mother, he knew only too well, had a mind of her own, and a great sense of fairness. She had, after all, taken in and raised as her own the baby girl her eldest daughter, and eldest child, Jeannie had scandalously produced without benefit of matrimony, and without ever disclosing the identity of the miscreant father.

Little Winnie was now six, and competing with the rooster for total dominance of the street. Her mother had made an early escape from her disgrace by running off to Belfast, and getting work in a hospital, and then marrying an understanding tram driver patient several years her senior. She had had little contact with Winnie since; Robert Hugh, while not turning her away from his door – it was not actually his door – had made it very clear she was not welcome, and she had gone about building a new life for herself which did not include Winnie.

Winnie was her grandmother's favourite. She went everywhere with her, around the farm to feed the hens or the pigs, to fetch water and to collect the eggs. Everything Winnie did, she did with great energy and little patience. So much so that she had to be diverted from egg collection, as she could not stop herself flinging each newly collected egg into the bucket with disastrous results.

Robert Hugh knew full well his mother worried about Winnie's future. At night, sitting by the fire in the candlelight, she sometimes mused aloud about what would happen to the little one with no father to look after her or fend for her. When she knew she was seriously ill herself she had made Robert Hugh promise he would be good to Winnie if anything happened to her. Her son had no intention of being anything else, but he began to wonder was his mother thinking of changing her will and making some provision in it for Winnie.

She might even leave the farm to Winnie, who was, after all, the first born of her own eldest child. Mary McMaster was no radical, but she had an independent streak in her. She had made up her own mind to go against her family's wishes when she had married, and for the past ten years she had been the head of the household, and the deciding voice in all matters relating to family and farm. Robert Hugh did not know if his mother had made a will; she had been a healthy woman of middle age when left a widow, with a large family around her, and might never have thought of it. Then again, she might have. It was another thing to worry about.

Winnie also had things to worry about. She knew her granny was sick, but being sick meant staying in the warmth of the big feather bed, and having others bring cups of tea and bowls of broth. It also meant her granny had even more time than usual to talk to her, and tell her stories of her own childhood, of a life that had more to it than baking bread, feeding hens and carrying water. She told her of the pony and trap that her father had had, that could carry you smoothly over the stony lanes without shaking the very bones out of you, the way it was in the high-sided cart pulled by Robert Hugh's mare, the way you would have to hold tight onto the sides to stop your bottom rising from the seat and smacking down on to it.

Winnie had long since stopped asking about her own father. When she was about three or four she had realised that, unlike all the other children she knew, she had no father. She was told he had gone away, and no one seemed to expect him to come back. As she had never had a father, she lost interest in him, and rather liked being just a bit different from other children. But as her granny talked about her home and her father, Winnie began unconsciously to invent a father for herself. Or rather, she simply took over the best points of her granny's father and constructed a rather superior model for her own use, which made her very happy.

But her happiness had been crushed in the previous winter. Her constant companion of the past few years, her older cousin by a year,

9

young Sandy, the son of Samuel Alexander from the lower farm, had started public elementary school in September and she had been denied his company for long dreary hours from Monday to Friday. At first she had not minded, for she still had Kate Wallace, the neighbour's child who had become her cousin when her Aunt Mary had married the widower. And anyway, Sandy had left Winnie lots of tasks to do while he was away at school. She had, for example, to feed his horses. His horses were branches of thorn which he stuck into the rough wooden hay cradles that still survived in the turf shed, and which he groomed and fed with a dedication that racing thoroughbreds would hardly have merited. When he started school, Winnie was instructed to look after them, make sure they had enough water and enough hay, and were given a bit of exercise to stop them getting fractious.

Everything went well enough, but Sandy was a real McMaster, and took his play very seriously. One afternoon in late June he had arrived home across the fields from school to find two or three of the thorn twigs had fallen out of their stalls. He accused Winnie of neglecting his horses, told her she could never be trusted to look after them again, and shouted and raged at her just as he had heard Robert Hugh raging at the mare for tramping on his foot, or at his sisters for some feminine folly or other. Winnie was also sufficient of a McMaster to resent such treatment, and the two inseparables were, for the time at least, semi-detached.

Much worse followed. Sandy caught a chill at school in early autumn, and was put to bed. The chill rapidly worsened into pneumonia, and just as Winnie ached to go and visit him, it was forbidden. Each night Samuel Alexander would walk up the loanin to his brother's house and report on the boy's progress. Winnie, already in bed, would hear his boots on the street, and creep out to the knot hole in the floorboards of the upstairs corridor which acted as spy-hole and listening post and allowed a child lying full length both sight and sound of the kitchen hearth.

On the night of November 10th Samuel Alexander's footsteps sounded even more deliberate than usual. By the time Winnie's eye was glued to the knot hole, Samuel Alexander's were streaming with tears. Standing with his back to the fire he announced to the kitchen that Sandy had gone. The Lord had taken him. "I begged him to take the two wee girls, and leave me the lad. But he took Sandy. He's gone".

Winnie had seen enough of death around the farm to know what it was, and just how final it was. But Sandy's death was different; it was unfair. He was only a year older than she was, and he was her friend; he had died before she could make up with him. Her sorrow was mixed with anger – anger at fate, anger at herself, anger at life, anger at her loneliness.

In the weeks following, she heard endless talk of God's will, and letting it be done, of the unfathomable goodness of God. No one but she seemed to feel any anger towards the God who had taken Sandy, who had even refused a father's request to take the two sisters and leave Sandy. Winnie, who had no liking at all for the elder sisters, Isa and Mary, thought the request had been very reasonable, and she found it hard to see why it had been refused. She was too young and too much a child of her upbringing to question all that she had been taught, but Winnie's God, whether he knew it or not, became a sterner, harder deity, at best a distant relation of the Gentle Jesus Winnie sang about in Sunday School.

It had been a dreadful winter for Winnie. Her grandmother and her Aunt Annie, however, shepherded her through her grieving and loneliness, and by spring she was almost back to her rowdy self, and if anything even more boisterous and wilful.

But now she was happy again because she had just acquired a ready-made cousin two years younger than herself, and while this new cousin had a father in good working order, she had no mother, and never had had one, or at least could not remember ever having had one. Winnie's Aunt Lizzie was going to marry a very handsome young widower, Bob Culbert. Bob's first wife had died tragically in childbirth three years earlier, leaving him with a two-year old infant daughter to raise as best he could. They were living in Cumberland in England, where his search for work in the linen trade had taken him, and he had had no way of bringing up the baby Lily.

So he had brought her home to his late wife's family in Lurgan, and there her grandmother and her aunt Maria had nursed her. Two years later Bob found work near Belfast, which meant he could visit his daughter, so he left Cumberland and came home to Ireland. Then, on a day trip to Portrush, he had met Lizzie McMaster who with her older sister was taking advantage of an LMS sixpenny excursion from Ballymena. Lizzie had recently left home at Kellstown to become a dressmaker, and had hopes of a job with a laundry in Ballymena, doing repairs and alterations.

The romance blossomed, and Lizzie counted the beautiful motherless little daughter as just as big an attraction as Bob's constantly smiling eyes and cheerful sense of humour. Three weeks ago Bob had come with Lizzie to visit her family, and he had brought Lily, now almost five. Bob had helped with the hay, but he was no farmer and his efforts to make a rick had had the McMasters in fits of laughter. Like his father before him, he was a block printer in the linen trade, and the only field he was at home in was the football field.

His young daughter and Winnie had taken to each other so much that it was agreed Lily would stay at Kellstown for part of the summer. Lily was a fair-haired beauty, almost as lively as Winnie herself but more than a little overawed by the strangeness of the farm, and barely able to understand the strong Ulster-Scots dialect, especially as spoken by Robert Hugh and the men around the farm. While she told everyone she was English – having been born in Carlisle in Cumberland – her Lurgan accent said otherwise and was as strange to Winnie as Winnie's was to her. She also told everyone her name was Cuthbert, not Culbert, at which they all smiled and thought she might have a lisp. So she wrote her name out for them, in a good firm hand.

The two little girls were thrown together, literally, in the small bed with the feather mattress they shared in their Aunt Annie's room, which was so soft that however far apart they began the night, they invariably ended up locked in each other's arms. They roamed the farm together, and now that her granny was in bed ill Winnie took charge of egg collecting and sundry other duties, with Lily as her constant companion. Kate Wallace made it a threesome, and they would have been four if Kate's young half-sister Mary had been able to toddle a bit faster.

The girls sat together on top of the five-bar gate at the back of the farmhouse which gave the best view of all of Slemish, less than two miles away, as the crow flies. It was a real mountain, not just a peak among others, but a solitary, self-contained, almost symmetrical mountain rising sharply from the surrounding countryside at the northern end, running up to a just perceptible crest at the centre and then sweeping down again at the southern end. From the gate its full elongated front closed off the horizon, and rose up towards the sky.

In the morning, with the sun rising behind it, it was sombre, a stark, even menacing, outline. But in the evening it caught, full on, the rays of the setting sun and looked both magnificent and inviting, warm and green with a touch of purple. First thing in the morning, Winnie and Lily had to run out of the farmhouse and round the corner to see Slemish. Depending on the weather, it never looked exactly the same, and once, early in Lily's stay, it had disappeared altogether as a morning mist blotted it out. Sometime or other later in the day, the two would be found side by side on the top of the gate gazing at Slemish.

Long after they were in bed, Robert Hugh would rouse himself from the settle in the farm kitchen and lean on the same gate, looking at Slemish in the moon light, and luxuriantly relieve himself through the bars of the gate, sharing a moment of intimacy with the mountain he loved in his own way every bit as much as Winnie did.

Winnie had climbed Slemish. Earlier that year she had gone with her Aunt Annie and Robert Hugh on the side-cart to the moss on the slopes of Slemish to bring home the turf, and while Robert Hugh had joined the other men in the bog for bread and buttermilk, Annie had taken Winnie scrambling up the heathery slope of the southern end of Slemish, and on to the grassy top along the length of the summit.

To the east they could see the long sweep of moorland, ending abruptly in the Antrim coast, and the deep blue of the North Channel. Beyond that, sharp and clear in the spring air, was Scotland. To the west the small fields and farms of the Braid valley were laid out before them. Annie picked out for Winnie the school at Racavan, and the graveyard near it, where Sandy lay. They could just see Kellstown, and the Currie farm, where Robert Hugh had found his wife Jane, and where Annie herself had hopes of taking charge as the wife of Jane's brother Jamsie, if and when he could bring himself to ask her.

From there they ran to St Patrick's wishing chair at the northern end of the summit. The chair was a narrow seat in one corner of a great slab of basalt that might have accommodated an appropriately emaciated slave fifteen centuries earlier, though not a portly saint. Everyone had to make a wish as they sat in the chair, but they could not tell anyone what the wish was, or it would not come true.

Lily was told all about the Wishing Chair and could not wait to climb Slemish and make her wish. Now she would not have to wait long, for Annie had promised to take the two girls and Kate with the men the following day when they started drawing the wood for the bonfire. They would have a picnic on Slemish if the weather was good.

2 CULBERTS AND CUTHBERTS

The weather was not good, but that was not the reason there was no picnic on Slemish. On the day before the coronation, the little world of Kellstown was shattered by the death of Mary McMaster. She had become very ill during the night, and the doctor had been sent for first thing in the morning. He knew the end was coming, and Robert Hugh and Samuel Alexander began their bedside vigil. It was their mother who brought up the question of a will. Always organised, she was alarmed at the thought of leaving loose ends untied, and she asked the doctor to draft a will, to be witnessed by Robert Hugh and Samuel, who were also the sole beneficiaries. She was too weak to sign her name, and managed only a cross, witnessed by the doctor.

There were no Coronation celebrations in Kellstown. Mary McMaster lay in her coffin in the upper room, and friends and neighbours came by to drink tea and say farewell. Winnie and Lily were taken in to the room, and in fear and trembling looked on the waxen features, Lily having to be lifted up to see the face. The farm work went on in silence, broken only by muffled voices and the rattle of cartwheels. Kellstown was always an isolated place, an island in the countryside. Now it seemed totally cut off.

The two girls spent most of the day sitting in silence on the five-bar gate gazing at Slemish. But they saw nothing of the celebrations. When the fire blazed out on top of the mountain at ten o'clock, part of a chain of beacons right around the county, they were already in bed, clinging to each other in stunned sleep. The next day Lily's father came to take her back to Lurgan; a death house was no place for a small and as yet unrelated girl. On the third day they buried Mary McMaster. The coffin was taken in the hearse, drawn by two black stallions with funeral plumes on their manes, around the Ballygelly Road and up the rough half-mile track to Racavan cemetery which was no church yard, but a non-conformist burying ground set in the middle of the countryside remote from any church or dwelling house.

Only the men went to the cemetery. The women stayed at home to mourn and prepare food for the mourners. Extra tables were brought

14

into the kitchen, and chairs borrowed from the lower farm, and as the mourners straggled back from the cemetery they sat in relays at the tables, quiet and sombre at first, but brightening as the tea warmed them and old acquaintance was resumed. After an hour or two the kitchen and the now coffin-less upper room resounded to loud voices and laughter as stories and jokes were told, and memories rehearsed.

A stranger from beyond the Braid stumbling in would have immediately known he was at a wake like any other across the breadth of Ireland; his only surprise would have been at the total absence of alcohol and tobacco.

Winnie spent the afternoon handing round sandwiches and cakes, and collecting cups and plates. Long after she had been sent upstairs to bed, she was still lying in the corridor with her eye to the knot hole, taking in the scene in the kitchen, not so crowded now as all but family and close neighbours had gone home. Once more she heard that it was God's will – God's will this time that her beloved Granny should, like her best friend Sandy, be taken from her. Even the new comfort of Lily had been removed. She did not think to question the rightness of God's will, but she felt the severity of it.

A voice asked Robert Hugh was there a will. Winnie heard him replying that there was indeed, but there was little enough to leave anyway. The solicitor was coming out the next morning and would read it to the family. She had heard enough gossip around the fireside to know that a will was a sort of letter from the dead person, and she was excited at this bit of news, and looked forward to hearing the reading of the will. Not that she had any expectation herself of a legacy; indeed she would not have known the word and would only have had the vaguest idea of the purpose of a will. But it meant she had still something of her Granny to cling to. She would hear from her at least once again, in the morning.

With that thought she crept back into the small feather bed in her Aunt Annie's room, and went to sleep, though not before she had cried bitter tears of sorrows, and of loneliness.

The solicitor was due at ten, and Winnie was on her best behaviour. Long before ten she crept into the upper room, used only at Christmas, or when the Minister visited, or for weddings and funerals. It had a permanent faint smell of damp, and its brocaded chairs seemed musty. The pedal organ stood, as usual, firmly closed, and beside it the plant stand had the pot of dried grasses on top and the large ostrich egg on the lower shelf. Winnie drew a small stool into a corner beside the organ and waited.

15

As the hour approached members of the family entered the room and filled the available seating with subdued expectation. At ten sharp Robert Hugh and Samuel Alexander entered, accompanied by the solicitor. Robert Hugh was just inviting the solicitor to open the will when he spotted Winnie; he walked across to where she sat, took her firmly by the hand and said "Winnie, this is no place for bairns" and brusquely ushered her out, shutting the door behind her.

Winnie stood in the middle of the empty kitchen, flushed with embarrassment and anger. She desperately wanted to hear again from her grandmother, and, and as the favourite grandchild, she greatly resented being excluded from the family gathering. She rushed upstairs to her bed in tears; the upper room, not being under the upstairs corridor, was out of knot hole reach.

She never did hear what her grandmother had written in her farewell note. In fact it had been no more than half a dozen lines, leaving her entire estate to the two older sons, with one farm to each. Winnie had no interest in such details anyway, but from that day onward she felt a constant resentment towards her two uncles, particularly Robert Hugh.

The rest of the summer passed in some gloom in Kellstown. The autumn was lightened briefly by another short visit from Lily and her father, as they made preparations for the wedding which was to be held on Christmas Day in Ballymena. The wedding itself was, for both girls, overshadowed by the knowledge that immediately after it Lily would be leaving for good.

Bob Culbert had heard that a firm in Kent was recruiting blockprinters for its linen factory in Crayford. This was a skilled trade and offered him the chance to earn a decent wage and get some stability as he set up home with his new wife. All his family had been involved in one or other aspect of the linen industry, and were well accustomed to migrating to wherever the industry was flourishing. His grandfather, Edward Cuthbert, had come originally from Cumberland in the north of England to a post as a land steward at Oldpark in north Belfast, but the title was much grander than the job and he had found he could make more money working as a printer in his master's linen mill than he could helping run his farm.

He also found that the name Cuthbert was almost unknown in Belfast, while there were lots of Culberts. After a time he gave up correcting people, and when he married a Belfast girl he did so as Edward Culbert. His son Walter followed him into the blockprinting, and when he in turn married Sarah Jane Ramsay in 1872, they moved into a small terraced house at Sullatober, a tiny linen village just above Carrickfergus, outside Belfast.

There Robert was born in 1875, and immediately called Bob. The family had later moved to Lurgan, and in turn the young Bob had joined a linen firm as a dyer in the block printing works, and moved to Belfast. The mixing of the dyes for the printing blocks was a skilled and essential part of block printing, and the distinction between dyer and printer was often blurred. For several years he worked as a dyer in a laundry in the village of Dunmurry, half way between Belfast and Lisburn.

Football meant more to him than printing and dying, and he lived for Saturdays. In Lurgan he and his brothers had played for Glenavon, and when he moved to Belfast he joined Dunmurry Recreation. A handsome young man with a growing reputation as a footballer, he never lacked for a girl-friend. One, in particular, was Sarah Campbell, whose family came, like his own, from Lurgan, but who now worked in a linen mill near Lisburn. But he was in no position to marry. One of the periodic slumps in the world market for linen had led to job losses in Belfast, and Bob and his younger brother Sammy had to take day work as labourers.

Then word came that there was the chance of a block-printing job in England, in Carlisle where his grandfather was still in touch with some relatives. Within days the two brothers were off. The relatives in Carlisle turned out to be Cuthberts, not Culberts. His grandfather, he remembered, had sometimes talked about the Cuthberts, but everyone had called him Culbert. Bob had been born Culbert, for it said so on his baptismal lines and on his birth certificate. All his uncles and cousins in Ireland were Culbert. In Carlisle, however, the remaining relatives were all Cuthberts, and they assumed he was one too.

From his cousins in Carlisle he learned a bit more about the Cuthbert family. A brother of his grandfather had enlisted in the 34th Cumberland Regiment, and gone off to fight in the Crimean War, where he had died at the siege of Sebastopol, though already family legend had changed that to the Charge of the Light Brigade. At any rate he had died in the Crimea, and his name, Robert Cuthbert, was there on a memorial plaque at the barracks, which Bob went to visit.

As all his relatives called him Cuthbert, he began doing so himself. He rather liked the sound of it, and as it really seemed to be his family name, he started signing himself Robert Cuthbert. Bob had a strong individualistic streak in him and rather liked the idea. He liked Carlisle too, but he was lonely, and found he missed Sarah Campbell far more than he had thought he would.

17

Their courtship continued via the Royal Mail, and in 1902 he asked her to marry him and come with him to Carlisle. Sarah readily agreed, though she was surprised to find she was marrying a Cuthbert, not a Culbert, but as the latter name was common as muck around Lurgan, she readily said yes to being Mrs Cuthbert.

It was a quiet wedding in Lisburn's Railway Street Presbyterian church which Sarah had joined when she came to work near the town. After the wedding they went straight to England to begin their married life in Carlisle.

It was to be a short one; in six years Sarah was dead. It began well, and a baby son was born to the couple a year after they had set up home in Carlisle. But little Walter, named after his grandfather, died of consumption when he was barely two. Lily, born in 1905, was the joy of her father and mother, and as healthy as they could wish. But the birth of a third child almost two years later brought disaster. Both mother and child died in the birth, and Lily was sent back to Lurgan to the care of her mother's family.

Now, four years later, she was delighted to be going back to England. She still insisted she was English, having been born there, and she talked about going 'home', though she had no memory at all of her early days in Carlisle, and no idea that Crayford in Kent was further from Carlisle than Carlisle was from Ireland. Her name, she insisted, was Cuthbert, not Culbert. She was sorry to be going away from Winnie and Kate, and even sorrier to have to put off once again her trip to climb Slemish. But she would, she told everyone, be back next summer.

In fact it was to be ten summers before Lily returned and Slemish was climbed. It was a decade within which empires crumbled and millions died, the world was changed beyond recognition, old countries disappeared and new ones emerged. Ireland saw an attempted revolution and communal violence approaching civil war, culminating in partition and the creation of two distinct oddities – the Irish Free State and Northern Ireland.

For Lily it was a golden decade. She loved her new mother, and Lizzie loved Lily. In rapid succession Bob and Lizzie produced three sons, Bobby, Alec and Hugh, brothers for Lily. They lived in a terraced house, number 3 Earlsfield Cottages, beside the railway – the loop-line that linked Crayford to the big wide world via Dartford. Lily excelled at school, and delighted in helping with the three brothers. She acquired new friends in Crayford, two of them the Lalliment sisters, evacuees from 'gallant little Belgium' at the outbreak of the Great War.

They roamed the countryside and the chalk pits that surrounded

Crayford. They learned to swim in the basin at the pits, and they were given rides on *Puffing Billy*, the little steam engine which drew the chalk. From school they were taken to see the nearby Black Prince's House – a granite pile said to be haunted by the ghost of the eldest son of Edward the Third, who had humiliated the French at the great Battle of Poitiers in 1356. Lily's father and stepmother took her up to London on the train to see the Tower of London and enjoy the delights of the Chamber of Horrors at Madame Tassaud's.

Bob Cuthbert – he had reverted to Culbert when he had returned to Ireland after his first wife's death, and then back to Cuthbert when he crossed again to England after his second marriage - was born a Presbyterian, but was by no means a religious man – his religion was football. In Crayford he, sometimes, attended the Church of England, but concentrated on football, and was soon a leading light in Bakers' works team. Lily was enrolled in the Sunday School. She was given a new Bible for attendance at the end of her first year, and she eagerly looked on the title page to see who the publisher was. It was Cambridge University Press, not Oxford, so each year for the week before the boat race she was a fervent Cambridge supporter, even though she had no idea where or what Cambridge was. All her friends were sharply divided between Oxford and Cambridge on the same scriptural grounds.

The war at first meant excitement, not least in the shape of the Lalliment girls, with their strong French accents lending a new dimension at school to 'O Mary, go and call de cattle home across de sands of Dee' and other aspects of English literature. Then people claimed that if you sat very quietly on the top of the hill above the chalk-pits you could actually hear the guns in France. So many hours were spent by the three of them on the hilltop; but no matter how hard they listened, they never heard the guns. But they did see the Zeppelins drifting noiselessly overhead on their way to bomb London, and they shook their fists at them in patriotic anger. At least they did until the night the Zeppelin came down in flames on Bexleyheath. At Earlsfield Cottages, as the humble terrace was grandly named, they had seen the burst of flame in the sky, and Bob Cuthbert had promptly herded the entire family into the tiny cupboard beneath the stairs, and insisted they stay there until the danger had passed. After that there was no rushing out to watch Zeppelins.

As the war went on, school-friends lost their fathers and brothers. Bob Cuthbert had no great tendency towards either patriotic or military zeal, and he never thought of volunteering for service. By the time conscription was introduced in 1916, he was already past 40 years of age and exempt from call-up. That same year the higher wages in the big Vickers munitions factory in Crayford attracted him away from the declining fancy goods end of the linen trade. His younger brother Sammy, however, had volunteered at the beginning of 1916, and was barely through his initial training when he was dispatched not to the front, but to the back – to Dublin, to help put down the Easter Rising.

Fortunately he arrived just as the rebellion was collapsing, and his active service consisted of helping put a stop to the looting which had become widespread in the ruins of Sackville Street, and indeed, if his dark hints were to be believed, of indulging in a little of it himself. Then he went to France, where for the next two years he managed to avoid both injury and capture. He spent his few brief leaves in Crayford, serenading his brother and family with a version of *Mademoiselle from Armentières*, and accounts of life in France.

He told nothing of the horrors of the trenches. His stories were all about the incidentals of war – of his attempts to speak French, of the strange food he ate during brief respites from the front line. He gave a long account to an entranced Lily and her mother of one afternoon in the Flanders countryside when he was sitting close to a massive tree, the branches of which were lined with crows. Suddenly a battery opened up nearby. The crows, as one, lifted off and the combined downward thrust from their legs snapped off two great branches with a detonation as loud as a shell. To Sammy it was the most remarkable thing he saw during the entire war, or at least it was the most remarkable thing he was ready to talk about.

To Lily, the years while the war was unfolding in all its grisly horror just out of earshot and not many miles away were ones of almost unblemished delight. She loved her new mother, she loved school and she most of all loved her three new young brothers. Her stepmother taught her dressmaking, and the high wages from the munitions factory meant some unexpected luxuries for the growing family, including rudimentary piano lessons for Lily from an enthusiastic young teacher in her school.

Slemish seemed a world away. Lily and Winnie corresponded after a fashion through postcards; Winnie's were always Slemish, the Giant's Causeway or the Glens of Antrim; Lily's were austere views of Station Road Crayford or the Black Prince's House. There was little room for news on the cards, though Lily learned that Aunt Annie had at last extracted a proposal from Jamsie Currie, and had married and moved a mile away to the Currie farm at Racavan. Winnie learned more than she wanted to about the three golden-ringleted young brothers, and the superiority of things English.

Kate Wallace was a more faithful correspondent than Winnie, and gave long accounts of everything that was happening in Kellstown. Her young sister Mary was growing up and had become a particular friend of Winnie. Her father, who had long since abandoned Presbyterianism in favour of the more serious pursuits of chewing tobacco and getting drunk, was ill and worse tempered than ever. Her brother Billy was threatening to run away. Lily had been terrified of 'Aul Jamie Wallace' when she had met him in the Wallace farm, sitting by the fireside and bombarding the burning turf with long jets of tobacco spit. It all seemed a very long way from Crayford, and the happy family in Earlsfield Cottages.

When the war ended Bob Cuthbert went back to his old employer and to the linen trade. As a block printer he was more than a labourer, though the work was physically demanding. His day was spent inking the heavy wood block, placing it exactly in the required spot on the long strip of linen cloth, tapping it with his hammer, then carefully lifting it again and moving to the next point on the repeating pattern. The block was solid, two inches thick, and usually almost two feet by two. The strain on the back was severe.

In the old days block printers had actually carved the patterns on the blocks themselves; they were the artists of the linen trade. But in modern factories, like Baker's, the blocks were prepared by specialists who did nothing else; Bob's skill was in preparing the dyes or inks that were transferred to the cloth by means of the blocks. His years as a dyer had given him a great knowledge of colour, and a mastery of the various ingredients that went to make up the dyes. But it had also given him chronic dermatitis.

During the war there was no question of travelling to Ireland, and the first years of the peace were just as difficult. But Bob and Lizzie were increasingly anxious to visit their families, to show off their three sons, and their beautiful teen-age daughter, and letters were written to Kellstown, to Lurgan and to two sisters of Bob who lived in Belfast and could provide shelter for weary travellers disembarking from the Heysham steamer at Donegall Quay.

But if the war had ended in Flanders, it was still raging in Ireland, particularly in Belfast, as the IRA, after the 1921 truce, and the creation of Northern Ireland, transferred its attention from the south and west of Ireland to the north and east. The visit was postponed for a year. But hopes of travelling in the summer of 1922 were crushed by some of the worst violence Belfast had seen. Perhaps 1923 would be better.

But Bob Cuthbert never saw either 1923 or Ireland again. In the autumn of 1922 his dermatitis was worse than ever, but he refused to let it interfere with his football. Though now 47, he was still playing for his work's team, not the dashing halfback he had been, but a rock solid fullback with hopes of lasting at least one more year. In late September he caught a chill; it was not serious, and it was certainly not the influenza which had killed forty million Europeans in 1918 and 1919.

There was no question of missing work, and in any case there was a vital football match against Erith the following Saturday. He said he would play. On Friday he fainted at work and was sent home. On Saturday morning he felt better, and despite the pleas of Lizzie, said he was well enough to play.

He travelled with his teammates to Erith on a wet, cold afternoon, and played the match in pouring rain. There were no changing rooms, just a store at the back of a pub, with several basins of water to wash off the worst of the mud. They trudged through the rain to the station, and sat in their already soaked coats. At Crayford, Bob had to be helped off the train, and across the road to his house just a few yards away.

There he collapsed and his companions helped Lizzie carry him upstairs to bed. He died in hospital three days later. The doctor said it was pneumonia. The death certificate added the information that his body had 90% eczema.

Lizzie was left with a 16 year-old stepdaughter and three sons, the eldest almost nine, the others six and five years old. Lily had had some part-time work, folding handkerchiefs and putting them in their boxes in a small linen factory, but without the breadwinner's wage there would be no bread, and no money to pay the rent. Her only relatives were in Ireland.

Within weeks of the funeral the family was on its way back to Ireland. First the train from Crayford to Dartford, then to Cannon Street, and across London by tube to Euston, and from Euston to Heysham. At Heysham it was only a few yards from the train to the *Duke of Lancaster.* They had no cabin; they sat up all night, finding what comfort they could in the angular seats of the Smoking Room. The excitement, and discomfort, of their first sea-voyage took the children's minds off the tragedy that had dismantled their lives in little more than a week.

3 DIVIDING LINES

It was a harsh homecoming in the cold, wet, early dark of a November morning on Donegall Quay. For Lily it was not a homecoming at all. More than ever convinced of her own Englishness she was shocked by the, to her, foreign, harsh accents of the dockers and porters who milled around the shed at the foot of the gangway, and horrified too at the foulness of their language – every remark sprinkled with four-letter words and their various declensions in a manner common enough in any port, but peculiar to Belfast in its intensity.

Shocking too, to her English eyes, were the heavily-armed RUC constables and B-Specials on security duty in the shed. Belfast was only now beginning to recover nervously from the appalling violence of the first half of 1922, when the IRA, no longer fighting its war against the British forces in the partitioned 26 counties of southern Ireland, had turned its anger and its guns on Belfast and on the new Northern Ireland. Fire had been met with fire, and at times murder with murder.

The outbreak of civil war in the south between supporters and opponents of the Free State Treaty settlement had brought some respite to the North, and the nightly exchanges of gunfire, and the bomb attacks on trams, had tailed off in the early summer, and it had now been two weeks since the last shooting in Belfast. But no one knew how long it would last, or how the civil war might end.

Lily and her mother led the three young brothers, each clutching his suitcase, out of the shed and through the drizzle, past the Custom House and up a dimly-lit High Street to Castle Junction. The first trams were just beginning to run, and they had a twenty minute wait before they could board one for the Grosvenor Road. They got off at Roden Street, and headed west along its rows of terraced houses, dwarfed by an enormous mill chimneystack and factory wall.

Lizzie could scarcely remember the house. She had been there several times before the war with Bob, to visit his sisters, who lived with an aunt under the shadow of the great chimney in a terraced parlour house. It sat right on the street, and at the back was a small yard with an outside toilet. But it was a parlour house, not a kitchen house.

23

To Lizzie, born and reared in the Braid countryside, the house in Roden Street had always seemed grim and dark. The front was overshadowed by the chinmeystack and the factory wall, and the back seemed to have no light at all. There was no area at the front, no buffer between the tiny house and the outside world. You were either trapped inside, or you were out on your own.

Lizzie rapped on the door, and in an instant it was opened and the two sisters were welcoming the bedraggled party with exclamations of surprise and admiration for the fine young boys and the lovely daughter. Sarah, as befitted a woman of her years, was dressed entirely in black, and wore her hair in a bun. Wooden clogs, the footwear of the linen mill worker, peeped out from beneath her floor-length skirts. Martha, her junior by several years, and unmarried, had not yet lapsed into black.

The gas was lit and the sisters fussed about making both tea and arrangements. The family was to stay in Roden Street for that night only. Tomorrow, Lizzie and the three boys would take the train to Ballymena and stay in the Braid at Kellstown until some permanent arrangement could be made. Lily listened in horror as the sisters explained that she was taking the train, not to Ballymena, but to Lurgan, where her own late mother's family had agreed to take her in.

She would be staying with her Aunt Hester and the grandfather she scarcely remembered from her childhood in Lurgan before the war. Her grandmother, who had looked after her as a baby, had died during the war; another aunt, Maria, whom Lily remembered with some affection, had left home to be married. Lily begged to be allowed stay with her stepmother and brothers; she argued that Lizzie needed her to help with the boys.

But she was told there was no room for her at Kellstown. Robert Hugh now had four children. It would be hard enough to find beds for Lizzie and the boys, let alone a girl of almost 17. There was nothing to be done.

That night Lily slept with her stepmother on a mattress on the floor of the front room at Roden Street. The musty cramped room was made even more prison-like by another mattress wedged up against the window that looked directly out onto the street. It was there to stop the bullets and the flying glass that were now more a possibility than a probability. Roden Street was solidly Protestant, but less than half a mile away was the Falls Road, solidly Catholic, and controlled by the IRA. Only a few months ago it had been a regular battleground. A neighbour had been shot dead at his own doorway. A curfew was still in force.

Upstairs the three boys crowded into one bed in the front room.

Sarah and Martha decided it was hardly necessary to drape a soaking wet blanket over the window – the form of defence that had become standard when no spare mattress was available. The heavy curtains were defence enough, and anyway the shooting seemed to be over, at least for the moment.

The house was wide awake at six the next morning. Martha had to be at work at the mill by eight o'clock, and the visitors had to be fed and prepared for their journeys. The bustle and the noise made the dark little house in the pitch black of an early November morning less forbidding than it might have been, and Lily was too busy helping with her three young brothers to think about her coming separation from them. Anyway, her stepmother had told her the night before that it might not be for too long – she would have to find a house in Ballymena to rent, as the farm at Kellstown was too small for them all. Ballymena would be better for schools and maybe for some dressmaking work for herself if they were in the town. Then Lily could come and join them.

Martha left them all with kisses and tears as she ran across the street to work. An hour later a procession of the three small boys with their cases, Lily and Lizzie with theirs, and Sarah in her black shawl and heavy boots, tramped along Roden Street, and down the Grosvenor Road to the terminus of the Great Northern Railway. Lily found she was to have a short reprieve; she would be travelling with the rest as far as Lisburn, eight miles from Belfast, but there she would have to leave their train and catch another to go a further 12 miles to Lurgan.

She studied the map on the station wall as she waited – geography had been one of her good subjects at school – and saw with despair that, after the parting at Lisburn, the lines she and the rest of the family were to take ran in opposite directions. Her route to Lurgan bent southwards to the bottom tip of Lough Neagh, while that of Lizzie and the boys turned sharply north along the east of the Lough to its topmost corner at Antrim. There they would have to take another train to Ballymena, and then go a further eight miles by road.

Her heart sank as she worked out that to get from Lurgan to Kellstown would mean changing trains twice and then finding some means of covering the last eight miles, and would take hours, never mind the cost. Half-formed hopes of being able to visit Kellstown, perhaps even the next weekend, died in the draughty, smoky and gloomy station.

But no journey by train is ever really dull, and for the three young brothers it was their first chance to see something of Ireland. They had heard lots about Slemish and the Braid from their mother, and a great deal about Lurgan and its famous football club, Glenavon, from their father. They had each other, and were not going to be separated. They peered eagerly through the grey November light at the back streets of working class Belfast as the train pulled out. Like most industrial cities, Belfast had turned its back on the railway, showing all the intimate details of its squalor to visitors.

But by Balmoral they were among trees, with glimpses of large prosperous houses, and from there to Lisburn the train scurried though villages with mills, over farmland, along high embankments giving distant views of much larger linen factories along the banks of the Lagan. The boys had shouted with delight when the train stopped at Dunmurry, for they all recognised the name, and knew that it was playing for Dunmurry Recreation that their father had won a cup-winner's medal as a young man.

The amputation at Lisburn was mercifully swift. Lizzie and the boys scrambled down with their cases, while Lily was left to continue the journey alone. The stop was a short one before the train busily huffed and puffed out along the line towards Lurgan, leaving the small group waving frantically from the disappearing platform.

Lily gazed mournfully at the flat, bleak, winter countryside. She felt no sense of homecoming, though she had spent the early years of her childhood in Lurgan. The names on the stations they stopped at – The Maze, Soldierstown, Moira – meant nothing to her. In little more than half an hour they had arrived in Lurgan; waiting on the platform was a tall grey-haired lady that Lily took to be her aunt Hester, though she had no recollection of her and would never have recognised her.

With the faintest suggestion of a smile the lady came towards her; "You must be Lily, poor child," she said in a strong, flat Lurgan accent. "And you must be Aunt Hester," said Lily in her sharply contrasting English accent. She said it without thinking, but the faint smile disappeared from Aunt Hester's face; she did not like being mocked by golden-haired young girls with outrageous English accents, especially when they were her own flesh and blood and had no business sounding like that.

It was a poor beginning. Lily's efforts to improve it, as they walked – marched might be a better term – up the street from the station to the centre of the town did not help. She chatted brightly about her brothers and Lizzie, and how she hoped they were all right on the journey to Ballymena, and how much she missed them already. She forgot completely that her Aunt Hester had barely known her stepmother, and had never met her three brothers, or that none of the four was any relation at all to Aunt Hester.

For eleven almost blissful years her own life had been lived in a land bounded by her happy, laughing father and her beloved stepmother, with the welcome additions of her brothers and her friends like the Lalliments. Her only contacts with her real mother's family, the Campbells, had been one birthday card and one Christmas card each year. Even those had been from her now-dead grandmother, and from her now-married Aunt Maria. None had been to or from her Aunt Hester.

She talked of England, of places around Crayford, and of her friends there. Aunt Hester said nothing. As the road rose up towards Lurgan's main street, Lily's spirits began to decline. It was cold and gloomy, and the wind hit their faces as they passed the church and entered the broad, long and bleak heart of the town. One or two of the shops had their windows boarded up, and at least one had recently been burnt. "The Troubles" was Aunt Hester's curt response when Lily asked what had happened. "Catholics own them", she added in explanation.

Lurgan had not experienced the levels of street violence and murder that had plagued Belfast for two years, or even the intensity of the religious rioting that had hit neighbouring Lisburn, but as Lily was to learn in the coming days, it was a bitter town, sharply divided between Protestant majority and substantial Catholic minority. One end of the town was almost entirely Catholic, but the division was more marked at street level – there was scarcely a mixed street in Lurgan, all were either one or the other.

The narrow street off the town centre into which Aunt Hester now led Lily was entirely Protestant. The house was rather impressive, three storeys, in a terrace of four, with a small garden at the front. After Crayford it seemed enormous, far too big for just Aunt Hester and Grandfather Campbell with whom she shared it. It was comfortably furnished, and why not, as Henry Campbell was a merchant with his own small business, trading in second-hand furniture, and with a shop in the town where he presided over Campbell Brothers.

It was the house she had lived in for almost four years before her father had remarried, but it was not the same house. Then it had been full of people – her grandmother and her Aunt Maria as well as her grandfather and Hester, and the frequent comings and goings of friends and relatives. Now there was no one but the stern-sounding Hester and the silent grandfather.

When he was not out at his shop, he sat in his chair close to the range in the kitchen at the back of the house, reading. When it was not a newspaper it was a book, often the Bible. He and Hester seemed to have little to say to each other, and he had almost nothing at all to say to the newly arrived 16 year-old granddaughter. It was Hester who told Lily that her grandfather had found a job for her, and that she would be starting work the following week in a small stitching shed attached to one of the town's many linen mills. Lizzie had written to say that Lily was practised with needle and thread, and had learned the basic skills of dressmaking.

It was still early afternoon when Lily had finished unpacking her suitcase and helping Hester with clearing up after the midday dinner. She said she wanted to go and explore the town, and see her Aunt Maria and her new baby. Hester reluctantly agreed, and issued a series of strong warnings about which streets had to be avoided, about how long the walk was to Maria's cottage on the edge of the town, and how Lily had to be back well before six, before her grandfather's return from the shop.

The visit to Maria was a success, and lifted Lily's heart, though the walk was long and meant passing through the meaner parts of the town. She had very warm, if by now also rather indistinct memories, of Maria. She could remember nothing of her own mother, but Maria had filled that role from Lily's first return to Lurgan as a two-year old until her departure for England some three years later. From the one or two photographs she had of her mother, she knew that she and Maria had been very alike.

Now Maria was a wife and mother herself, with a young baby on her lap. She hugged Lily, and wept as she listened to the story of the sudden death of Bob Cuthbert, and of the three young sons who has lost their father. She told Lily all about her husband, about her wedding two years earlier, and married life. By the time Lily had to leave to walk back to the town centre, she had begun to feel she was part of a family again, and the dreadful sense of isolation that had come over her as she had parted from the others at Lisburn was beginning to lift. But it descended more bleakly than ever as she hurried back towards what she could not bring herself to call her new home.

4 LURGAN

Lily's stay in Lurgan lasted three weeks. She soon discovered that any visit to Kellstown was out of the question; by the time she finished work at the stitching shed on Saturday evening it was far too late to catch the two trains and get from Ballymena to the farm. Even if, by some miracle, that had been possible, there was no way she could make her way back to Lurgan on the Sunday night to be ready for work the next morning. That was a crushing blow. Now she could only hope that a visit would be possible at Christmas, when she would have two days off. But that was still many weeks away.

The stitching shed was another disappointment. Lily was not afraid of hard work, and had no difficulty mastering the simple skills required in hemming handkerchiefs. She had looked forward to escaping for ten hours a day from her gloomy grandfather's gloomy house, and expected she would soon make friends with the other young girls in the workroom.

It was not to be. For a start, her English accent was both ridiculed and resented. Why was she speaking like that when her grandfather was old Campbell from the junk shop, and when she herself had grown up in Lurgan? It was clearly put on; Lily Cuthbert was a swank and a snob. Lily hardly helped herself - she spoke like that, she told them, because she was English. She had been born in England and so was English. She constantly told them about England, about Crayford, about school there, about the Lalliments, about London.

By the end of the first week it seemed no one wanted to talk to her. Even those who had, at first, taken to the pretty new arrival and tried to befriend her, turned their backs. They mocked her accent, and shouted her down when she mentioned anything about England. Only one girl continued to show any interest in her, and her interest was entirely in Lily's eternal soul. She had soon discovered, by dint of very direct questioning, that Lily was not saved. The questioning had to be direct, for Lily had no idea what she was talking about, and was blissfully unaware of the dire necessity of being saved.

It was not something that the Church of England Sunday School in

Crayford had spent much time on, nor did it come up in the liturgy and sermons of the Sunday services which Lily had attended with Lizzie. Her stepmother knew all about being saved, but as neither her new husband nor her new church had seemed too bothered about the matter, she had happily left such worries behind her when she left the Braid and moved to Kent.

But it mattered in Lurgan. In fact it mattered all across the north of Ireland, for something akin to the 1859 revival was again sweeping the land. For the most part, being saved had been something left to the frequenters of gospel halls and tin tabernacles; nothing so embarrassingly emotional and public was expected from the inherently upright members of orthodox Presbyterian or Methodist congregations, and certainly not from members of the Church of Ireland.

Salvation, if such crude terminology could be used in their cases, was ensured by the infinitely more discreet and respectable pathway of rigorous attendance at public worship and avoidance of public scandal. (Roman Catholics, blissfully lost in the utter darkness of Rome, were spared any involvement in the issue.)

The gospel-hall irregulars had long maintained a steady sniper fire against such mainstream Protestant complacency, and sought to breach its defences by means of tent missions, open-air oratory and forays into the public distribution of gospel tracts. But such futile assaults had little impact on the armour plate of church respectability. That was until the advent of two remarkable preachers, each of whom, in different ways, was making being saved a matter of central concern, an issue for the church-going middle classes and professional people, as much as for the godless factory workers.

The first of these was W P Nicholson. A former seaman from County Down, he had undergone his own dramatic conversion as a young man in his 20s and had taken to preaching. He had had some theological training in Glasgow, enough to get him a post as an assistant minister in the Presbyterian Shankill Road Mission in Belfast, from where he had progressed, first to Scotland, and then, in 1914, to Pennsylvania and later to Los Angeles, all the time gaining in reputation as a fearless preacher of the gospel.

He had returned to Ireland in 1920 for a short private visit, but had responded to invitations to preach. The visit lasted several years, and from October 1920 onwards W P was drawing crowds of thousands, and people were being saved in their hundreds - in Bangor, Ballymena, Lurgan, Newtownards, Lisburn, Carrickfergus and especially in Belfast. Nicholson's missions were not tin chapel affairs; many were organised jointly by groups of Presbyterian and Methodist Churches, carefully prepared and advertised, and his message was specifically and sharply directed at the church-going classes. Established churches noted significant increases in both membership and attendance as a result.

There was a marked absence of the mystical manifestations of the 1859 revival. People did not swoon at Nicholson's meetings, but they did get saved. They hardly dared not to, for Nicholson was feared for his 'terrific severity', and he was not above singling out individual members of his audience if he thought they looked particularly guilty and in especially urgent need of salvation, or were simply not paying adequate attention. He was very much against the cardinal sins of drinking, smoking, gossiping and thinking church membership got you a ticket to heaven. He was very much for being *Washed in the Blood of the Lamb*, being *Free from your Burden of Sin*, coming to Jesus for his Cleansing Power, and being baptized in the Holy Ghost.

Also preaching at the same time and in the same towns was a very different apostle of salvation. George Jeffreys was a frail young Welshman, with a quiff of curly back hair and a lilting south Wales accent. Not robust enough to follow his father into the mines, he had combined a shop job with preaching in chapels, and had had some Bible-college training. His reputation as a preacher reached as far as Monaghan in the heart of Ireland, and early in 1915 a small group of men there, presumably Presbyterians, invited Jeffreys to come to their small market town in southern Ulster to conduct a mission.

This he did with immediate impact, and his fame spread to Belfast, where he was invited to conduct another mission, this time with such success that he soon established a permanent church with himself as Pastor. The church was in Hunter Street, not far from the Donegall Road end of Roden Street.

It was to be the first Elim Foursquare Gospel Church, a new denomination that spread rapidly across Northern Ireland, and then into London, throughout England and into Scotland and Wales. George Jeffreys, or Principal Jeffreys as he was termed as head of the new church, did not, like Nicholson, try to bully people into salvation. Instead he wooed and courted them, talked endlessly about the love of Christ, about the Saviour's ability to heal the sick, and his readiness to fill the believer with indescribable joy through the charismatic experience of baptism in the Holy Spirit. By 1922 he had churches in Belfast, Ballymena, Bangor and Lurgan.

This was the strange world that Lily found herself plunged into in 1922. Nothing she had known in England prepared her for it.

Attendance at church and Sunday School, and religious teaching in school, had been part of her life, but in a very general way, all part of being English. There was nothing personal about it; the church spire was part of the landscape, so familiar you rarely noticed it. In Protestant Ulster it was very different; religion dominated the landscape in the way Lindsay Thompson's enormous factory chimney towered over Roden Street. There was no escaping it.

Something special had happened in the years up to 1922. The war, with its terrible losses at the Somme and elsewhere, had brought tragedy to most streets and many homes. Those who returned from the trenches, and the families of those who did not, had seen the horror and depravity of war, not the glory. The bombings, murder and arson fuelled by the hatred of Troubles had left few families unscarred, and the Protestant community felt isolated, betrayed and insecure. That man was a fallen creature, born in sin and shapen in iniquity, was established orthodoxy, but the proof of it was now all around.

Into this morass of fear, doubt and disillusionment stepped the preachers. Neither Nicholson nor Jeffreys touched politics. Nicholson, unlike his predecessors and successors in the pantheon of firebrand Ulster preachers, had nothing to say about nationalism or unionism, nor was denunciation of Rome any part of his weaponry. He was busy enough lambasting the Presbyterian establishment, the complacency of churchgoers and the evils of drink. In the tradition of the 1859 revival, his chief concern was convincing his hearers of their guilt and sin.

But what both Nicholson and Jeffreys promised the individual was redemption, a better way, a chance to wash off the mud and blood with which man had bespattered himself in both Flanders and the streets and ditches of Ulster, and to start afresh. Nicholson promised it through discipline, unwavering faith and pursuit of an intense and elevated spirituality through baptism in the Holy Spirit.

Jeffreys promised an escape from misery to joy. Proof that the Saviour could restore the fallen spirit was there to be seen in his physical healing of the sick. The guilt and sickness of the soul could be gloriously swept away in the ecstasy of the Pentecostal experience, the pain, squalor and hatreds of daily life buried in the fathomless sea of God's love.

For both preachers the admission price was the same. You had to be saved. The response was phenomenal; in Belfast and other towns people came in droves. Men, mostly working-class men, were saved in their hundreds. Three thousand shipyard workers marched from the yards in east Belfast at the end of their shift to the opening night of Nicholson's mission at Ravenhill Presbyterian church. At the entrance the crush was so great the brick pillar holding the gate was moved off its base.

These things were happening in 1922, the year of the worst violence of the Troubles, when fear and hatred poisoned the streets of the towns and the hedges of the countryside. In the first six months of the year more than 200 people died in violence in Belfast and the surrounding area. With the IRA mounting a sustained campaign against the new Northern Ireland, which in turn produced retaliatory violence against the Catholic community, many saw a real danger of full-scale civil war between Protestant and Catholic.

As violence dramatically subsided towards the end of the year, even those sceptical of the preachers' evangelical fundamentalism began to suggest their missions had played a significant part in helping divert large sections of the Protestant working class away from hating their neighbours to loving God. The fact that the IRA had been diverted into a real civil war in the south of the island against the provisional Irish Free State was a more likely explanation for the drop in the murder rate in Belfast, but one less easily attributable to the direct intervention of Jehovah in the affairs of the six counties of north east Ireland.

Lily was seriously deficient when it came to any sense of guilt or sin, and felt no great urge to respond to her workmate's repeated invitations to attend the mission being conducted in Lurgan by the great Nicholson himself. But there was no escape from the blanket of religious enthusiasm that had descended over the town. She fobbed off her workmate and found excuses for not going to the mission, but she still had to listen to repeated urgings to get saved, and non-stop warnings of the hellfire and damnation that awaited her if she did not.

And not just at work; neither her grandfather nor her aunt was fanatic, but both were saved, and both were shocked to find that Lily was not. Lily was obliged to attend not just one church, but two. Her aunt was Presbyterian, and Lily was marched to morning and evening service. Her grandfather, she was amazed to find, attended the Salvation Army, and she was obliged to accompany him to an afternoon service in the local citadel.

The explanation for this odd state of affairs, odd even for Lurgan, was that the elders of the Presbyterian Church he had attended for years had expressed their concern when they heard that he was taking into partnership one of his employees in the shop – a Catholic. He was called to a meeting of elders and reminded of the scriptural injunction to come out from among them and be separate, that light had no fellowship with darkness.

"That's what you think, is it?", he had said, thanked them for their opinion, and left the meeting. He never turned up again in the Presbyterian Church, and a year or two later, when he moved into a new shop in Lurgan's Market Street, the sign over the door read Campbell and McGibbon.

Three church services on the Sunday, even if one of them was enlivened by a brass band and the availability of tambourines and thus somewhat different from the endless dreariness of the Presbyterian services, cast Lily into ever-deeper gloom. The services were bad enough, but attendance at them meant she had no time to visit her Aunty Maria, and no time to make other friends.

Life was miserable, and meaningless. She longed to visit her brothers and Lizzie; she longed to escape from Lurgan, even just to escape from the stern aunt and the silent grandfather. She feared Christmas would never come. Worn down by her workmate's coaxing, or perhaps by the efficacy of her prayers, she agreed to go to the Nicholson mission on the first Monday of her third week in Lurgan.

It was being held in the largest Presbyterian church in the town, and Lily and her friend were lucky to find two seats together in the gallery, even though they were there a good half hour before the service was due to start. It was a wet night, and the packed church smelt of saturated wool and cheap clothing, all beginning to steam in the heat inside the building. It was not church as Lily had known it in Crayford, and she did not like it, nor feel in the least comfortable.

Soon a figure appeared in the pulpit and began to lead hymn-singing. No it was not Mr. Nicholson, a whisper from her friend informed Lily, just one of the local men. Lily rather liked the hymn-singing. She was instinctively musical, and the hymns were not the usual Presbyterian dirges but the mission hymns, lively, and owing more to the musical hall than to the Covenanting tradition in their tunes if not their words.

The words somewhat mystified Lily. She was not at all sure how she herself might answer the repeated questions – *Are you washed in the blood of the Lamb? Have you been to Jesus for the cleansing flow? Have you any room for Jesus?* – but she liked the tunes.

After several rousing hymns a murmur of excitement ran round the congregation as a burly figure entered the pulpit and eased aside the local man. It was WP himself. He was no more than medium height, but was sturdily built and had a massive head of curly black hair.

"Call that singing?" he challenged the congregation, "I've heard better from the seagulls that used to follow my boat when I was a sailor."

He took charge of the singing. First the gallery had to sing against the downstairs, verse about; then the women had to take on the men, and after that, amidst much tittering, the married folk against the single. Between hymns the singers were urged to greater efforts by a barrage of criticism, even abuse, and biting humour, though WP never relaxed his stern expression.

Late-comers hoping to slip in unnoticed and squeeze into the end of a row did not escape lightly. Each arrival was remarked on from the pulpit in unflattering terms. One bald-headed gent was greeted: "Hey, you, you're late. What kept you? It certainly wasn't combing your hair". The crowd exploded. The result was electric - the singing echoed round the church, people smiled at each other and tried to outdo their neighbours. Lily relaxed a little.

Then, suddenly, Nicholson grasped his Bible and launched into his message. His approach was severe, and his language rough, often using words that many in his audience would have disallowed in their own homes. An audible intake of breath followed the preacher's denunciation of those who relied on church membership for their salvation – they thought because they had been baptised, catechised, vaccinated and confirmed they were all right. "Bastard theology. Bastard religion" thundered Nicholson.

He raged against the evil of drink, against tobacco, against women who had bad tongues and spent their time nagging and gossiping. Redemption from such gross iniquities could come only through being washed in the blood of the Lamb, being saved. Even the Old Testament Patriarchs could get a touch of WP's tongue. Jacob, he told the congregation, was so crooked he could hide behind a corkscrew; he could steal the eye out of your head and spit in the hole and you would know nothing about it.

At times in his preaching Nicholson would fix his eyes on one section of the congregation, and seemingly address his condemnations and his forensic questions to one unfortunate individual. Sometimes he even singled out a man or woman – "You at the end of the back row", or "Yes, you missus with the big hat and the black coat. What about you?" Everyone except the victim enjoyed this immensely.

Along the gallery from Lily and her friend, a group of young girls started giggling and whispering among themselves. Nicholson broke off in mid-sentence and glared at the gallery. 'You bits of girls' he declared "You would do better to stay at home than come here and play the whippersnapper. Do you want me to put you out? No? Then shut your mouths."

Lily was horrified. She had loved the singing, but she hated W P Nicholson. He frightened and offended her, particularly when at one point in his sermon he stopped to order a window to be closed, complaining that there was a draught blowing round him like a stepmother's breath. Lily saw nothing funny in this, and did not join in the roars of laughter. She thought Nicholson was rough and coarse, and he talked on and on about sin and guilt. Life had dealt Lily enough severe blows in recent weeks – her father's death, the flight from England, separation from her brothers and stepmother – to make her feel miserable. She did not need any preacher to pile on the agony. Nicholson seemed to embody all that was dark and hostile about her life in Ireland, a life totally removed from the sunny, happy days in Crayford.

Nicholson had urged his listeners to make a decision – had ordered them to, on pain of eternal damnation or worse. That night Lily made a decision, but not the one WP had in mind.

Up early the next morning she put her few belongings into a small bag, and smuggled it out of the house under her coat. Instead of heading for the stitching shed, she went to the railway station. She had enough money for the fare to Belfast, but not much more. She boarded a crowded morning train, squeezed into a compartment jammed with workmen and cigarette smoke, and began to think about what she was doing.

She knew she was running away. She had read lots of stories about young people who had run away. They always ran away to escape from someone or something, a wicked stepmother perhaps, though Lily could never quite envisage a stepmother who was wicked as she loved her own so much. Sometimes it was from poverty or disease or some great threat.

In Lily's case it was nothing so particular. It was much more; she was running away from fate, away from life as it had become. She was running away from Lurgan because it was a foreign place, because being there meant separation from her stepmother and brothers, from her Lurgan relatives because they were strangers, and from a life that constantly echoed with guilt and sin and the threat of damnation.

She had no idea where she was running to. She would have loved to run to her stepmother and brothers, but that was impossible. She doubted if she had enough money to get there, and she was not at all sure she knew how to reach them. She knew too that she might be sent straight back to Lurgan. So she was running to where the train took her, and that was Belfast.

As the train pulled into the station, the workmen finished their last hand of poker, and grabbed their 'piece' tins. The one nearest the door hoisted the leather strap that allowed him to drop down the window, and then leaned out and grasped the brass handle, opening the door and skipping out from the still moving train. His workmates tumbled out after him; it was a point of honour to hit the platform running, and not face the humiliation of descending from a stationary train.

Lily, who was in no hurry, waited until the train had stopped, and descended from the empty carriage. It was still early when she walked out of the Great Northern Station into Great Victoria Street. She knew nothing of Belfast, so she simply followed the crowds as they streamed out of the station, across the road and into the city centre. After five minutes she found herself in a large square, dominated by a vast domed building, with lawns and trees and statues in front of it. Under the trees were park benches, and Lily gratefully seated herself on one of these.

She was cold and frightened, but determined never to go back to Lurgan. The only people she knew in Belfast were her aunts Martha and Sarah, with whom she had spent one night. She knew their address. But she dreaded turning up on the Roden Street doorstep and being put on the next train back to Lurgan. Roden Street might be a last resort, but not just yet.

From her bench she looked around Donegall Square, with its impressive buildings, clanging trams and bustling crowds. Across to her right was a particularly striking sandstone building four or five storeys high, with tall ornate chimneys and dormer windows in its steep roof, capped by a fine wrought-iron balustrade. She thought it looked very pretty. As she admired it she noticed a number of girls of about her own age going up the steps to the large front door and disappearing inside.

After a while she realised she could not sit on the bench all day, so she hoisted her bag and walked across the square. Her path took her past the door of the building she had been looking at, and as she came level with it she saw a notice pinned to it: *Girls Wanted. Apply Within.* Without thinking enough about it to lose her nerve, she walked in.

Four or five girls were sitting on a bench at the side of the tiled hallway. Lily joined them and asked what the job was. The building belonged to a linen company and girls were needed for various tasks associated with the Christmas trade. They were called in one by one to an office beside the hall; Lily was asked for her name, age and address. "68 Roden Street" she replied quickly. Had she any experience? She told them she had had a job in England folding handkerchiefs, and that she had been working at stiching in Lurgan.

That was exactly what they needed. Could she start right away? By ten o'clock she was installed in a large workroom, busily folding and pinning delicate lace handkerchiefs to a card, attaching a small blue ribbon, and placing them in a cardboard box. The work was tiring, for the girls were on their feet, lifting the hankies from the piles that were constantly replenished on the long trestle tables, and taking them to a side bench to fold and pin them onto card. Even so, running away seemed the best idea she had ever had.

During her midday break she spent a few more pence of her dwindling capital on a cup of tea and some bread and butter in an eating house behind the City Hall. At six o'clock she found herself on the pavement in Donegall Square, wondering what to do next. On the spur of the moment she had given Roden Street as her address, because she knew to get the job she had to have one, and it was the only address she knew in Belfast.

But giving it had made it, in a way, officially her home. So with little or no hesitation she set out to find the tram that would take her up the Grosvenor Road to Roden Street. The tram was crowded with factory and office workers, and as it was already dark she had to peer carefully out of the windows to watch out for the tall factory chimney that would tell her she was at Roden Street.

She was as relieved to find her aunts at home as they were amazed to see her. Long explanations amidst floods of tears followed. Having listened to how unhappy and friendless Lily had been in Lurgan, to how much she longed to be nearer to her own family, and, not least, to how she had already found herself a job in Belfast and completed her first day's work in it, the aunts' shock softened into sympathy.

A telegram was sent to Lurgan to reassure the Campbells that Lily was safe and well, and staying for the moment in Roden Street. Then supper and the spare room were prepared, and plans discussed. First, and the aunts and Lily were at one on this, they had to make contact with her stepmother in Ballymena. It was agreed that the younger Aunt Martha would accompany Lily to Ballymena that Saturday. Recent reforms in the hours of work in Belfast meant that most factory workers finished early on Saturday, some even as early as lunch-time. Martha would be free to travel after three o'clock, and Lily would find out the next day when she finished on a Saturday. Once they knew the train times, they would send a letter, and hope that someone could meet them at the station.

So almost without any discussion it was agreed that Lily would be staying, both in her job and in Roden Street, at least until Saturday. It was a short week. Her working hours from eight in the morning until six, with 45 minutes break at midday, left her no time to explore Belfast, and with no energy to do so if she had had the time. The thought of meeting her brothers and stepmother again on Saturday was enough excitement.

On Friday a letter arrived from Lizzie saying she would meet the train and take them back to Kellstown, where they could stay the night, returning to Belfast on the Sunday.

Early on Saturday afternoon Martha and Lily took the longer tram ride from Roden Street through the city centre to York Street and the Northern Counties station. The NCC route to Ballymena was shorter and quicker than the GNR line via Lisburn and Antrim, and they were in Ballymena before four o'clock. Despite her Aunt's protests and predictions of disaster, Lily had the window down and the door open before the train had stopped and was skipping on to the platform like a seasoned traveller, peering into the gloom of the November afternoon for a first glimpse of her stepmother.

Lizzie was there, and alongside her, Bobby, the eldest of the three brothers and Lily's favourite though she would never have admitted to any such preference. The reunion among the three was extravagant enough to suggest a separation of several years rather than a few weeks. Tears and hugs took priority over questions and explanations until Lizzie extracted herself to greet Martha and urge the little group to waste no time as they had to find a jaunting-car to take them to Broughshane. After that they would have to walk the remaining three miles.

The station yard was crowded with jaunting-cars – the ubiquitous Irish 'outside car' with its high wheels and two outward facing seats to which the passengers – two or three to a side - clung in varying degrees of terror related to the speed of the horse and the quality of the roadway. Lizzie quickly negotiated a fare to Broughshane, and they were soon bouncing their way out the Broughshane Road. Half an hour or so later they were dropped in the broad main street of Broughshane and began their long walk home by way of Lisnamurrican and the top road towards Buckna.

Bobby insisted on carrying the small suitcase Martha had packed. At first he and Lily walked ahead as he told her about the two younger brothers, and how he and Alec had started at Lisnamurrican school, how no one could understand them and their English accents, how hard it was to follow the teacher's broad Ballymena-Scots, how he could never understand a word his Uncle Robert said to him, and how all three had to share a room with their mother in the crowded farmhouse.

He told her all about the farm, about the excitement of the threshing the previous week, about a visit to Slemish – not the top, just the slopes, with Uncle Robert to bring home the turf from the peat-bog. Behind them, Martha explained to Lizzie how Lily had turned up out of the blue on their doorstep on Tuesday night, announcing that she had run away from Lurgan that morning, and had got herself a job, and was not going back to Lurgan. She gave it as her opinion that there was no point sending her back to Lurgan, that the only thing that would satisfy her was to be nearer her brothers, and that if nothing else could be arranged, they would be happy to let her stay in Roden Street meanwhile.

Lizzie confessed she was at a loss as to what to do. She knew that she herself and the three boys could not stay indefinitely at Kellstown. There was simply no room, and, buried in the depths of the country at the foot of Slemish, she had no chance of earning money from her dressmaking skills. She could not expect her brother to feed four additional mouths for ever, never mind five. Certainly there could be no question of taking Lily in. There was simply no room, and anyway there would be no chance of her finding any sort of job in such a remote place.

It was getting quite dark as they passed Lisnamurrican school and turned left along the road that ran towards the now dimly visible Slemish. The rough surface and sharp stones on the road made walking difficult and they slowed their pace, Lily insisting on taking the case off a protesting Bobby. Lizzie assured them it was no more than a mile to the turn off up the back loanin that led into the McMaster farms, first Samuel Alexander's lower farm, and then, just beyond it, Robert Hugh's, now home to Lizzie and the boys.

A turn in the road and overhanging trees obscured the entrance to the loanin, so that they did not see the welcoming committee sitting on the ditch around a storm lantern. The two younger boys, Alec and Hugh, threw themselves at Lily with cries of delight, while their two McMaster cousins who had brought them down the loanin, hung back shyly, having no memory of the Lily who had left for Crayford before they were born.

"Hello Lily, welcome back to the Braid", said a voice from the shadows, and a sturdy figure stepped forward. It took Lily a second or two to recognise the voice, rather than the person. "Winnie", she cried and the two girls, both now young ladies, hugged and kissed and cried tears of joy. Then Kate Wallace ran forward, and the whole performance was repeated. For the first time since stepping off the boat a month earlier, Lily had a feeling of coming home. In the pain and sorrow of her father's death and the sudden return to Ireland, she had not thought of Winnie and Kate. She knew from a letter that Winnie was starting to train as a nurse, and had left the farm, so she had no expectation of seeing her at Kellstown.

Yet here she was, and in the cold dark of a muddy lane overhung with bare hawthorn bushes, her presence brought memories rushing back of the blissful week they had spent together, when her father was about to marry Winnie's aunt, and when the greatest challenge facing the two young lives was when would they climb Slemish.

Despite the distressing circumstances that had brought them there, it was a happy band that followed the swinging storm lantern up the gloomy, overhung loanin, past the lower farm and into the street. With a promise of seeing them all again in the morning, Kate waved goodbye and skipped over the plank bridge and through the trees.

5   TOGETHER

A powerful tea of eggs, bacon and freshly baked soda bread awaited them in the farmhouse. Mercifully, Robert Hugh's grace had become even shorter and more rapid in the intervening years and was over before they had settled in their chairs around the kitchen table. With pitch darkness now outside, and the lamps lit inside, with only the sound of the wind in the fir trees across the burn, and an occasional lowing from the cows in the byre next door, the world seemed not just a better place than it had since that fateful day when Bob Cuthbert had been brought home semi-conscious by his team-mates, but also a much more distant place.

"Boys oh, Lallie" boomed Robert Hugh from the top of the table, "Where did you get those blond curls? There maun be a wheen o fellas across in England greetin their hairts oot that ye hae left them."

"Just the one or two, Uncle Robert", replied Lily, more guessing than understanding what had been said, and blushing modestly to take the edge off her boldness. It set the tone for the evening. Instead of a mournful counting of the catastrophes that had overtaken the family and the world since they had last sat around the same table, there was nothing but happy reminiscences and much joking. Even Robert Hugh's dutiful reading of one of the shorter Psalms in a rapid, unintelligible mutter through his moustache did little to dampen their spirits.

But reality could not be entirely excluded. What were they going to do with Lily? Lizzie repeated, more for Robert Hugh's benefit, than to reopen the matter, that there was no question of her joining them in Kellstown. She knew her stepdaughter well enough to realise there was no point sending her back to Lurgan. Behind those angelic curls and sweet face there was a stubbornness that came from who knew where – perhaps even from the Campbells from whom she had just fled.

Lizzie was sensitive enough, too, to understand that it was not just the separation from her brothers and herself that had made Lily run away. Whatever the full story, it was clear she had been deeply unhappy in Lurgan, and would never go back. Martha again repeated her offer to have Lily live with them in Roden Street; after all, she already had a job, and she could travel up to the Braid the odd weekend to see her brothers. It was the best they could do until something was sorted out.

For Lily there was the added consolation that Winnie would also be in Belfast, and she would not be friendless.

It was already late by normal Kellstown standards, and Martha had to be walked down the loanin to Samuel Alexander's where she had been offered a bed, there being no more available in the already overcrowded upper farm. So Lily and Winnie linked arms with Martha and set off down the rough laneway, alongside the burn and under the tall dark fir trees. They greeted Samuel Alexander and his two still unmarried daughters, and Lily was pressed to take another cup of tea and see the visitor settled in the spare room.

By the time they set off on the short walk home the skies had cleared and a partial moon was shining. "Will we have a look at Slemish?" suggested Winnie as they rounded the bend into the street in front of the farmhouse. "Indeed so", replied Lily and the two girls linked arms as they veered around the corner of the farmhouse, up the few yards to the gate into the field behind the farm. There was Slemish, massive, silent and eerie in its stark outline in the moonlight. It was exactly as Lily had remembered it from a decade earlier. Here, in the half darkness with just the wind in the trees and the quiet clucking from the henhouse ark in the field, she again had a feeling of great safety. There were no boarded up shops, no burned-out houses, and no preachers shouting about blood. Together they gazed at Slemish.

"I don't know why, but I love that mountain", said Winnie. "I miss it in Belfast, and I sometimes come home more to see it than to see my Uncle Robert or Aunt Jane or my cousins. And I've climbed it at least once every year since I last saw you. We'll have to go to the top together next spring, and bring the three boys with us."

With that, and a farewell glance at the mountain, she led Lily back to the house, and into the soft feather-mattress bed they had shared briefly as children. The aunt with whom Winnie had shared a room was now married, and Winnie had the luxury of a small box-room to herself. She and Lily lay awake well into the night, while Lily talked of her life in Crayford, of the Lalliment sisters, of Lucy Rollins and Carrie Simmons, and of the terrible sudden death of her beloved father.

Winnie told her of how happy she had been to start training as a nurse in Belfast, and to get away from Robert Hugh. She felt he resented her being there, and though her Aunt Jane was as nice as ever, it had never really been home to her since her grandmother had died. She had a secret to share too. It was not just Slemish that drew her back to the Braid on many weekends, but a tall young gamekeeper who worked on Lord Rathcavan's Cleggan estate near Broughshane.

Winnie had met him at a church social in Buckna, and they had been walking out whenever the chance presented itself. No one knew about it, and Lily was sworn to secrecy. Jim, the gamekeeper, was talking of emigrating to America, where he heard there were posts for gamekeepers in the big estates on the Hudson River north of New York. A cousin of his had emigrated there some years earlier, and wrote regularly to Jim urging him to follow his example.

While Jim was much too shy and too circumspect to mention marriage, he had told Winnie that many of these jobs in America carried a house with them, and how grand it would be to walk straight into your own place, and not spend years sharing with your father and mother, or renting some tumbledown damp cottage at the butt end of a mountain or bog. Winnie was in no doubt at all that, once asked, she would buy the whole package – Jim, America and a place of their own. She could barely wait.

Though now sixteen, Lily had never really had a boy friend. In Crayford she had been very busy helping her stepmother with the three boys, and while she had been an enthusiastic part of every picnic, outing or swimming party organised by her friends, and had flirted with their brothers and developed crushes on most of them in rapid succession, she had never had a particular friend.

She talked long about Lurgan and how awful it had been. She described the long broad main street that seemed permanently swept by wind and rain, the cold house she shared with her silent grandfather and stern aunt, the cramped little stitching and folding shed she worked in with girls who either ignored her or mocked her English accent. And she told Winnie about her one friend who worried far more about Lily's eternal soul than ever Lily had.

"Don't tell me you're not saved", said Winnie sitting up in the bed. "You must be as bad as myself. Aunt Jane is always at me about it. Uncle Robert never says anything but he makes me go to the meetings he holds every month in the barn. He has had a wee pulpit built out of plywood, and there's a harmonium up there behind the corn that they pull out. And five or six times during the winter some minister or missioner comes and preaches. That funny Welshman Jeffreys who does the miracles and heals the sick was here once, though I saw nobody healed.

"I suppose I'll have to get saved one day. You have to or you'll go to hell. Not that it does them much good as far as I can see. Uncle Robert has a wicked temper and most of the women have fierce tongues. Still, it would be terrible not to be saved in the end. We'll have to get round to it, the pair of us." On which inspirational note, they fell asleep.

Sunday was a rush from beginning to end. It began with Winnie and Lily taking their toothbrushes and soap and towel down to the spout and washing in the icy water of the burn before rushing back to the warmth of the kitchen. Kate was over almost immediately for endless chatter over cups of tea. She brought with her her younger half-sister Mary, a growing teenager and a full cousin of Winnie. At mid-morning the entire household apart from Aunt Jane and Lizzie were loaded into the high-sided carts of Robert Hugh and Samuel Alexander which lurched off down the loanin to bounce and jolt the three miles to Buckna Presbyterian Church.

Lily found the sermon boring, the hymns mournful and the whole service dreary beyond words. The high point was when Winnie poked her in the ribs and pointed to a tall, amiable, young man who smiled at Winnie as he took his seat in a pew near the back. "Jim", she said, and smiled.

It was almost two o'clock when they reached the farm again, and there was time only for a quick meal before Lily and Martha had to set out for Belfast. There was the long walk, almost to Broughshane, before they said goodbye to Winnie and the three brothers, and clambered up onto a lorry with wooden benches in the back that ferried country people into Ballymena station on their way back to Belfast.

At the station they sat on the windy platform in the dwindling light, waiting for the train from Derry. By now Lily regarded herself as a seasoned traveller by train. She knew that if you watched carefully as the locomotive lumbered past, you could see the glowing flame from the firebox. This time the *Dunluce Castle* did not disappoint her, and she had a great view of the sweating face of the fireman as he bent to stoke the flames. The little cameo reminded her, not, as perhaps it should have done, of the fires of hell that awaited the unsaved, but of the warmth and safety of the Kellstown kitchen.

It was dark by the time they reached Belfast and took the tram across the city to Roden Street. Another working week awaited Lily.

6   WORKING GIRL

The routine of work, the cheerful friendliness of her two aunts, and the chance to meet Winnie when she had time to spare from her nursing duties, plus the knowledge that almost every weekend she would be able to travel to the Braid and spend at least an evening and a morning with her brothers and her stepmother, helped slow down and then reverse the spiral of almost hysterical unease that had swept Lily along since the day her father died.

The working hours were long and the work itself repetitive and boring, but the room she shared with the other girls, folding and packing the linen handkerchiefs, was clean, warm and bright. They talked all day and about everything. Lily had learned from her Lurgan job that Irish girls were not over-interested in the Black Prince's House or refugees from Belgium, or how wonderful a place Kent was. So she said less and less about life in England, and soon the other girls took her English accent in their stride and mostly ignored it.

The endless chatter covered boyfriends, preachers and film stars. The newspapers were full of Lloyd George and Bonar Law and the General Election, and of the final act of the establishment of Northern Ireland – the formal opting out from the Irish Free State as provided for in the Government of Ireland Act – but of what interest was all of this to working girls, even if, as someone had heard, Bonar Law's father had been a Presbyterian Minister, and his grandfather an Ulsterman?

Bonar Law was no Rudolf Valentino and was soon forgotten. Besides, a woman had to be 30 years of age to have the vote, and only the supervisor was that ancient. The girls' votes, had they had any, would have gone elsewhere; some of them could switch easily from a breathless rehearsal of the entire plot of the latest film at the Picture House to a verbatim account of W P Nicholson's sermon at St Enoch's in Carlisle Circus. To all of this Lily had little to contribute, though she did say she had found WP very rude and boring.

She could display some authority on the subject of her own favourite film star, Charlie Chaplin – who was English, she would add - as before she left England she had already seen one or two of his reels which had not yet arrived in Belfast. On those evenings when she could meet Winnie after work, they spent as much of their time as they could in the company of Mr. Chaplin, or even of Mr. Arbuckle, rather than that of Mr. Nicholson. (Since his acquittal in America on a charge of murdering an actress earlier that summer, Fatty Arbuckle had never ceased to fascinate the girls. Already anyone displaying the slightest tendency to overweight was jeered at as a Fatty Arbuckle.)

WP Nicholson, however, was harder to avoid than Bonar Law. Both he and George Jeffreys seemed to have followed Lily from Lurgan to Belfast. Jeffreys had opened a new church – or 'tabernacle' as it was called – quite close to Roden Street, and Nicholson was packing in the crowds every night at St Enoch's. Several of the girls in work were saved, and Lily had plenty of invitations to go with them to meetings, all of which she managed to decline. But the gloom of religion hung over Belfast and was unavoidable.

Roden Street had been close to the worst of the sectarian violence just a few months earlier, and Lily soon learned that everyone, and almost everything, was either Protestant or Catholic. She noticed how the girls at work were sometimes quick to add 'She's a Catholic', when a new employee arrived, and how the new employee would always find a workplace beside other Catholic girls. There was no obvious bitterness among the workers, and no confrontation, but you kept to your own.

She learned that streets too were either Protestant or Catholic, that picture houses, while they might show the same films, had their religious allegiance. At first she found this obsession with religion, and the repeated attempts of the saved girls to give her tracts to read or entice her to meetings, just odd, or even funny, but soon it depressed her. So, too, did the relentlessly damp weather and the grim greyness of the streets. Everything was redbrick, but rain and smoke and winter gloom made Belfast more grey than red.

Even the prospect of Christmas, and a longer visit to the Braid, was marred by the knowledge that her job would end a few days before Christmas, when all the temporary girls would be laid off.

Still, there was the excitement of searching out suitable, and affordable, Christmas presents for the boys. Her stepmother, her aunts and Winnie were all to be the happy recipients of boxes of linen handkerchiefs which the girls in the factory were able to buy at a discount. But the boys were special, and Lily spent all her spare time trying to find suitable toys or books.

Just before Christmas there was good news, of a sort. Christmas Day was on a Sunday and the factory was closing from Friday to

Wednesday. On Friday morning the overseer of the folding room took Lily and another of the temporary girls aside and asked them if they would stay on after Christmas on a weekly basis, as the company had received additional orders.

It was one thing less to worry about, and lifted Lily's spirits higher as she set out for York Street station late on Friday afternoon. She had arranged to meet Winnie at the station and they were to travel home together. The station was crowded, and the train packed. There was no chance of a seat, and the two girls sat in the corridor on their suitcases. But by now nothing could worry them; they would have four full days together at the farm; it would be the longest time Lily had had to spend with her brothers since their father's death.

Their plan was to race from Ballymena station to the middle of the town and catch one of the Broughshane side-cars, though, with it being Christmas, they were not sure if they would be able to get on one. They joined the crush of people off the train at Ballymena and hurried through the barrier, where the first of several pleasant surprises awaited them.

Standing there, where he could not possibly miss them, was Winnie's Jim, nervously clutching his cloth cap, blushing and smiling away like mad. He knew who Lily was, for Winnie had told him all about her, but now he had to be introduced for the first time. What was he doing here, asked Winnie. He had a wee surprise for her he said, as they walked into the yard outside the front of the station.

The surprise was a handsome pony and trap, waiting patiently among a dozen others, but outshining them in the brightness of its paintwork and the stylishness of its pony. With matching style, Jim unlatched the door at the back of the trap and handed the two young ladies up the step and into the upholstered seats. Grasping the reins he settled himself into the driver's place at the rear and they set off through the streets of Ballymena and out the Broughshane road in something approaching splendour.

The trap, Jim soon admitted, was Lord Rathcavan's. A package had needed urgent delivery to an address in the town that afternoon, and no one could be found around the estate except Jim. When he had completed the delivery he realised the Belfast train would be arriving in ten minutes at most, and he knew Winnie would be on it. He said he couldn't resist waiting for her and taking her home in style; he would be able to drop them on the road at the end of the loanin and have the trap back at the estate in plenty of time.

It was a famous journey, clipping through the frosty evening with just a touch of moonlight. The well-sprung trap eased the ride over the rough stones of the country road and in less than an hour Jim had dropped them at the foot of the loanin – he dared not risk the pony and trap up the rough path, and anyway he was beginning to feel guilty about making so free with his employer's possessions, though he knew no one would mind him giving two young ladies a lift home at Christmas. Lily had enough sense to jump down first from the trap, grab her case and set off up the loanin, leaving the dark, deserted road to Jim and Winnie.

She went no more than a few yards, for the loanin was almost pitch black, and no one had come to meet them, as they were not expected for another hour at least. She had to wait for what seemed ages for Winnie; she could hear some squeals of excitement, and the quiet rumble of Jim's voice, and long intriguing periods of total silence. Then Winnie was springing lightly up to her, grabbing her free hand and almost dragging her up the loanin.

Jim had had more than one surprise. He had asked Winnie to marry him. Lily was sworn to secrecy, for it might be years yet before they could get married. But Jim had been writing to his cousin in New York and had been sent the addresses of several big estates and he was going to write to them. If he could find a position with a house attached, they could marry and go out to a new life in the new world.

"And you said yes", said Lily. "Heth and I did not," replied Winnie. "I told him I would have to think about it. I didn't want him thinking he just had to ask and I would come running. But of course I'll say yes when he has some definite word from America. If I said it now, he'd want to marry me next week, and we'd end up stuck round here for ever. No, it's America for me and Jim."

Lily had to laugh at Winnie's coolness, but she was delighted for her, and happy too that there was no immediate danger of Winnie disappearing out of her life, as so many others had done recently. She promised to keep the secret.

Their early arrival at the farm added surprise to the warmth of the welcome. There was a long explanation of why they were early, and a detailed description of the grand manner in which they had been conveyed from Ballymena station almost to the farm door. A degree of embroidery was required to place Jim and his trap at the station at the precise moment when their train had arrived, but the assurance that he had been delivering a package to the station and just happened to see them as he was unhitching the pony satisfied everyone, and drew a remark or two on the obliging nature of Jim.

Winnie clearly wanted Robert Hugh and his family to know as little as possible about Jim. The less the better, for then the less likely he was to be drawn in and made part of something that Winnie could not wait to be free of. Lily smiled to herself at Winnie's determination. Nor could she help thinking wryly that, just as Winnie had found the ticket out of Kellstown that she so eagerly wanted, she herself would have given almost anything to find a ticket in.

As they sat around the kitchen table there was another surprise to come, and to Lily it was the best news of all. There was a chance that her stepmother would be able to rent a house in Ballymena; if she got it, she would move in with the three boys, and she would want Lily to come and join them, to help mind the boys as Lizzie set about earning a living for them as a dressmaker. Robert Hugh had a friend called Davidson who worked as a builder in Ballymena, and he had asked him to keep an eye open for a house his sister might rent. Nothing was settled, but through Willy Davidson she had a half-promise from one landlord that if one of his houses fell vacant in the next half year, as he expected, then Lizzie could have it.

It was not clear exactly which house it might be, but it would be in the Moat Road, and, according to Lizzie, most of the houses the landlord owned there had three bedrooms. Some were even parlour houses, with a front room downstairs, considerably up-market from the standard kitchen house where you walked straight in off the street into the one main living room. Harryville School was just round the corner, which would mean the boys would have a five-minute walk to school, not the near hour-long hike that they now faced each day. And just around another corner an aunt – the sister of Robert Hugh's wife Jane – lived in a small rented house.

The few days passed like a dream for Lily. She had come happy that she would have those few days with the boys, and with her stepmother and Winnie and Kate, never expecting the great news that she might be able to join them, and leave Belfast and the handkerchief factory behind.

7   HARRYVILLE

It was another six months before she escaped from Belfast. There was no word from the landlord about the house in the Moat Road. Lily's job at the handkerchiefs was only part-time, and then only when there was a rush and word would be sent to her to come in. Sometimes this meant working all day Saturday, which made it impossible to travel to Kellstown. Her visits were much less frequent than she had expected.

Her aunts in Roden Street were kind enough, much more agreeable than the Campbells in Lurgan, and she saw Winnie every now and then, but she still felt desperately lonely. She kept returning in her mind to Crayford and the happy times there with all her friends and her father and stepmother. She treasured the photographs her stepmother had given her when they had hurriedly packed up their belongings in the house in Earlsfield Cottages, particularly the one taken in a studio in Dartford of her three young stepbrothers in 1920, three young faces staring solemnly at the camera, the youngest still with his childhood ringlets. She knew Lizzie still had the ringlets from all three boys, solemnly wrapped in tissue paper and kept as souvenirs.

The more she dwelt on these memories, the less she liked Belfast, the less she felt at home in Ireland, with its 'troubles' and its hatreds and suspicions, and with its army of preachers.

Then, at the end of May, a letter arrived from Lizzie saying the house would soon be vacant; she was to move in sometime in the second half of June, and she wanted Lily to come and help with the move and live with them. She had already been given some dressmaking commissions, and was working at home on clothing sent out to her from Ballymena. She would be very busy and it was essential that Lily should come the moment the word was sent.

The word came in the middle of June, and before the end of the month the little family was reunited in Number 19 Moat Road, Ballymena. The Moat Road was a long, unsurfaced street that curved upwards through Harryville, from near the bridge over the Braid river, following the line of the river, but rising sharply above it to the motte, the giant earthwork from which the street had taken its name, the spelling more accurately reflecting the Ballymena pronunciation of motte.

The terraced house gave directly onto the roadway, but it had a yard at the back, with a toilet, which, remarkably, had a proper flush lavatory in it, not the dry closet that was standard for most of the neighbouring houses. Downstairs it had two rooms and a scullery, and upstairs two bedrooms, the smaller just big enough to hold a double bed. The larger bedroom was to be shared by Lily, her stepmother and the Singer sewing machine which was going to have to pay most of the rent.

The smaller room was for the boys. They were well used to sleeping three to a bed, and soon settled on an arrangement whereby the two younger ones had their heads at the top, and Bobby, now growing rapidly, slept at the bottom, with his feet on, or under, the bolster. Nightly their bedtime prayers were supplemented by expressions of amazement and horror at the pong from the feet thus placed, a topic that never failed to send the two younger ones into paroxysms of laughter.

To Lily it was a palace. It was even smaller than Roden Street, but it was bright – the sun streamed in through the ever-open front door, down the hallway and into the kitchen. The yard at the back was whitewashed and cheerful, and behind the back wall the ground fell in a grassy slope down to the River Braid, beyond which rose the great trees of the Lord Waveney's demesne surrounding Ballymena Castle.

The next month was spent whitewashing and distempering. Lily was already well able to handle a whitewash brush, and now she acquired the additional skill of wallpaper hanging. Furniture was acquired; the loft at Kellstown yielded up two bedsteads and a kitchen table. Second hand furniture shops and an auction house provided the rest. Lizzie's Singer sewing machine was installed in the bigger room upstairs, well lighted by a window onto the street.

The Singer was crucial; it represented their only source of income, and now rent had to be paid, as well as the bills for groceries to feed five mouths, three of them belonging to energetic and rapidly growing boys. Lizzie already had some steady customers for her dressmaking, and now she set about winning more. Lily had to find a job. She was seventeen, and had had experience of factory work in the linen industry. Soon she was taken on as a packer by a laundry on the Larne Road, within walking distance of the Moat Road.

The three boys had all of July and the first half of August to make friends with their contemporaries in the Moat Road, to explore the delights of the motte and the wooded slopes that surrounded it and stretched down to the river, and beyond that to the demesne, and to steel themselves for their first encounters with the master of Harryville School, whose reputation went before him. The boys were now eight, seven and five, and there was no escape, not even for Hugh the youngest, from the terrors of education.

Meanwhile they rapidly established themselves in the Moat Road. Three brothers, so close in age, were a formidable unit. Anyone taking on one of them, took on all three. The mocking of their English accents stopped abruptly after the locals were sent sprawling in sharp encounters. Inspired by their father's exploits, all three were mad keen on football. At school in Crayford, Bobby, the eldest, had learnt something of the rules of the game and acquired the basic skills, which he soon passed on to the other two.

On the stony and either dusty or muddy slope of the Moat Road, the three brothers were a match for all-comers. When they first arrived they were allowed, as shy strangers, to play together on the same side when teams were picked. Soon they simply refused to be separated, and after that there was competition among the others to be on their team.

That summer the games of football were interrupted only by the occasional passage of a coal cart or other horse-drawn vehicle, and by the rare spectacle of a motor vehicle churning up the dust – or by the unavailability of a ball. No one in the Moat Road was well-off. Many families were very poor, and none had good money to waste on anything like a proper football. Every now and again the supply of assorted rubber balls, superannuated tennis balls and spheres of unsure origin would run out, and the footballers of the Moat Road had to resort to a tightly tied bundle of newspaper or some other improvisation.

About half the men were unemployed, and most of them had run out of the new insurance cover for the unemployed and were dependant on the local Board of Guardians for outdoor relief. In many households the only wage-earners were the wives and daughters, for there was a steady demand for female workers in the many linen factories around the town.

There was poverty, but not the grinding deprivation of an industrial slum, for Ballymena was a country town, and almost every family in the Moat Road had close relatives farming in the neighbourhood, who regularly brought in eggs and butter, and the occasional fowl for boiling. The farms also offered some seasonal work for unemployed men, saving the hay in early summer, later harvesting the corn, pulling flax or cutting turf.

Nor were the unemployed idle; some men took a great interest in racing pigeons, and the back yards of many houses had white-painted wooden lofts perched on their walls. Others were handymen of one sort or another, getting odd jobs here and there in the town.

Just across the road from Number 19, Mr. Wright had set himself up as a carter when his job at the mill disappeared. His farming relatives had let him have a small two-wheeled cart, and had sold him, at a knock-down price, a very small and very venerable horse. He was soon busy enough delivering bits of furniture for the auction-rooms, and transporting this and that around the town. In the evening the cart rested, shafts high in the air, on the roadway outside his house, and the horse was stabled in his back yard.

Hugh, the youngest of Lily's brothers, had soon made friends with young Billy Wright, and spent almost as much time in the Wrights' as he did at home. While, like the rest of the family, he thought Number 19 was great, the Wrights house had something extra. "Mammy, mammy, guess what's in Billy's kitchen?" he had shouted dashing into Number 19 at teatime one evening in their first month in the house.

"Now what could it be?" Lizzie had replied "I bet it's a cat, or maybe a ferret." "Nothing silly like that," interrupted Hugh, "It's a horse." "You mean a clothes horse for the nappies and the washing," said Lizzie. "Don't be stupid. It's a real horse, a real big horse".

And so it was, for Mr. Wright lived in a terrace house with no way into the backyard except through his own kitchen. He could leave the cart in the road all night, but not the horse, so each evening and morning the horse ambled through the kitchen on his way to and from its shed in the yard. Hugh had been paying his first visit to the Wrights' kitchen at the horse's knocking-off time, and had had the shock of his life when Billy's father had led the horse into the kitchen, pausing to pick up a bucket of water. Hugh had shot out of the house and dashed across the street bursting with this tremendous item of news, that the Wrights had a horse in their kitchen. There had been nothing like this in Crayford.

With the family reunited, together in their own small but clean and bright house, the boys adapted easily to life in Ballymena. The camaraderie of the street merged quickly into the solidarity of attendance at Harryville school and organised resistance to the menaces of the Master. In a few months they were part of a community, and had regained much of the happiness that had been wrenched away from the by their father's sudden death.

Their English accents began to weaken, and soon all three were picking up the distinct tones of Ballymena-Scots and its rich vocabulary of dialect words. Frequent weekends and holidays back at the foot of Slemish, where the dialect was markedly richer than in the streets of Ballymena, speeded their linguistic reorientation. With the English accents all but gone, there was nothing left of their accidental English birth. They were Ballymena men, though with a lingering loyalty to Lurgan's football team, Glenavon, for whom their father and uncles had played.

For Lily it was different; Crayford had been her golden age. She guarded her English accent, and tried not to slip into the style of her workmates or, indeed, of her stepmother, who had never really lost her accent while in England, and who now had reverted entirely to the manner of speech in which she had been reared near Slemish. But Lily clung to her English accent as if it were a lifeline to her very Englishness. As she kept reminding herself, and her friends, she had been born there, had gone to school there, and all her best friends were there. She was English.

She wrote regularly to three or four friends in Crayford, and eagerly awaited their replies with their accounts of what was happening in their world, her world, the real world. Their letters meant she could continue to live in that world, and stay aloof from Ballymena, Northern Ireland, strange accents and endless gospel preachers. Life at home, inside Number 19 Moat Road, was different, for everything there had been part of Crayford – Lizzie, her brothers, the dressmaking, even some pictures and photographs of Crayford that she had hung on the walls. At home she was happier than she could ever have imagined after her father's death.

But a pretty seventeen year-old girl, now almost 18, could not exist only within her immediate family, no matter how devoted they all were. Other avenues inevitably opened. Winnie became a regular visitor, sometimes staying overnight and sharing Lily's bed. Jim too was a frequent visitor and Number 19 became a regular trysting spot for the two. There was no word of the job with the house in America, and they were now talking of getting married in Ballymena and going out after that. Through Winnie, Lily made other friends in Ballymena, and made regular trips to the picture houses to renew acquaintance with Chaplin, Arbuckle and others.

The Moat Road had another unexpected bonus. The aunt, Minnie Currie, who lived nearby was a music-teacher. She was unmarried, and took a stream of students in her own house. The front room had a piano, and was reserved for lessons. The back room had a harmonium. The aunt soon discovered Lily's passion for music, and her great desire to learn to play the piano, and was delighted to give occasional lessons. Lily was an eager pupil, and happily pedalled away at the harmonium when she got the chance. It was clear she had a good ear for music, and though the lessons were casual and infrequent, and Lily had no instrument at home on which to practise, she began to grasp the rudiments of piano playing.

The family attended West Church, one of Ballymena's several Presbyterian congregations. This meant morning and evening service on Sundays, and Sunday School for the boys. Lily was relieved to be too old for Sunday School. She took church going as a normal part of life, and never resented the time spent at West Church, nor even the length of the sermons. Anything less than 40 minutes and the congregation would have felt short-changed. But she resisted all suggestions that she should teach in Sunday School or join the choir.

She joined in church socials, gatherings held in the church hall for the younger members of the congregation, and consisting of games, singsongs and a large supper, but never dancing. Badminton was another activity in the church hall, and she once or twice was persuaded to try that. One great attraction of the church hall was that it had a piano. It was an elderly upright, standing unused except when needed for games or singsongs, and Lily was able to slip away from her friends and sit at the piano, picking out the simple pieces she had learned from Minnie Currie.

Lily, had she been asked, would have said that morning and evening services at West church – every Sunday without fail – were ample spiritual exercise for a girl of her age, but now her new friends were urging and expecting her to accompany them to special meetings and missions. A new regular non-denominational Sunday evening meeting had begun in a hall in the town and was drawing crowds of young people from many of the established churches.

Sunday evening after church had long been the social highlight of the week for the God-fearing working-class young of Ballymena. Summer and winter they would walk out in droves along the roads into the country, with ample opportunity for much joking and teasing and matchmaking. Particular groups of friends would return to one or other of their houses for a supper of tea and a vast array of sandwiches and fancy cakes.

The new after-church meeting seriously interfered with this socialising, but it did not stop it. It meant the walk was later and shorter. But for Lily it also meant that if she wanted to go on the walk, she had to embrace an additional hour and a quarter of worship, exhortation and that apparently most desirable of activities, fellowship. Added pressure on her to attend came from the cheerful enthusiasm of her brothers to add this final church attendance to their Sunday already crowded with Sunday School in addition to morning and evening service.

Their enthusiasm stemmed more from the fact that they and their many pals from Harryville took over the back gallery of the hall and spent most of the service inflicting subtle tortures on each other, in circumstances that allowed neither vocal expression of pain nor robust retaliation. When they were not doing that, they were flicking small pellets of paper, sometimes, it must be admitted, manufactured from pages detached from their hymn books, over the edge of the gallery and onto selected targets down below.

A weekend break at Slemish meant a welcome reduction in the devotional regime, for even Presbyterian farmers could find time for only one long round trip to hear one long sermon each Sunday. The MacMasters attended morning service only. Unless, of course, one of Robert Hugh's occasional loft meetings was on. Then the corn loft above the byre would be swept clean, the pulpit erected and the harmonium dusted down.

A congregation of family and neighbours would sing psalms and hymns, and hear the word of God expounded, at some length, by the visiting missioner, who always, despite the small and highly select nature of his congregation, was clearly convinced that he had in front of him some of the most stalwart and resolute sinners in the entire county, and that he was therefore presented with a challenge and an opportunity that might never comes his way again, or theirs, as he kept reminding them.

Lily, looking around the twenty or so faces in the loft, reckoned that most of them, if not all, were already saved, and that she alone must be the cause of the heavy burden on the preacher's heart, a realization that greatly added to her already considerable discomfort. Occasionally Winnie would be with her, and her unsaved solidarity provided much appreciated immoral support. Kate and Mary Wallace, who were becoming her inseparable companions on visits to Kellstown, always braved the plank bridge to come to the loft meetings, but Lily was never sure whether this was due to spiritual zeal, or the desire for company.

Fortunately for Lily, the missioners were usually accommodated in the farmhouse, which meant there was no room for Lily or her stepmother, so visits to the farm rarely coincided with the high season for preaching.

Another form of religious exercise for Lily and her brothers, and this one did amount almost to torture, was the tent mission. It was Winnie who, rather surprisingly, introduced Lily to the tent mission. A large tent or marquee, though that term was never used, had been erected in the corner of a field on the Broughshane Road on the outskirts of Ballymena, big enough to hold a hundred people or more. It was already filling up one early June evening when Winnie and Lily slipped in. A flat wooden platform stood at one end, rising to about one foot above the grass. There was a harmonium to one side, and the congregation sat on backless wooden benches. Tent missions were held at carefully determined times of the year. They could not be in winter, because the cold would be too intense and the tent might be blown away, nor could they coincide with periods of high activity on the farms. So they tended to be in late spring or early summer, before the haymaking season, or in autumn, after the harvest had been saved.

The exquisite nature of the torture of the tent mission, not just for Lily and her brothers but for all the younger people bullied, persuaded or otherwise pressured into attending, stemmed from the thinness of the tent walls. Sitting imprisoned inside on a lovely May or June evening, every delightful sound from the free world outside was excruciatingly audible. Bird-song, the sounds of farm animals, the occasional cheery greeting of passers-by on the road, odd snatches of conversation – a never ending flow of evidence that life with all its outdoor pleasures was racing ahead without them - penetrated the canvas of the tent. Inside the pervading and unforgettable smell of damp grass trampled underfoot spelt decay.

In autumn it was not so bad; on dull evenings the light would be fading outside, and inside the bright glow and hissing of the paraffin lamps gave an air of warmth and even cheerfulness. Moreover, some of the preachers were well aware that their audience was not entirely captive, and that many of their younger listeners would bolt at the first opportunity if the strain became too great. So, as with the great Nicholson himself, hell fire and damnation often came with a leavening of comedy.

Sermons were laced with jokes and stories; the preacher and his fast-pedalling harmonium player cum soloist might operate as a double act, one telling tales out of school about the other and the digs they were staying in, about how the soloist, with his big brown eyes and soft voice, always got three sausages instead of two from the landlady at breakfast, always had the room with the feather bed while the preacher slept on straw. Preachers could sometimes make themselves the butts of their own jokes; an exceptionally long sermon might be ended with the preacher looking at his watch, sighing, and remarking, "As the Buckna man might say, yin or twa o those would fair shorten the winter."

The Almighty himself was accorded at least a sardonic sense of humour, as in the Ballymena preacher's account of the Last Judgement, when the folks from the Braid confronted Jehovah and sought to escape damnation with a plea of ignorance;

"Lord, wa didna ken, wa didna ken," they cried. And the Lord looked down in his infinite mercy and replied "Wall ye ken the noo, ye ken the noo.'".

When Lily heard that story at that first mission, she did not laugh; it portrayed just too accurately the God of her new homeland.

But most of her new friends had no such misgivings. Fearless preachers, particularly if they could make their congregations laugh before they made them tremble, were enormously popular, and Lily found herself tagging along with her friends to mission after mission. Not all her friends were saved; some, like Winnie, had no doubt that, one day, they would be, but meanwhile were happy enough outside the fold, and actually enjoyed the thrill of being the object of thundering appeals and menaces at gospel meeting after meeting.

So church services and missions, and talk of salvation and damnation, became part of Lily's life on the Moat Road. But it was part of the background, not the foreground. That was occupied by the immediate family, and by the pleasant home. Her stepmother was finding plenty of work, Lily was content enough with her job at the laundry, and the boys were blissfully happy.

They had the open ground behind the houses that ran down to the millrace and the river Braid, or the Braid water as everyone called it. A series of precarious foot and hand holes in the stone facing of the wall that held the sluice gate feeding the millrace meant they had access to the grounds of Ballymena Castle on the other side of the river. The Castle, a gloomy 19th century Scots Baronial pile, was unoccupied, and the gardeners had long given up trying to keep the boys from Harryville at bay.

There was also the dream playground of the motte, a double earthwork right alongside the top of the Moat Road. Beyond the motte the ground dropped precipitously through trees to the river at its wide point close to the weir, and beyond the river was the romantic tower of Ballymena Castle. Hours were spent, summer and winter, in defending the motte against an endless variety of red Indians, black savages, and brutal Huns.

The raucous happiness of the three young boys was a joy to their older sister. As Lizzie became busier and busier at her dressmaking, and was often away from Number 19 attending customers in their homes, Lily took an ever greater share in the upbringing of the boys. She made most of their clothes, leaving their mother free to work on profitable orders. She made most of their meals, rushing home at dinner time in the middle of the day, and again after work to prepare the tea.

She helped them with their schoolwork. Even though the concept of homework for public elementary schoolboys had not then reached Harryville, Lily made them read aloud, and go through their spellings and tables. At school at Crayford she had shone at verse-speaking, and had often been brought to the front of the class to recite. At home these poems had frequently replaced bedtime stories for the three brothers, and they still loved to hear *Abou Bin Adhem may his tribe increase, awoke one night from a deep dream of peace...* or *Mary call the cattle home, across the sands of Dee...*

It was clear that all three were bright children and would have little serious problem with schoolwork. Lily was determined, and had persuaded her stepmother to be of the same mind, that they would all go on to the Technical School, and learn a trade instead of heading straight for a job in the mill at the age of 14.

The bond between sister and stepbrothers became ever closer. For Lily, though she would never have thought so, it was a way of preserving her world of Crayford and England. Her work at the laundry, and the growing friendships with girls there and at church, her stepmother's rapid embracing of her family and friends in Ballymena, her brothers' immersion in all things Ballymena, and above all the inescapable menace of the preachers and their gloomy message, made Lily feel at times that she was drowning in a sea of Irishness, or to be more precise a lint dam of Ballymena Presbyterianism.

Her regular, and very good, renditions of *Abou Bin Adhem,* and *Mary call the Cattle Home,* always in her very best English accent – except when she made the brothers laugh with her broken English version of the Lalliments' attempts at 'Maree call de cattle home across de sands of Dee..' – were part of her mainly unconscious, but sometimes deliberate, determination to be, and remain, different. So, too, was her totally deliberate refusal to allow herself to slip into the Ballymena accent. As the years passed, her English accent modified but never to the point of disappearance – and never in the direction of Ballymena-Scots.

8 DECISION TIME

Time flew; the boys were growing up, her stepmother was doing well at the dressmaking, and between her income and Lily's wage the little family at 19 Moat Road steered clear of poverty and kept a reasonably firm grip on that quality most highly-desired on the Moat Road – respectability.

Respectability consisted of two key elements. The first was sobriety; any suggestion that the head of the household drank was a threat to respectability, while public drunkenness, such as rolling home roaring or singing late at night, meant instant loss of respectability.

The second was not being 'poor'; poor people were not respectable. To be really poor was not just to be unemployed or heavily in debt, it was to be poor in a much more profound sense, to be slovenly, lazy, to have the house dirty and the children unwashed. To Lizzie McMaster the key test was the state of the kitchen sink; anyone who 'kept a dirty sink', that is one permanently clogged with tea leaves and scraps of food, was dismissed as 'poor'. As the kitchen was the room where all visitors were entertained to cups of tea, the kitchen sink was visible to all callers.

As the 1920s progressed, not a few families in the Moat Road slipped down and off the ladder of respectability, and were 'poor'. Lily had a horror of being poor, and even of poor people themselves. She was determined that neither she nor her brothers would ever be poor.

She was, by now, not just pretty, but strikingly beautiful, slim with wavy light brown hair. Her English accent made her stand out even more from the cheerful circle of friends that surrounded her, and she was not short of admirers, though few had the temerity to ask her out, fearing her grand accent and her sharp temper.

One who was beginning to worship her from a distance, and in silence, was Jack Kennedy. He was one of a family of nine, and, aged 18 when he met Lily in early 1925, was a year younger than her. He was working in a chemist's shop, and attending classes at the Technical School with the aim of becoming a pharmacist. They met at a church social in West Church which the Kennedys also attended. The Kennedys were regular attenders, too, at the Sunday night after-church meetings for young people. Jack's older sister Ena was Lily's age, and one of his younger brothers, Willy, was just a year or two older than Bobby, and another, Alfie was one year younger. As Lily and Ena became friends, a small network of friendships began to develop between the two families.

The Kennedys lived in a terrace house on Waveney Avenue in the heart of Ballymena, just across the river from Harryville Bridge. Robert Kennedy had moved his large and still growing family from Cullybackey into the town a few years earlier, when he had found a job as a bread-server with the town's main bakery. A dour man at the best of times, he had become even dourer following his conversion at one of W P Nicholson's missions in Ballymena in 1923. He had arrived home and ordered his older sons to leave the Orange Order, have nothing to do with the Freemasons, and stop playing football. The pictures, dancing and smoking were all banned.

His wife Jane, a saintly, God-fearing woman, smiled and told her children to obey their father. It was something she herself had learned to do over many years, to the extent that that particular duty now eclipsed those others she had undertaken – to love and honour. Robert's conversion had one material benefit to it; he became even more careful in his handling of money, and more assiduous in his devotion to work. Bread servers were not well paid, in fact they were not paid at all, but worked under a contract with the bakery, effectively buying their daily cartload at cost and depending on their own sales to make a profit.

Robert worked long hours and built up his rounds. Like other breadmen he used his cart and his contacts to develop sidelines, and by the mid-1920s was well able to support his large family, and to put aside some savings. In part he was driven by fear of poverty, remembering how hard times were in the cottage at Dunnygarron outside Cullybackey where he himself had grown up as part of a large family.

His grandfather had crossed to County Antrim from Ayreshire sometime in the first decades of the 19th century, under circumstances which were unclear and probably unsavoury. He had found work as a farm labourer, and died as such, leaving no land to his own sons. His eldest son, Robert's father, had in turn worked as a labourer, but had managed to acquire a cottage and a smallholding as tenant of the local big house landlord. After the Land Act of 1903 he had purchased the holding, but continued to work as a labourer.

Robert had no taste for farm labouring, and found work as a carter in Cullybackey, changing to breadserving for a local bakery before moving to Ballymena. By 1920 he was well established; a photograph of that year shows him as a highly respectable *pater familias* surrounded by his wife and nine children, aged from one to 18, all well-dressed and looking proudly if not defiantly respectable.

A sharp reminder of the family's precarious status, however, came less than two year's later. Hubert, the second son, lost his job in a linen mill, and had to go on Outdoor Relief, paid at the discretion of the Ballymena Board of Guardians. (The eldest son, Robert, known as Bertie, had joined the Flying Corps in 1918, and had stayed on in the Army.) One Saturday in the summer of 1922, Hubert paid his sixpence and went on a half-day excursion on the train to Portrush. While strolling around that bracing resort he had the misfortune to be recognised by a member of the Board of Guardians, who was also taking advantage of the sixpenny excursion.

When Hubert appeared before the Board the following week to have his relief extended, he was told that the Ballymena Board of Guardians had better things to do with its money than subsidise excursions to the seaside, and he was struck off. Hubert immediately presented himself at the Wellington Street office of Wilson McKeown, agent for emigration to the USA, Canada, South and East Africa, Australia and New Zealand, and signed up for an assisted passage to New Zealand, which, he was assured, was the furthest place from Ballymena on offer.

Within months Hubert had gone, and his father had been saved at Nicholson's meeting; a tight ring of religious and financial rectitude was now fastened round the remaining members of the Kennedy family.

Lily's friendship with Ena meant she was a regular visitor to the Kennedy house, and Bobby soon struck up close ties with both Willy and Alfie. As the three Cuthbert brothers were still inseparable, Alec and Hugh usually tagged along. Lily's visits would have been more frequent had it not been for an instinctive dislike of the father of the house; she found him gruff and ill-tempered, on top of which she could not understand a word he said, for his Cullybackey accent was made even more incomprehensible by a slight defect which made him sound as if his voice was coming, not from his mouth, but from somewhere south of his Adam's Apple.

The visits continued because the father was offset by the mother. Jane Kennedy was a gentle lady who took immediately to the strange, lovely, English-accented, young girl her family had befriended. She saw too, long before Lily did, that her young son Jack was badly smitten, and she could think of nothing she would like more than that the two might, some day, become a pair.

Friendship with the Kennedys had for Lily, however, one major drawback. They were fierce churchgoers and attenders at missions. This was partly at the dictate of their stern father, but their mother was also deeply religious. Her cousin, Jim McWhirter, was beginning to make a name for himself as one of the evangelistic band George Jeffreys had built at the heart of the Elim movement. Mrs Kennedy, despite her husband's frowning disapproval, was a frequent attender at Sunday evening services in the Elim Tabernacle that had opened in the town.

For the Kennedys there was no question of going to the pictures or dances; their father would not allow it, and for the girls the decree was absolute. Church socials were tolerated with reluctance, on account of the church connection, but permission to attend was subject to a strict curfew, which none of the children would dare infringe. The term social did not mean, as the name might suggest, some sort of party, for most of the time was taken up by what were called 'devotional exercises', including a lengthy address from a visiting speaker. But they always started with a vast tea - a good spread which left plenty of time for socialising before limbering up with the devotional exercises.

The faithful to be found at Christian Endeavour socials were unlikely to share Lily's continuing enthusiasm for the pictures. Her only partner in pursuit of the company of Charlie Chaplin and his worldy like was Winnie, though she was now spending nearly all her spare time in Belfast in the company of Jim. Winnie had another distraction in Belfast; Mary Wallace, at the age of 18, had come to the city also to train as a nurse, and the two became inseparable friends.

In 1923 Jim had joined the B-Specials, the auxiliary police service that had been set up at the time of the troubled origin of Northern Ireland, and whose part-time members mounted regular patrols around the countryside. The workers at the Rathcavan estate had been encouraged to sign on as reservists, and Jim had jumped at the chance to earn some extra money to add to his savings, and possibly bring closer the day he would marry Winnie. He also had an elder brother in Canada who was a policeman in Toronto. As no progress seemed forthcoming on Jim's cousin's plans to find a gamekeeper's job for Jim with a house in New York State, he was now thinking of Canada as an option, and perhaps a job with the police there.

Winnie encouraged him. Times were now quiet in the Ulster countryside, particularly around Ballymena, and Winnie was in little danger of losing her young man to a sniper's bullet. Neither had she any real worries when Jim had the chance to enlist full time as a Special Constable and leave his post as a gamekeeper. It was a real bonus when he was posted to Belfast, and he and Winnie spent most of their spare time together, far from the prying eyes and reporting tongues of Ballymena and the Braid.

But she was beginning to lose patience with Jim and his cautious approach to marriage. She was now in her twenties, and that was old enough to be getting married. As she confided to Lily on a rare visit to 19 Moat Road early in 1925, she would be married before the year was out.

And so she was, if only just. Number 19 saw very little of her during the year. She still wrote to Lily, but the overnight visits ceased entirely, and Lily was thrown for companionship more and more on her local friends, particularly the Kennedys.

Winnie's letters were full of her life as a nurse in the new Royal Victoria Hospital, and of Jim, tall handsome Jim in his black uniform, and his boisterous friends in his platoon and their round of night patrols and guard duty. But there was no mention of wedding plans. As autumn drew on, the letters became shorter and less frequent.

It was a real surprise then, when Winnie arrived late one Friday evening without warning at Number 19. Lizzie and the family welcomed her as warmly as ever, established immediately that she would stay until Sunday evening, and set about preparing as celebratory a supper as they could devise. It was a happy evening, with the three boys bombarding Winnie with questions about Belfast, and about Jim and the Specials, and Lily and Lizzie wanting to hear everything about life in the hospital.

Winnie in her turn gave them a great account of life in the city, and told them Jim had heard again from his brother in Toronto, and now that Jim was a full-time policeman there was a real chance he could get a job on the Toronto police and they would at last be going to Canada.

Only Lily noticed that Winnie seemed a bit quieter than usual, as if her mind was elsewhere, and not just on Canada, or on Jim back in his barracks in Belfast. She wondered why Winnie was not going out to the Braid to visit her uncle and aunt and the farm at Kellstown. She helped Winnie make up the make-shift bed in the front room that was used for visitors, and stayed for a few minutes to see that Winnie was comfortably tucked in. She suggested that the pair of them might take the new bus service out to Broughshane the next afternoon and take a look at Slemish and have tea at Kellstown.

There was no reply. Then a loud sob, and suddenly Winnie was weeping into her pillow.

"I couldn't face my Uncle Robert and all that crowd. I daren't tell him, and I know if he got one look at my face he would know."

"Know what? What are you talking about? Do you mean going to America?"

"No, not that. I think he knows I'm pregnant."

"But you're not. How could he be so silly?"

"I think I am. In fact I know I am. I missed in September, and again last month and this. I was so frightened I said nothing to Jim, but I made him promise me we would get married as soon as possible. And now we'll just have to."

"But how can you be pregnant? You're not married and you're not living with Jim, and Jim's not like that. Are you really going to have a baby?"

"Oh Lily, you're a great wee innocent. It's away far too easy to have a baby. The easiest thing in the world, and I think Jim and I have just managed it, even though we thought we were being very careful. I have told no one, though Jim guessed soon enough, and feels terrible. He's sure Robert Hugh will be after him with a pitchfork. I've told nobody except you. I think the baby won't be born until June, and by that time we might be in America. So not a word to anyone, ever."

Lily had not been reared on a farm, and lacked the easy familiarity with the mechanics of reproduction acquired by someone like Winnie. But like any young girl of almost 20 she knew the basics from a theoretical point of view, and was genuinely shocked when she thought what Winnie and Jim had been up to, to bring about Winnie's current state. Truth to tell, she was more shocked at strong, shy and gentle Jim than at Winnie, who had always been headstrong and rebellious.

Winnie had stopped crying and only an occasional sob now punctuated her tale of woe.

"I know what they will all be saying and thinking, that I am turning out like my mother. Every bit as bad as her, and bringing disgrace on the family all over again. Robert Hugh wouldn't even have to say it, it would be all over his stupid face. And, do you know Lily, he's right isn't he? How could I be so stupid?"

The girl now sobbing into the pillow seemed neither headstrong nor rebellious; she was fearfully embarrassed at her predicament, but she was even more angry with herself, and genuinely remorseful that she had proved her Uncle Robert right, that she had gone to the bad as he had always predicted she would. What would her grandmother have thought of her? But no one would know; she would defy them all and be married properly, just as she and Jim had long intended. And then it would be America.

Winnie knew, though she could not bring herself to admit this, even to Lily, that Robert Hugh had always found her somehow an embarrassment. He had never treated her like any of his other nephews and nieces, and she was not going to go to him now to ask for his help with the wedding. She told Lily she had thought of getting married in Belfast, but that would be difficult, and would look like running away. No, she said, they had hopes of persuading the minister in Broughshane, where Jim had belonged to the congregation, to marry them quietly as soon as possible.

She promised to let Lily know when it was to be, but there was no talk of bridesmaids, or wedding gowns, and Lily was sworn not to tell Lizzie. Much as she liked her, Winnie did not want any McMaster to know.

Lily thought it was wonderful that Winnie and Jim were to be married. She was very happy for her friend, but at the same time more than a little upset at the circumstances. She had long supposed that she would be Winnie's bridesmaid, but there was no such invitation. Winnie had become a rather special friend; they had both felt a common bond from the day they had found out that while one had no father, the other had no mother. They both felt different, set apart somehow from their friends and contemporaries – Lily because she was English, Winnie because she was illegitimate, though such a word was never used by her nor spoken in her presence.

But she was old enough now to know that the reason she had no father was that her father had never married her mother. Nor would anyone tell her who her father was, so she really had no father. That was why her name was McMaster, even though it was her mother, not her father, who was McMaster. She had taken to Lily at first because Lily's mother was dead, and she liked her even better when Lily's father married her favourite aunt, and Lily became a ready-made cousin. Winnie's mother had eventually married a tram driver she had met while nursing in Belfast, and had had a son and a daughter – step-brother and sister to Winnie – and her life was now built around them. There was never any question of bringing Winnie back into her family.

Lily and Winnie told each other secrets they would have told no one else. They talked about boy friends, and about God and religion. They laughed together at things too sacred to mention to anyone else. Now Lily realised that she was going to lose Winnie. Once married to Jim, Winnie would certainly still be a special friend, but things would be different. Lily knew just how determined Winnie was to leave Ireland and go to America, and nothing would stop her now.

Thinking of Winnie as a married woman reminded Lily that she herself was no longer a girl. She would be 20 by the time of Winnie's wedding. She had been sixteen when her father died, and a very young sixteen, living happily within a close family and almost entirely occupied with her parents and her three young brothers and her girl-friends in what was little more than a quiet English village.

When she had had to leave Crayford almost immediately, she had believed it would be just for a short time, that somehow or other things would work out, and she would be back with Lucy and Carrie and the others. The sudden separation from her stepmother and brothers, the unhappy time with her Campbell relatives in Lurgan, the flight from Lurgan and the job in Belfast had been one long nightmare.

Now she was recovering from that nightmare to find that she had grown up, and that some time soon, like Winnie, she would be expected to marry and settle down. That would be in Ballymena; there was no way out, no route that could lead back to Crayford.

In fact she already had settled down. Winnie often talked about her future in America, with her own children around her. Lily, though she was only slowly and dimly realising it, already had 'settled down'. She was a bread-winner – her small wage was much less than the money earned by her stepmother's dressmaking, but it was an essential part of the household income, and the only part that came in a regular pay-packet. She never thought of it as her own; its entire contents were handed over each week to her stepmother, and Lily got some back as spending money, but had to ask for extra amounts to buy clothes or pay for outings.

She had also become a parent, almost without knowing it. Because her stepmother was so busy earning an income, and often had to go to clients' homes out of working hours, Lily was often mother to her three young brothers. The youngest was not yet five when his father died and the small family returned to Ireland; the oldest had then been nine. She worried about them when they were out too long playing by the river; she put them to bed more often than their mother.

All daughters in working class homes did their large share of the housework, and older daughters in large families had to undertake much of the rearing of younger brothers and sisters. But that was the inevitable lot of daughters; it was what being part of a family meant, and it would soon be over anyway. Daughters dreamt of the day when they would marry, leave home and do their own housework and have their own children.

Lily had no such dreams. From the age of sixteen on she had looked on her three young brothers as her own children, and the housework she did was not helping her stepmother, it was her own housework. As she left her teens and entered her twenties she had no dreams of marrying and leaving home. With three young boys to be reared and with her stepmother busy earning money to keep them, not only could there be no question of that, but no such thought ever entered Lily's head. She wanted nothing more than to be at home with her brothers.

The two girls talked long into the night. Winnie, tying to put her own troubles aside for the moment, wanted to know about Lily's boy friends, and was she looking forward to getting married. It was only after she had laughingly dismissed any such notion that Lily herself began to think seriously, for the first time, about her future.

For three years the home at Number 19, and the three brothers, had been Lily's lifeline to the real world of her girlhood. That had been her escape from the smothering embrace of Ireland, and of Ballymena in particular. But Ballymena, she now saw, had invaded Number 19 and largely taken it over. Her stepmother and her brothers knew only one real world, and it was the one with the Moat Road at its centre. Crayford had been a short interlude, now largely forgotten by all of them except Lily.

Winnie was full of plans for the future. She and Jim would be in America one day, and that day was not some distant date, but as soon as they could arrange it. Jim's brother in Canada was urging them to come out to him, where he was sure Jim's service as a full-time policeman would help him secure a place with the police there. This would be their last Christmas in Ireland.

But Winnie had been talking of America for three years, and now she was getting married and having a baby. Was it all talk? Did Winnie and Jim really have a choice? Could they decide themselves to change everything and start a new life? Lily knew that people emigrated all the time. She knew some families in the Moat Road who had gone to Canada or Australia, and many others had a son who, like Hubert Kennedy, had left Ireland for some distant colony.

She had never met Hubert, for he had gone to New Zealand before she had known the Kennedys, but she knew about him. The other Kennedys talked about his latest moves and his frequent changes of job. But over time his name cropped up less and less. He had a new life; he was gone from theirs. He was a memory from the past, like someone who had died.

Yet, Lily thought, he had not died. He had simply decided himself to go to New Zealand. No one had forced him. Could people really make decisions like that and change everything? Everything in Lily's life had been changed often enough – when her mother had died and she had been sent to Lurgan, when her father had remarried and taken her to Crayford, when he had died and she had been sent back to Lurgan. Yet in all these earthquakes in her life, Lily had had no say; no one had asked her what she wanted to do. All the decisions had been taken for her.

Then she remembered her flight from Lurgan to Belfast. That had been her decision, and it had changed her life for the better. Would she now be living happily with her brothers and stepmother if she had not caught the train that morning from Lurgan to Belfast? With a little thrill of excitement she realised she really had changed her life by her own decision. It might have happened anyway after a year or two, and Ballymena was only 30 miles from Lurgan, and she was still with her own family. But she had helped make it happen. Yes, Winnie was right; she would soon be in America, because that was her decision.

One day she herself might make an important decision like that, but for the present she was content. The boys were growing up, but the youngest was still barely nine; her stepmother, to Lily's relief and some surprise, showed no interest in re-marrying, though she was still in her forties, and was very popular. She was what was termed a great laugh, always ready for a joke and an exchange of repartee. It was only when she thought about it that Lily realised no man would want to marry a widow with not just three young sons, but a stepdaughter too.

The world of Number 19 was safe for a while yet.

9   RAISED HANDS

Winnie and Jim Greer were married on the morning of Christmas Eve 1925 in Second Broughshane Presbyterian Church. It was a quiet wedding; Mary Wallace, who had long been privy to Winnie's secret, stood witness, alongside one of Jim's friends. Robert Hugh and his wife Jane were there, and Winnie's Aunt Lizzie and one or two relatives and neighbours. Winnie had been talked out of her determination not to tell her relatives at Kellstown about the wedding or invite them to it.

In the end, they were told at least part of the story. Winnie said she and Jim were going to Canada, and wanted to be married before they left. It was easier to travel as a couple, and as Jim might be offered a post as a policeman in Toronto any time now, they had to get married as quickly as possible. No mention was made of the most common reason for quick marriages in the Antrim countryside.

Lily was not at the service. She had gone out to Kellstown to help prepare the meal for the wedding party, for Robert Hugh had insisted that they would all come back to the farm. He had no doubt that Winnie was pregnant, and that was the sole reason for the quick wedding on the most unlikely day of the year – Christmas Eve. But he had asked no questions and made no insinuations. Winnie was no favourite, but he was not totally insensitive to her circumstances, and at times felt sorry enough for the young girl who had no real home, no father, and almost no mother. And he was certainly not going to give the neighbours any more grounds for gossip than they already had.

Four traps were enough to take the whole group the few miles up from Broughshane to Kellstown. Lily, with the help of Robert Hugh's young daughter Minnie, a cheerful seven-year old, had laid out a big table in the middle of the kitchen, added some decorations, and made sure the turf fire was blazing in the hearth to welcome the party after its chilly ride.

The warm kitchen and the ready conversation took the chill out of the atmosphere. Robert Hugh, in an extended grace, prayed for the blessing of God on the marriage, and on the future life of the young couple, wherever they might pass it. He then read Psalm 127, beginning 'Except the Lord build the house, they labour in vain that build it...' which he had always liked, and which he felt was most appropriate for a young couple, whom he suspected of being no better than they ought.

He read it, as ever, in a low rapid mumble which added no significance whatever to the injunction that 'Lo, children are an heritage of the Lord, and the fruit of the womb is his reward...' though, had he looked up, he would have seen Winnie blush bright red as he did. The Psalm ended the serious business, and thereafter was a hubbub of conversation, reminiscence and joking, until the bridal couple departed in a trap driven by Jim's friend and best man, bound for Ballymena station, and a train to Portrush for the short honeymoon. Both were due back on duty in Belfast immediately after the Christmas break.

It was an odd Christmas Day in the Moat Road. The three boys, who had never been to a wedding, first wanted to know all about it, but then lost interest entirely as they opened their presents. Lily and her stepmother had talked about Winnie and Jim for weeks, and had sat up late the previous night going over the events of the day, and the tiny, lonely wedding with so many missing guests. There was so much that could not be said in front of the boys.

In February, Winnie lost her job. She had not told the hospital she was getting married, or that she was pregnant, and when both facts emerged she was asked to leave. Her digs in Belfast had been arranged through the hospital, and she was given notice to quit her room.

The baby was due in May, and Winnie, now obviously pregnant, at first tried to find a room in Belfast for herself, where Jim could join her when off-duty, though most of the time he lived in the barracks. Very little was on offer, and the one she took in desperation was so miserable she felt she could not face long days on her own waiting for the baby to be born.

All this was related to Lily in the letters that came weekly. At the beginning of April, Lizzie said the only thing for Winnie was to come to Ballymena, and if she still refused to go back to Kellstown, they might be able to find a decent room for her to rent in Harryville. At the very worst she could stay in the Moat Road until the baby was born. It would be difficult, with only the two bedrooms, but they would manage somehow.

The plan was put to Winnie, who would not hear of it. She was not coming anywhere near Ballymena and its gossips. She had left it for good. And anyway if she stayed with Lizzie, it would cause trouble with Robert Hugh and the family at Kellstown. It was out of the question. A week later, having talked it all over with Jim, she reluctantly changed her mind. She would come until the baby was born, though after that she wanted out of Ballymena as fast as possible.

So once again Lily was sharing her home and her thoughts with Winnie. Lily watched at close-quarters her friend's transition from tom-boy, sharp-tongued, single girl to married woman and mother-to-be with fascination. In many ways she had not changed at all, seemed just the same, just as bold and uncaring of the opinion of others, while at the same time she was no longer a girl. She was a woman. She was reluctant to visit the farm at Slemish. She said the only McMaster she wanted to see was her Aunt Lizzie.

Winnie told everyone in Harryville that the baby was not due until the autumn, and everyone smiled and said it was great, just great; it was the best way to start a marriage, with a baby in the first year. She was reluctant to go with Lizzie to look at rooms she might rent for later. She was not going to bring up any child of hers in one room in Ballymena. Jim had been in touch with his brother in Canada again, and with his cousin in New York, and one way or another, they would be off to America once the baby was born.

Lily knew she meant it, and she began to dread Winnie's departure, knowing it would leave her without her closest friend. She had plenty of other friends; some were her work mates, others lived on or near the Moat Road, and there were the Kennedys and others she knew from church or from the Sunday night meetings. She had one or two boy acquaintances who had taken her to the pictures, or on long-walks on summer evenings, but no one who could be called a boyfriend.

She was teased from time to time about Jack Kennedy, for his devotion to Lily was now obvious, at least to his own family and to Lily's, but she just laughed. He was thirteen months younger, and to a 20 year-old young lady there could be no one more immature and less interesting than a 19 year-old tongue-tied youth. Jack was not only tongue-tied in that sense, his slight stammer carried his gabbled Ballymena accent far beyond Lily's comprehension. She would do better than that, she promised herself.

Though defiant, Winnie was not proud of herself for getting pregnant before marriage. Like anyone else brought up in the evangelical Protestant tradition she could not rid herself of the vague idea that sex was the original sin. It was what Eve's temptation of Adam, and Adam's fall, was all about, ever since permissible only within marriage, and even then of doubtful propriety. And she had committed that sin, and had been found out.

73

Her guilt was mixed with anger at herself, because she knew she had lived down to Robert Hugh's worst expectations. While never openly unkind to her, he had made no secret of his continued disapproval of her mother's disgrace, and combined earnest expressions of concern for Winnie's welfare with repeated expressions of pious hope that Winnie would turn out better than her.

Now Winnie had given him every excuse to say he had always feared things would turn out this way. That made her very angry with herself, and the anger made the feeling of guilt even stronger. Why had she been so weak? What was wrong with her? Was it because she was unsaved? If she had been saved she would have been going to meetings with Jim in Belfast instead of to the pictures, and she would have had different friends in the hospital.

Just as she was determined to start a new life with Jim and the baby in America, she wondered could she start a new life in a different way, here and now. She tried once or twice to talk to Lily about these things, but was too embarrassed, and too ready to make a joke of her feelings. Lily was surprised to hear her friend mention such worries, and put it down to the mysteries of pregnancy. But it all made her think a bit. It was not possible to live in Ballymena and not be keenly aware of being, or not being, saved. Even if you did not go to meetings, open-air preachers at the Fair Hill were loudly reminding you of the question mark over your eternal destination, and the stark options open to you.

In the streets people were forever handing out tracts, which you could never be rude enough to refuse, or to throw away. Even if lightning did not strike you dead on the spot, you would not want to meet trouble halfway. And you would find the tracts at night at home in your coat pocket, and start to read the dire tales of *The Man who Forgot God,* or *Eternity Where?* Lily had no idea what she believed, but she knew God existed, and that the Bible was his Holy Word. Was something more required of her?

The impending arrival of Winnie's baby in May drove all such thoughts from the minds of both. A healthy son arrived on time and was named Samuel James. Winnie had her hands full, and Lily was delighted to devote as much time as she could to helping. The comings and goings between 19 Moat Road and Winnie's new digs, a few streets away, were non-stop.

Then something happened which clouded out the early summer sunshine and plunged both addresses into grief and despair. Mary Wallace was taken suddenly ill and collapsed while returning to Belfast after a weekend at home. She was rushed into the hospital where she herself was training as a nurse. Appendicitis was diagnosed, and she was operated upon as soon as possible. But it was too late, and she had died of peritonitis before her friends and relatives in Ballymena had even heard she was ill. She was barely 18.

Winnie had lost the lively and lovely young girl who had become her closest friend. As a nurse she was no stranger to death, and she still remembered her own grief over young Sandy, and later over her grandmother, but this was different. Fortunately the demands of her infant son reminded her on an hourly basis that life went on, and left no time for despair or self-pity.

For Lily it was also different. Mary's older half-sister Kate had become her particular friend at Kellstown, so she bore a double burden of grief – her own which was real enough, and that of Kate. Death had already been a visitor in her life; though she remembered nothing of her mother, she had always had an awareness that her mother was dead. She knew too that she had had an infant brother, Walter, who was also dead. Her father, the centre of her world, had died too.

Life was fragile. She worried when the three boys played down by the weir on the river and when they came home wet with rain and sweat from playing football. She bullied and badgered them into changing out of their wet things before they caught a chill. The spectre of pleurisy was constantly paraded before them. They were too young to realise that their sister was haunted by the memory of her father coming home, shivering, from a football match, and being dead within a week.

Within another month Winnie was saved. She and Lily had talked long about Mary's death, and about the awfulness of death itself. Winnie wondered aloud if it was not time she was saved, but the way she said it made it sound almost as a joke, or as if she was talking about having one of the radical new hair styles that were all the rage. So Lily was dumbfounded when Winnie confessed that she was saved.

It was indeed like a confession, as if getting saved was something more to be ashamed of than happy about. She and Jim and the baby had gone to stay with Jim's parents near Portlglenone for a weekend, and while there had been taken to a tent mission. Winnie said she could not remember much about the sermon, but it was full of the threat of damnation, and where would you be if the Lord called you home. She had sat there thinking of Mary, and of her own shame at having to get married.

For years she had known that sooner or later she would have to get saved, and suddenly she decided now was the time. She was among strangers; there were no neighbours watching, and no one in the tent knew her except Jim and his father who had brought them. When the appeal came at the end of the meeting, she slipped up her hand and joined the elect.

Her feelings were almost entirely of relief. She had done something important which, for years, she had known she had to do, and she was happy that she had done it. She knew her life would change, and that there would be no more pictures, and no thoughts of dancing, that she would have to spend time reading the Bible and praying and going to meetings. But she was happy about that too.

Lily listened, a bit embarrassed to hear her friend talk like this, and expecting Winnie to throw in a joke about herself and what she had done. But there was no joke, and Winnie even rather shyly asked Lily would she not like to be saved herself. Lily avoided the question by telling Winnie she was glad to hear the news, she was very happy for her, and she hoped it might improve her temper and blunt the sharp edge of her tongue.

After that they talked very little about matters metaphysical and spiritual. Winnie did go to church meetings a lot, and severed relations with Messrs Chaplin, Arbuckle and their like. But she still spent a lot of time at Number 19, and showed no tendency to allow her new state of grace inhibit her natural irreverence or readiness to remark upon, and laugh uproariously at, the foibles and weaknesses of the neighbours she was now under a scriptural injunction to love as she would herself.

She talked a lot about the Promised Land. But this was Canada, not Canaan. Each week she read the front page of the *Ballymena Observer* with a zeal more appropriate to the gospel itself. 'An Opportunity for Irish Families' was the heading on one regular advert; it declared that 3,000 improved or partly improved farms were ready for occupation in Canada by emigrants under the Empire Settlement Act. Money to pay for passage, and for stock and equipment on the farm would be provided, repayable over 25 years.

Winnie had a horror of debt, and did not like the idea of being deep in it for 25 years. She was more taken by the offer from Nova Scotia; 'Experienced or Partly Experienced Farm Workers Wanted; Good Wages; Assisted Passage'. Jim was an experienced farm worker, and it was a good omen that the agents for Nova Scotia in Ballymena were Greer's Shipping Office.

But Jim had his heart set on the police, and against going back to being what he insisted on calling a farm labourer. So together they concentrated on the adverts by Cunard, White Star, Canadian Pacific and other shipping lines, all promising passage to Canada for £3, for 'approved settlers'. The word from Toronto was that there was now a real chance of a place for Jim in the police early in 1927.

Lily listened to all these plans and wondered from time to time what sort of future lay ahead for her in Harryville. Her long-held assumption that one day she would be able to go back to where she really belonged – to Crayford – never disappeared, but alongside it was a competing realization that she was taking root in Ballymena, and that those closest to her, her stepmother and her three brothers, had forgotten all about Crayford, and thought of nowhere but Ballymena as home.

As her 21st birthday passed in November she began to contemplate a future in Ballymena without Winnie as a friend, and with no real prospect of herself ever returning to England. Like every young girl of her age and class she had been educated for little other than marriage. Despite her love of poetry, and her desire to be able to draw and paint, and to play the piano, she was now working as an unskilled assistant in a laundry, and had never worked as anything much better.

She could, of course, wash and cook and tend children. Not only could she sew and mend, she had learned to dressmake. She was eminently marriageable, and even if she had no interest herself in marrying, there were plenty who had an interest in marrying her. But she gave them little encouragement, finding safety in numbers, content to be part of a crowd of people, fellows and girls, of her own age.

Among these were the Kennedys. Her friendship with Ena, the oldest Kennedy girl, had developed, despite Ena's religiosity. But Ena, circumventing all her father's injunctions and regulations, had first become engaged to, and then, that September, had become the wife of her boyfriend Dave. They, too, were talking of moving to Canada. More fun than Ena was her younger sister, another Lily, also 'saved', but a chatterbox with a quick temper. Friendship had grown too between Bobby Cuthbert, now 15, and one of the younger Kennedy boys, Alfie. As ever, there was Jack, still worshipping Lily from afar.

Ena sometimes spoke to Lily about her eternal welfare, and urged upon her the need to be saved. But she did so rather gently, and as a friend, and while Lily always felt uncomfortable and embarrassed, she did not let it damage the friendship. However, she found herself bothered by Ena's regular invitations to attend meetings and missions at the Elim Assembly in Ballymena, where Ena and her sister Lily, and their mother, were enthusiastic adherents.

Right at the end of 1926, in the week after Christmas, she agreed to go with Ena to the final night of a three-day Elim convention, being held in the Protestant Hall in High Street. She agreed partly because she had run out of excuses, partly because the meeting was in a large public hall, not the small Elim 'tabernacle', as it was called, in Castle Street. She had been to the tabernacle once or twice and had felt uncomfortable with the enthusiasm and informality of the services. But most of all she decided to go because the speaker was to be Principal George Jeffreys, the founder and leader of the Elim movement, and the young Welshman she had already heard so much about in Lurgan and Belfast before she had come to Ballymena.

For moral support she dragooned her three young step-brothers into coming with her. In the case of the older two not much persuasion was needed, but the youngest, Hugh, just past his tenth birthday, objected to having his face and hands scrubbed and his hair brushed on a Tuesday evening, and complained bitterly that it was too cold to go out, and that he had no overcoat. Nor indeed had he, for he had outgrown his first such garment, and would not have another until money could be found to buy a new one for Bobby, when his could be handed down to Alec, and Alec's to Hugh. Neither Lily nor her stepmother could contemplate buying a second-hand coat, of which there was a plentiful supply at the Fair Hill every market day. Only poor people bought second-hand clothes.

Coat or no coat, Hugh was told he was going, and the four set out to walk the half mile or so to High Street on a clear frosty night. Hugh insisted on running ahead and kicking every stone or tin can he found on the street. It was his way of keeping out the cold. There was almost a full house at the hall when they arrived. Ena Kennedy was waiting for them inside the porch and guided them into a bench near the back where her sister Lily had kept seats for them all.

The congregation was already singing choruses, led by a red-faced, bald-headed little man with great reserves of energy, a fund of humorous exhortations and a strong Ballymena accent. The crowded benches responded with lusty and fairly tuneful singing of 'Coming by and by, tis coming by and by, a better day is dawning in yonder sky' and 'Every step of the way, my Lord yes, every step of the way' and 'Hallelujah to His Name'.

Though she loved music and singing, Lily had no taste for choruses. She thought them a bit disrespectful. She found the jocular approach of the bald man leading the choruses both hard to follow, due to his Ballymena accent, and hard to swallow. Jokes from the platform and roars of laugher from the pews jarred with her ideas of worship, learned first in the austere respectability of the Church of England, and confirmed in the sobriety of Presbyterian churches.

Her mood changed when the service proper began. It was led by the recently-arrived resident pastor of the Ballymena Assembly, an engaging young Englishman. In fact he was not exactly an Englishman but came from the Channel Islands. He sounded English, though if you listened carefully you could catch the suggestion of a French intonation in his voice. And certainly there was not the slightest trace of either a Ballymena accent or a Ballymena vocabulary.

The service moved from choruses to the majestic hymns, starting with Wesley's *O for a thousand tongues,* which stimulated the congregation to great musical heights. Lily and her brothers knew the hymn, and were soon singing their heads off with the rest.

Stand up, stand up for Jesus, ye soldiers of the Cross was not quite in the same league, but it was again familiar from their Sunday School days, and it was less of a strain on the vocal chords than *A Thousand Tongues.* The hall vibrated to its military beat, and the voices roared in triumph 'This day the noise of battle, the next the victor's song, to him that overcometh a crown of life shall be.'

There were Bible-readings and a soloist, a young man with a beautiful tenor voice who sang *The old rugged cross* and *Will your anchor hold in the storms of life?.* Then the Pastor introduced their speaker for the evening, Principal George Jeffreys. He told how the young Jeffreys had first come to Ballymena in 1915 and begun the work of Elim there; now, still a young man, he was beloved leader of the most dynamic religious movement in the British Isles, with churches throughout England, Wales, and Scotland as well as in Ulster where it had all begun just a decade ago.

Jeffreys, who had been sitting quietly on the platform from the beginning of the meeting, now stepped forward, Bible in hand, and began to speak. Thirty-seven years of age, he looked even younger with his thin, pale, earnest face and high forehead under a shock of dark curly hair, combed to one side. His voice belied his youthful appearance, for it was deep and resonant, with a distinct Welsh lilt. He spoke with measured authority, never shouting, though at times giving his words a remarkable emotional intensity in their delivery.

He took as his text the raising of Jairus's daughter, as told in Matthew Chapter 9, how a certain ruler came to Jesus and worshipped him and said 'My daughter is even now dead, but come and lay thy hand upon her and she shall live'. Lily knew the story well enough, but it came alive as Jeffreys recounted how Jesus had cleared the mourners from the house and declared that 'the maid is not dead, but sleepeth', and how, while the by-standers laughed at him, he went in, took her by the hand and raised her up.

The maid in Lily's mind was Mary Wallace. How she wished Jesus had been in Ireland, not Canaan, when Mary had died. He could have raised her up. If he had been in Crayford he could have stopped her father's fever and restored him. Almost as if he was reading her mind, the preacher was now telling the congregation that they should not think of the raising of Jairus' daughter as a story from the past, as a miraculous event that happened thousands of years ago in a distant land when the Son of God walked upon the earth.

No, he said, it was a miraculous event exactly the same as had been happening in Birmingham, in Glasgow, in Swansea, in Exeter and even in Ballymena. He told of healings that had been worked by God under his own humble hands not centuries ago, but weeks, even days, ago. He patiently explained what he called 'the ministry of the miraculous', the use of divine powers of miraculous healing both to show the mercy and kindness of God towards his people, and as proof that Jesus was indeed divine.

Nothing had changed in 2,000 years – through the Holy Spirit, Jesus was still walking the earth, still had the power to heal, and was providing evidence of the truth of the Gospel through miracles. Despite what people had written about him, the preacher continued, he was not a showman doing tricks to win public acclaim. The message he preached was as old as the Bible itself, and others had brought it throughout the centuries. He rejoiced in the healing of the sick, but that was as nothing to the healing of the soul.

Tonight, he said, he was not going to call for the sick to come forward for healing. He felt the Lord was telling him to talk to the people in Ballymena about spiritual, not physical healing. He would, before he finished, offer a general prayer for all who needed physical healing and those who heard that prayer with faith could indeed be healed. But the burden on his heart tonight was the soul, not the body. Jairus' daughter was healed, he said, because of faith – the faith her father showed when he went to Jesus fully believing that He had the power to heal her. So a soul afflicted by pain and suffering, a soul that was only too aware of its imperfections and failures, could be made whole, healed, transformed and made healthy by a simple act of faith. And if the soul was saved, the life would be transformed. Joy would replace sorrow, glorious certainty sweep away doubt and worry.

The audience sat spellbound; the strong, even tones of the speaker, at the same time both warm and grave, had nothing of the pulpit rhetoric about them. He was not hectoring or bullying a congregation, but conversing earnestly with each individual. His message had little of the threat or menace so favoured by most preachers; instead of warning of unspeakable punishments, it promised golden prospects of joy and transformation.

To young men and women whose childhood had been overshadowed by the Great War with its appalling loss of life and destruction of dreams, who in Ireland had lived through the nightmare of sectarian violence, and who, in many cases, had reached adulthood barely evading the clutches of poverty, it was an almost irresistible message.

No one in the hall, not even the preacher himself, could even have begun to articulate the impact the cataclysmic events of the previous decade had had on them as individuals. Certainties had been swept away, society's belief in the triumph of reason, its acceptance of authority had been fatally undermined, and all sorts of ties and bonds had been dissolved. Instead, there was a flickering, still vague but growing awareness that anything, indeed everything was now possible.

Across Europe, philosophers and writers were exploring the potential of the individual, the power of personal decision, each man's ability to shape his own future by his own choices and actions. No one in the Protestant Hall in Ballymena had ever heard of logical positivism or existentialism let alone thought deeply about them, but the forces that prompted the philosophers were the same forces that had overturned the chessboard, and radically altered the lives of the pawns as much as those of the kings and queens, knights and bishops.

The idea of the individual answerable for himself before God was, on the other hand, nothing new. Justification by faith – the faith of each man himself – was the essential keystone of fundamental Protestantism, and that was obtainable, everyone knew, through the individual's own decision – getting saved, coming to Christ, being born again. But it was known in the sense of something one had to do, not least in order to avoid the flames of eternal damnation.

Now George Jeffreys made it sound like a wonderful opportunity that anyone would be delighted to grab. It was not about escaping hell, it was about entering a sort of earthly heaven here and now, where happiness would be the order of the day, and ills of the body as well as the soul were curable.

Lily had never been too impressed by the Gates of Hell. Her early years in the Church of England Sunday School had given her a distaste for anything that smacked of severity in the matter of religion, or of enthusiasm. But the enthusiasm she felt in the speaker, and in the people around her that night, was attractive, infectious. It seemed to offer something more in life than working at a manual job in a laundry. It promised her a purpose, a role beyond that of mothering her brothers, for she had begun to realise that they would not be boys for ever. Winnie was going off to Canada, and Ena Kennedy might soon do the same. Could she, by her own decision, begin a new life?

The preacher closed his Bible and called for prayer. Lily had sat through plenty of 'appeals' at tent meetings and missions and had always been uneasy at the idea that a 'decision for Christ' could be accomplished by raising one's hand in public; to her, religion was a very private matter. It was all a bit too simple. After all, the preacher had spent the last hour telling you this was the most important decision of your life – this life and the next one.

But Jeffreys' quiet melodious voice seemed to be speaking to her alone, and before she knew it she had slipped up her hand in response to the appeal. A movement beside her told her two of the brothers, Bobby and Alec had done the same. Then all around hands were being raised, and people were crying Hallelujah and Praise the Lord, and Jeffreys was quietly thanking those who had done so, and calling for more.

Two seats back, out of Lily's vision, Jack Kennedy's hand shot up. Whether he had seen Lily's hand minutes before no one knew, and he never said. Neither of them realised it that night, but the raising of their hands had enormous significance for both their lives, a lifelong impact that was, for them and for others around them, tragic.

The Moat Road did not instantly start flowing with milk and honey, but for Lily at least part of her life was now lived in something approaching the promised land. She immediately joined the Elim Assembly, as did Bobby, though Alec, a quieter, shyer lad, stayed with the Presbyterians and continued to attend West Church with his mother and younger brother. But separate ways on Sunday mornings did not mean schism in the family – Lily still went occasionally to West Church on Sunday evenings, and the rest of the family often accompanied her and Bobby to special events at Elim.

The Assembly in Ballymena was young, and many of its members were young too. Lily found herself part of a band of twenty or so aged between their late teens and early thirties, mostly unmarried, who saw each other at least three times on Sundays – morning service, Sunday School and Bible Class in the afternoon, and gospel meeting in the evening – and as often again during the week. Tuesday night was Bible Study, and Thursday was Prayer Meeting.

Shortly after Lily joined, the young people formed their own group, called the Crusaders, which met every Monday night. As winter gave way to spring the Crusaders organised outings on Saturdays. These were often little more than a picnic in a field outside the town, but occasionally they would take the train to Portrush, or the new bus service down to Carnlough on the Antrim coast.

In June of 1927 they took the narrow-gauge railway that ran from Ballymena to Parkmore, high on the Antrim plateau, and from there by jaunting-cars to the Glens of Antrim. One glen, Glenariff, had been developed by the railway company with a tea house at the top, and a path down the glen alongside the river as it spilled over rocks and tumbled down waterfalls, to another café at the bottom. By 1927 Glenariff had become the Glens of Antrim, relegating the other eight glens to comparative anonymity.

The path down was dramatic. Wooden walkways and bridges took the visitor across waterfalls, almost underneath some of them, and over tumbling rapids. Overhead, giant trees formed a canopy penetrated by shafts of bright sunlight. The Crusaders jostled and joked as they meandered along the path, pausing to read aloud to each other the signs giving the names of each waterfall – *The Tears of the Mountain,* or *The Mare's Tail* or *The Fall of the Hoof.*

The names were also given in Irish, and the bolder souls did their best to manoeuvre their Ulster-Scots tongues around *Ess na Larach* and similar mysterious formulations, raising a good-natured laugh from their companions. They crowded in to the little thatched hut right under the tallest waterfall, with small windows of coloured glass that allowed them to see the cascade in deepest red or coolest blue.

At the bottom of the glen, tea and buns in the café fortified them for the ascent back to the railway, this time by road and jaunting-car clinging hysterically on as they bounced along the stony surface. The café also sold post cards of the Glens, and no trip anywhere really counted unless several post cards were sent. These were hurriedly filled out and left at the Parkmore Post Office. The ride in the train back to Ballymena was an ecstatic mixture of lusty hymn singing and discreet flirting, with ample opportunity for stolen glances and secret squeezings of hands, and for the really adventurous, of slim waists.

Another Saturday the trip was on the railway to Portrush, from where the electric tram took them down Causeway Street then into the countryside and across the fields by way of Dunluce Castle, the MacDonnell fortress perched on its rocky base jutting out into the Atlantic waves, to the Giant's Causeway. The crowded seating on the narrow wooden benches of the tram as it lurched the seven miles to the Causeway meant much throwing together and more familiarity than decorum normally permitted.

At Jack Kennedy's suggestion, before boarding the tram, they had all trooped into a photographer's to have 'film star' portraits taken. Lily had bought herself a paper parasol and insisted on being photographed with it. The small cigarette-card sized prints were ready for collection before they caught the train home, and they all did look just like film stars, particularly Lily with her parasol resting on her shoulder.

Between Sunday services, week-night activities and outings, the younger element of the Assembly were living an almost communal life. They spent more time in each other's company than many of them did with their families, for long working-hours meant time at home was limited, and much of it devoted to sleep. They participated eagerly in the services and meetings, but all of these also provided ample scope for socialising. The young people tended to arrive early and linger long to enjoy the company all the more.

For the first time since leaving Crayford, Lily was wholeheartedly immersed in a community far wider than her family. She liked the ability of the Elim church to combine intense religious fervour with cheerful informality in a way that contrasted greatly with the sternness of Presbyterianism.

And while Elim might have been founded in Ulster, there were constant reminders that it was a much broader church, with its headquarters now in London. Its pastor in Ballymena was the Channel Islander, Mr. Le Tissier, and it had a stream of visitors from across the water for special occasions – Englishmen, Scotsmen and, of course, the great Welsh leader, Principal Jeffreys himself. To her surprise, Lily discovered than being saved, far from burying her ever more deeply in the provincial gloom of Ballymena, was proving a lifeline to the outside world.

Not that such thoughts were ever clearly formulated in her own mind. She was simply very happy in a new world. But it also brought her closer to old friends, like the Kennedy family, and in particular to Mrs Kennedy, who, despite her husband's stern lack of approval, was deeply involved in Elim. Lily found her a kind and intelligent lady, with a great love, and much knowledge, of gardening – not an activity much practised in the Moat Road, but which Lily remembered from Crayford.

Lily was delighted too at the way Bobby was joining in all the activities of the church, and already emerging as a leader among those of his own age. Yet another bonus was the presence of a piano in the church, and frequent opportunities to sit down at it and try to play while the others were busy elsewhere, or just to sit and listen to some of her friends who were accomplished pianists.

A black spot in the middle of all this was the departure of Winnie and Jim and their infant son to Canada. At least it would have been a black spot if Winnie's unalloyed delight at the event had allowed any regrets, on her own or anyone else's behalf. The job in the police in Toronto had finally materialised, and no Irish emigrant ever took ship with a lighter tread. Lily and Kate Wallace travelled to Belfast with the emigrants. They helped with the three large suitcases that contained all that the Greer family possessed, and with which they would start their new life. With so much to carry, along with the baby and his small pram, the two additional pairs of hands were welcome, particularly in negotiating the tram from the York Road terminus of the Northern Counties Railway to the dockside at Donegall Quay.

The transatlantic shed was crowded with people and with mountains of luggage and crates and bundles of merchandise. Through a partly open, massive door they could catch a glimpse of the tender which would take the travellers out to the mouth of Belfast Lough for transfer to the White Star liner en route from Liverpool to Halifax, Nova Scotia, and onward to Montreal.

There was little time for tearful farewells. Tickets were quickly checked, and the suitcases piled with others on trolleys by porters. Then a sudden call for all steerage passengers to proceed to the gangway meant quick embraces and barrages of good wishes and promises to write. Then Jim, Winnie and the baby were up the gangway, through the shed doorway and had disappeared into the tender.

No one had cried, though they had all felt like it. Winnie was so delighted, and so relieved, that she and Jim were at last heading for the promised land, that her spirits held up, and neither Lily nor Kate dared give way to the sorrow of parting. Half an hour later the tender's hooter sounded, and the shed doors were pushed wide open to let friends and relatives onto the quayside to wave goodbye as the tender, which to Lily seemed almost as big as she imagined a transatlantic liner would be, slipped away from the quayside and down the lough. At the crowded stern of the ship Winnie and Jim waved frantically, and Lily and Kate wept unrestrainedly.

Soon after, Ena Kennedy married her Dave, and they too disappeared to Canada. Canada held no attractions for Lily. The only boat she was interested in was one that sailed east, and would take her back to England, to Crayford, and to her girlhood friends with whom she still exchanged letters, and who now also had a growing archive of postcards of The Tears of the Mountain, Dunluce Castle and The Pentagon, as the five-road junction at the Adair Arms Hotel in Ballymena had been named more than a century before Washington acquired its Pentagon.

Lily could no longer think of Ireland and Ballymena as an unfortunate interruption of her real life in England, which would one day be resumed. Five or six years had passed since that hurried journey from Crayford, but it was not just the passage of time. All her connections were now in Ireland, her immediate family, her friends, almost everyone she knew. The girls in Crayford were no longer school girls; one of them was talking of getting married, and they had lives that Lily knew nothing about.

All of this, however, heightened her sense of being English. Her English accent was the most distinctive thing about her, and she guarded it zealously. In her dreams she planned a return visit to Crayford, not to move there, but as a holiday, and she would take the three boys with her so that they would not lose touch with their real roots, as she regarded them. But for the moment it had to remain a dream, for where would she find the money, or the time, to take the boat and train to London?

After Winnie's departure Lily's friendship with Kate Wallace became more important to her. Kate, a nurse like her sister, was often home for the weekend when Lily visited Kellstown, and was soon skipping across the plank bridge over the burn for long chats and much tea. For Lily there were occasional trips to Belfast on the train to visit the aunts in Roden Street, who were always ready to welcome her. Lily liked the aunts, but found the dark house under the shadow of the mill chimney a gloomy place.

The gloom was only slightly lifted by the arrival of Dinah, a cousin of Lily and the daughter of her father's younger brother, Walter Culbert. For reasons that were never too clearly explained, Dinah had come to Belfast to live with her aunts when her mother had died. She was several years younger than Lily, and while the two became friendly enough, Dinah had the double disadvantages of being one of nature's born pessimists, and of coming from Lurgan.

In her flat Lurgan accent Dinah ritually predicted the worst possible outcome to whatever matter was under discussion, whether it was the likelihood of rain, the development of a slight cough into pleurisy, or the collapse of the linen industry and inevitable unemployment for both Culberts and Cuthberts. Lily could have tolerated that, just about, but Dinah also talked incessantly about Lurgan, reminding Lily of painful days, and also of her neglect of her own Lurgan relatives.

She resolved to make a real effort to remedy that, and her chance came in the autumn of 1927, when the Ballymena Crusaders organised a coach trip to the Lurgan convention. It was the custom of the Elim assemblies each to hold an annual convention, a spiritual blow-out covering a Saturday and Sunday, beginning with a service at 3.00 on the Saturday, another at 7.00, with tea provided in between, and two more services on Sunday afternoon and evening. Members of other assemblies would travel to one or other of the days' meetings, making it a big family occasion. The teas provided between the services on each day were magnificent in the wealth and variety of the sandwiches and in the splendour of the tarts, flans, pies and buns.

Food was not the only sustenance in abundance. Each service included not one, but two sermons, often delivered by visiting speakers who had travelled from England or Scotland, just as Principal Jeffreys had for the Ballymena convention the year earlier. The thought of four sermons in one day would have horrified Lily a year ago, but these sermons were different. The conventions were not gospel missions – though the final evening service always included an element of preaching to the unconverted – rather they were designed to nourish and inspire the believer.

They gave the speakers the chance, and the time, to explore personal religious experience, and to articulate the special message of the Pentecostal movement which they firmly believed was a latter-day, divinely inspired reawakening of New Testament Christianity. The speakers at conventions were never, or rarely, ranters and Bible-thumpers. Often they were well-educated, some had been formally trained as ministers in established churches before joining Elim. Others had professional backgrounds. Even those who lacked formal education had read and studied so intensely that their presentations were no less scholarly.

Not all the Ballymena faithful could grasp the subtleties of 'ecstatic religion', or the intricate relationship between sinful nature, bodily frailty, faith and divine healing. The mysteries of the charismatic experience, the speaking in tongues, the prophesying, perplexed and even frightened some so much that the careful expositions of the scriptural bases for these phenomena passed them by.

But Lily was drinking at the fountain-head. She was too shy, too private a person, not to be nervous at, and to shy away from, the public emotionalism that characterised the Pentecostal pattern of worship, but she was fascinated and inspired by the careful explanations of the speakers that linked eternal mysteries to human experience, and seemed to bring a touch of the divine into ordinary lives.

Some conventions had bookstalls at the back of the hall, and Lily, when she could afford it, was an eager customer. Often a book written by one of the speakers would be on offer, and Lily had to buy it. At home she read these books carefully, and tried to understand them. Often she could not, but this made her all the more eager, as if the ideas she could not grasp were the dim outlines of distant mountains set in a wonderful landscape which she passionately wanted to explore.

The fact that many of these speakers had distinct English accents did them no harm in Lily's ears. This was a reminder that the promised land into which she had now entered was not centred on Ballymena, nor bounded by Ulster.

Rather reluctantly, Lily slipped out of the Lurgan church at the end of the afternoon service and across the road to the Campbell house, for the new Elim church was in the same avenue where Lily had lived before her sudden flight in 1922. Her Grandfather and Hester were waiting for her, and to Lily's relief and delight, her Aunt Maria was also there, with her two children.

The meal was passed in a flurry of questions and answers, an unending exchange of information on who and what and where. Lily was brought up to date on births, marriages and deaths among the Campbells and allied families in Lurgan, most of whom Lily had never even met. The Campbells were given endless details of the three half-brothers, of the stepmother and of all the McMasters, none of whom was in any way related to them.

This comprehensive sharing of mostly meaningless information ensured that the short time before Lily had to dash back for the evening service raced by without any awkwardness. There was no time for anyone to ask what had brought Lily to a convention in the Elim church, but just enough to elicit a promise that she would be back soon to see them again, and to meet at least some of the cousins and other relatives who had featured in the news round-up.

She was glad she had gone to see them, for though Lurgan had few happy memories for her, she could not forget that her Campbell relatives had twice taken her in, first when death had left her motherless, and then fatherless. She could remember nothing of her mother, and the fact that these Campbells were the closest blood relatives she had meant little, but she was fond of her Aunt Maria, and something inside her made her resolve that she would indeed come back; she would not forget her Campbell connection.

Times were changing, even in the Moat Road. In 1928 Bobby had his 15th birthday. Not only had he left the public elementary school to enrol in the Tech, he had almost finished there and was already talking of a job and even a career. He wanted to be a chemist. He had been told he could work as an assistant in a chemist's shop and take night classes in pharmacy, and correspondence courses too if he wished.

Alec was due to move from the Harryville school to the Tech. Hugh, who was to be 11 in November, was more than content with a life that included Harryville school, the Moat Road and kicking a football up and down it, the river, the weir and the Castle demesne. The mysteries of life and eternity worried him less than they did the more spiritually-minded members of the family, though Lily had begun to remind him that he was not saved, and that many young boys of his age were already inscribed in the Lamb's Book of Life.

Still, his interim state of unbelief was handy enough on Sunday mornings, when he could be left at home to put on the Sunday dinner while the others were busy at their devotional exercises. The twin fundamental essentials of the Sabbath in the Moat Road – attendance at morning service and a fully cooked meal on the table as close to one o'clock as possible – were as important at Number 19 as at any other house.

In other homes, however, these conflicting obligations were usually resolved between husband and wife. Most often, the wife stayed at home to discharge her prime responsibility of ensuring a proper Sunday dinner on time and well-cooked, while the father marched his scrubbed and combed offspring to the family pew. In some houses afflicted with a Godless, or, even worse, drunkard husband and father, good could be extracted from evil by ensuring that the father was up from his bed of sloth in time to put on the dinner before the mother returned from church with her charges.

As Number 19 had no husband or father, a rota system had been instituted among the boys as soon as they were all old enough to take on responsibility for boiling potatoes. Now that Bobby and Alec had fallen into a state of grace, and were enthusiastic attenders at their respective places of worship, Hugh was happy enough to take the role on full-time.

Potatoes were at the heart of this problem of getting Sunday dinner on the table at the designated hour. Almost anything else could be cooked either very quickly or very slowly, or just warmed up prior to serving. But potatoes had to be boiled for at least 40 minutes, and brought to the right state of floury readiness immediately before their arrival at the table. Hard potatoes, or potatoes reduced to mush, could not be contemplated. So someone had to be at home to stoke the fire and put on the pot, or, as in the Moat road, light the gas, just at the time when the rector, minister or pastor was opening his Bible and letting the congregation in on the secret of the first of his three points.

This happy arrangement had to be reviewed at the end of 1928 when, to the delight of Lily and the surprise of everyone else, Hugh got saved. He went through the usual procedure of putting his hand up in response to an appeal at a gospel meeting in the Elim Church. He was not too sure why he did this, but he knew it was what his big sister desperately wanted him to do, and it was what his oldest brother Bobby had suggested he might think of doing.

Bobby was Hugh's idol. Bobby was a good-looking, gentle youth who was just brilliant at football. Since he had gone to the Tech he had been playing real football, on a team, on a pitch with goalposts, and wearing his own football boots. Hugh went to watch him play for the Tech whenever he could. Bobby had not let being saved interfere with his football, indeed he was even trying to organise the younger boys in the Elim Assembly into a team.

This was a great relief to Hugh, for he had heard so many preachers denounce football as a sin almost on a par with dancing, smoking and the pictures, that he feared Bobby would give it up entirely, and that he himself would have to choose between hell and a heaven where football was barred. That dilemma removed, he could think of no great argument against getting saved.

Lily's happiness was almost complete, or as complete as she had any right to expect living in a small, overcrowded house in Harryville, with money in short supply and what was really a menial job. But, for the moment at least, life was lived more in the Elim Assembly and among her friends there than it was in the Moat Road or the laundry. And with the three boys now saved, what more could she ask?

She had plenty of admirers among the young men of the Assembly. Jack Kennedy was still passionately in love with her from a respectful distance, and having passed the age of 21 could no longer be dismissed as a love-struck youth. There were stronger runners, however, and Lily knew well enough that she could almost have her pick from among the eligible bachelors of Ballymena Elim.

But she had no intention of marrying, or of going steady with any of them. She still harboured the vague hope of escaping from Ballymena and from Ireland, and she could never do that if she married a local. At times she dreamed of falling in love with one or other of the young English pastors who were posted to churches in Northern Ireland, or who came as speakers to missions and conventions. But that was little more than a dream, for it seemed you had to be a brilliant pianist, or a gifted singer, to qualify for a pastor's wife, and she was neither.

Besides, she could not think of marrying and leaving her stepmother with the three boys. They were all still at school, and Lily's wage was a vital part of the family support. Bobby would soon be leaving and getting a job, but the wage he could expect as a shop assistant would make little difference to the household budget. Marriage would have to wait for several years at least, no matter how ardent and impatient the suitors.

Bobby did get a job, and in a chemist's shop in the town. And he enrolled in night classes and proved a dedicated student. He took to studying, and signed up for several correspondence courses on matters as varied as theology, and Sight Improvement by Natural Methods. At the same time he was more and more involved in the church, and had begun teaching in the Sunday School.

Lily's delight at his progress, and at that of the two younger brothers, was mingled with the inevitable sadness of watching children leave their childhood. She would go from time to time to the bottom of the wardrobe in the bedroom she shared with Lizzie and take out the shoebox where, wrapped in tissue paper, were the golden ringlets of the three boys, preserved from the day when each had been first taken to the barber before entering school.

As she fingered the tresses she always thought of her favourite story from among those she had learned at school in Crayford, how Pope Gregory in the sixth century had visited the slave market in Rome and admired some golden haired young boys. 'Where were they from?' he had asked. 'They are English', he was told. 'Non Angli sed Angeli', was his reply. Not English, but angels, the teacher translated for them.

Lily thought it was a beautiful story, especially as Gregory had been so taken by the beauty of the young English boys that he had authorised Augustine's mission to England, with the resultant conversion of the English and the foundation of the Church of England. Or so the story was told at Crayford School. In Lily's mind's eye the slaves in the Roman market were Bobby, Alec and Hugh, beautiful in their golden ringlets.

She constantly said thanks in her prayers for the health of the boys. Boys and young men were often among the victims of consumption - as tuberculosis was invariably called - the most common cause of death in Northern Ireland, and rampant among the poorer working classes. Pleurisy leading to pneumonia was common enough too, so Lily's obsession with not getting wet, and above all of getting out of wet clothes as quickly as possible, was not without cause.

Unemployment and tuberculosis seemed to be in league. The numbers out of work in Ballymena and other towns in Northern Ireland remained stubbornly high during the 1920s, and increased as world conditions meant much less demand for a luxury product such as linen. As the mills began to shed jobs in 1929, the cases of TB appeared to multiply. One house on the Moat Road, mercifully at the end far away from Number 19, saw three deaths inside six months. It was at the low end of the road, a small damp terrace house with a dry outside privy. First the eldest daughter was taken into hospital, followed in weeks by two younger brothers. All three died.

Consumption did not necessarily mean a death sentence. With early diagnosis and proper treatment, people could be cured. But early diagnosis would have meant giving up work immediately and going into hospital or a sanatorium. There was some public support available for victims of the disease, once diagnosed, but it fell far short of a wage, and no working man could dream of giving up his job when he still felt well enough to carry on.

Then, to the anguish of his mother and the dismay of the whole family, Willy Kennedy collapsed on his way home from work. He had developed a cough, and had complained of tiredness, but had otherwise seemed fit enough. He was soon diagnosed with consumption. He was 20, two years younger than Jack, and a friend of the three Cuthbert boys. Much quieter than the rest of the family, he was the apple of his mother's eye. It seemed he had probably caught the disease through close contact with his workmates in the ill-ventilated wholesale warehouse where he had been employed.

Soon he was taken to a sanatorium in Belfast. Prayers were offered at every service in Elim for his healing; the pastor went to the hospital and anointed his body with oil, and claimed healing in Jesus' name. But he continued to decline. The Cuthbert boys had, at first, gone to see him at home, but Lily had become almost hysterical about the risk of infection, and Mrs Kennedy too had begged with them not to put themselves in danger. There was no question of visiting him in the sanatorium, and anyway, as complete rest was the first stage of treatment, visitors were not encouraged.

As sometimes happened with TB, he rallied and was sent home from the sanatorium for a few months. But there was no miracle for Willy, and he died in the early summer of 1930. Mrs Kennedy had raised nine children, and though she had lost Hubert to emigration, they had all survived and the youngest, Jean was now a bonny nine-year old. While she grieved over Willy, and desperately sought in her prayers and devotion some understanding of why he had not been healed, she knew in her heart that God was not at her or anyone else's beck and call, that healing was not for everyone, and that her own submission to the Divine will was all that mattered.

She and Lily became much closer at this period of grief. Lily had begun to look to Jane Kennedy for help in matters spiritual, to see her as someone to whom she could talk, and ask questions she would not have dared raise in a group or with people of her own age. At the same time she began to see a lot more of Jack Kennedy.

Jack was now trying to make a career for himself as a chemist's assistant. He had had a job in a shop in Ballymena as a trainee, but then had had to seek a succession of temporary posts as a locum. This had meant travelling further afield - at first to nearby places like Ballymoney and Antrim, but more recently to County Cavan – to Cootehill. He stayed in digs, and could rarely come home at weekends, as the locum invariably had to do the Sunday duty which was a vital part of the chemist shop's weekly routine.

But in the latter stages of Willy's illness he had come home at every opportunity, and near the end had given up his last temporary job to stay at home. His mother could not speak warmly enough of the great help he had been to her.

When he was at home he made sure never to miss the meetings at the Elim Church, in particular the Crusader meetings where he was sure to meet Lily and have a chance to talk to her. He had lost most of his teenage shyness and awkwardness. Working behind the counter in chemists' shops had taught him how to befriend people, to put them at their ease and talk to them about their problems. Going to live in digs in strange places had also made him much more gregarious, ready to mix with whatever company was available, and to enjoy himself whenever he had the chance. He had added badminton and strumming the banjo-mandolin to his social skills.

Lily could see just how much his mother looked to him for support, and how genuinely he comforted her and shared her grief. He took charge of all the funeral arrangement, as his father, dismayed and bewildered by the tragedy that had befallen his family, temporarily lost his customary authority. Lily saw Jack in a new light.

But she had little time to think of Jack or anyone else apart from her three step-brothers. If TB could strike down some one as healthy as Willy Kennedy, why would it spare Bobby, Alec and Hugh? Had they been infected? She listened to every cough and sneeze, and became even more obsessive over wet clothes or shoes, over getting overheated and standing around in the cold, about going bare-headed. Her stepmother told her to stop scolding or she would turn into a tartar.

12   GRIM REAPING

But the blow fell, not on them, but on someone no one had worried about, who had never been anything but a bundle of good-natured energy - their mother. In the middle of 1930 Lizzie, for the first time in her life, began to complain about tiredness, about a lack of energy. She was as busy as ever at her dressmaking, but was finding it difficult to keep up with her orders.

"Heth, Lily," she declared one night pushing aside a coat she was altering, "'I dinna ken whats th' matter wi me, but I'm nae use to ony yin or ony thing th' night. I'm goin to the dispensary th' morrow."

From the following day, Number 19 and its inhabitants were engulfed in a flow of events that left them all powerless, and their lives disrupted as they had not been since the dark days of Crayford in 1922. Lizzie saw a doctor and was sent to see another. She was told to take immediate bed rest and await the result of tests. Two weeks later the doctor came to visit her at home – a sure sign of serious trouble – and told her she had cancer. It was as if cancer had meanly sneaked in at the backdoor while they were all keeping watch for TB at the front.

In August she was taken into hospital, and in September she was sent home to die. Before the end of the month, Lizzie was dead. Lily and the three brothers survived her last days and the funeral almost in a trance. They could not believe what had happened, that the nightmare of 1922 was being repeated, and that the happy home and family they had so enjoyed would now be destroyed.

In her grief Lily began to realise that she was left as the head of the household, and the breadwinner. Her small wage was the core of the household income, with some help from Bobby and a token contribution from Alec, who, while still at the Tech, was earning a few shillings a week as a part-time messenger boy in a grocer's. Hugh was still at the public elementary school in Harryville.

After the funeral, relatives descended on the Moat Road from the Braid and from Belfast. Letters and offers of help arrived from Lurgan. No one could see how, with the little that was coming in by way of wages, Lily and the boys could afford to pay the rent and stay in

Number 19. Even if by a miracle they could, it was out of the question that Lily could work full time, run the house, and be both mother and father to the three boys, particularly to young Hughie still at first school.

Robert Hugh immediately offered a home for Hugh at Kellstown. With Bobby already in work, and Alec about to leave the Tech and get a full-time job, the house in the Moat Road could be kept on, at least for a while. And if not, the two boys could find digs in Ballymena. Hugh would not be far away.

Lily would not hear of it. Whatever happened, the family was not going to be split up again. Bobby and Alec agreed; they would both be paying their wages to Lily. And all three agreed that Hugh was going to have as good an education as he could get, and that meant going soon to the Tech. Living at Kellstown, eight miles out of Ballymena, would make that very difficult, if not impossible.

So they stayed in the Moat Road. Alec left the Tech and found a full time job as an assistant in a grocer's. Both he and Bobby handed their wage packets unopened to Lily every week, and accepted whatever pocket money she could afford to give back to them. The collective belt at Number 19 was tightened a few notches.

Lily was now the wage-earner, housekeeper and mother to three young brothers, one still at first school. She knew just how difficult it was going to be, and how uncertain the future had now become. She was not short of moral support – her friends at the church, and at Lizzie's Presbyterian church – were frequent callers, often with gifts of food and clothing. Boiling fowl, ham and sacks of potatoes were delivered regularly by Robert Hugh or one of the McMaster boys.

Jack Kennedy became a welcome visitor. He was always ready to organise trips with the three brothers, and was particularly kind to Hugh, who missed his mother most of all. One day Jack arrived with a kite for Hugh. It was a box kite, made of light wood and fabric which he had bought in Sligo, where he had found a job in a chemist's shop – it was not permanent, but neither was it a short term locum, and his wage was more than the minimum usually given to locums.

Jack and Hugh put the kite together and flew it on the grassy slope behind Number 19, where the ground fell steeply down towards the Braid water. Despite the gap of ten years, a friendship of sorts developed between the two. Jack now began to drop in at Number 19 whenever he was at home to see the boys. It meant he could see much more of Lily, and she of him, without a formal courtship.

She welcomed his company as much as the boys did. He was an uncomplicated young man, generous and full of good humour. On an odd Saturday evening he would bring his banjo-mandolin and they would all sit in the front room and listen to, and laugh at, his inexpert strumming of anything from *The Old Rugged Cross* to *Danny Boy*. He knew he played badly, but didn't care.

So Number 19 Moat Road continued in business, however precariously. Over it hung the constant threat of disaster in the form of the loss of one or more of the weekly wage packets. Lily's job was in ever increasing danger as the slump cut more deeply. Bobby and Alec both knew that they would have to find new jobs at some point. Shopkeepers took on school-leavers and paid them minimum wages on the grounds that they were actually helping them by giving them a training in the retail business. Some of the grander shops in Ballymena still expected their young recruits to work for nothing, just for the privilege of being 'trained' as gents' outfitters or grocers' assistants.

After a couple of years, young men felt they were trained enough, and expected something more like a proper wage. But that almost invariably meant finding another shop to work in, unless their luck was in and someone above them was retiring or dying. Bobby had completed two years in Woodside's, the shop he had started in in Ballymena, and had passed several examinations. He could now expect a proper wage, if he could find a proper job. He tried every other chemist in Ballymena without luck, so he began looking elsewhere.

He had become friendly with some of the visiting reps who called regularly at Woodside's, and he asked them to keep an eye open for him. As their work took them around chemists' shops in the whole county, and sometimes in several counties, they were not just aware of any vacancies, but could be relied upon to offer some personal details as to what sort of an employer this or that shop-owner might make, or even what such and such a town might be like to live in.

His hope, at first, was that he could find a job in one of the small towns close to Ballymena, like Cullybackey or Portglenone, or even Antrim town, all of which could be reached by railway. But nothing was available. Then, one day, a rep finishing his business with Mr. Woodside, nodded to Bobby to come to the door for a word.

"What would you think of Lisburn?" he asked. "Moody is looking for someone like you, with a bit of experience, and on his way to getting qualified. He's a grouchy old fellow, but very straight. You could do worse. Will I put a word in for you?"

"Yes please. I have to find somewhere. Should I write to him myself?"

The rep suggested he wait a week or so, by which time he would have been himself to Lisburn and would have had a word with Mr Moody, so that when Bobby's letter arrived it would not be out of the blue.

That night at Number 19 they had the nearest thing to a family row they had had for years. Lily was aghast at any suggestion that Bobby should leave home and go into digs in Lisburn. She would not listen to any of his arguments – that he had not got the job, but was just hoping he might be offered it, that he had to find a job somewhere and if it meant going to Lisburn, he would have to go.

Rational debate had never been one of Lily's strong points. She held fast to key points of principle and would not be budged from them. One point of principle was that she had kept the family together and it had to stay together. Another was that anyone living away from home in digs would be poorly housed and badly fed, and sure to fall victim to any and every disease around. Besides, how would she manage to keep Number 19 going without Bobby's wages?

Raised voices led to tears, and it was late that night before Bobby had forced his sister to sit down and listen to all sides of the question. The job in Lisburn was a chance, nothing more, and it might never happen. But if it did, it would mean a permanent place with a proper wage. Even after paying for his digs and his spending money in Lisburn, he would be able to send home more money than he was contributing now.

In digs he would have time and quiet to study and take on additional courses that might mean he could qualify earlier than he had hoped. He pointed out that Number 19 was overcrowded, and that the three brothers were now under each other's feet so much that it was hard for him to study. He reminded Lily that Lisburn had a thriving Elim Assembly which he had visited with the Crusaders, and finally he pointed out that a train from Ballymena to Antrim connected with the GNR to Lisburn, and you could do the journey in little more than an hour.

He suggested they should all pray for guidance as to what to do. He certainly meant to do so himself, though he had already decided that the offer of the job would, if it came, be more than enough guidance for him. He received more encouragement the next day when Jack Kennedy, home for a few days, called at Number 19. Ballymena, he told Bobby, was just hopeless for jobs, and life in digs was not at all bad. He had funny stories to tell of life in Cootehill, Sligo and other parts, and of the variety of digs and landladies he had experienced.

He was very proud of having represented Cootehill in the mid-

Cavan badminton league, and of being a member of the Sligo Camera Club. Both he and Bobby were enthusiastic photographers, and he promised to bring round his latest set of pictures from Rosses Point. He made living in digs sound the greatest fun a young man could wish for.

His intentions were the best. He knew the job was indeed a great chance for Bobby, but he also realised that Lily would desperately want him to stay, and would worry night and day about him if he went. Jack wanted to make as light of the move as he could, to reassure Lily that it was indeed for the best, and that Bobby would be fine and well, and not very far away.

With or without divine intervention, Bobby was offered the job, and within six weeks had shaken the dust of Ballymena off his sandals and was installed in Lisburn. He found digs through a member of the Elim Assembly, within easy walking distance of Moody's Medical Hall at the top of Bridge Street, right in the centre of the town. Moody himself was a stern employer who expected his staff to put in long hours and be both polite and efficient, but he also paid decent wages.

Most of Bobby's wages were sent back to Ballymena, where Lily was beginning to realise just how hard it was going to be to keep Number 19 afloat. Her stepmother had managed the household economy, and while Lily always knew there was no money to spare, she had never thought of the family as poor. Lizzie had always been able to find little bits of extra work when money was specially needed, but now there was no such chance; Lily's own wage, and the contributions from Bobby and Alec were more likely to go down than up.

For the first time since the family had been reunited in Number 19 almost a decade earlier, Lily knew real fear. She tried to draw comfort each night from the Lake District scene with the text *Jehovah Jirah* inscribed across it that hung above the bed she had shared with Lizzie. She tried to believe that the Lord would indeed provide, and her new faith helped her find assurance that they would not starve. But she also knew there was no guarantee that they would be spared real hardship, and that the responsibility for making sure such hardship and harm did not befall them rested more with her than with Jehovah.

But what could she do? Winnie and Jim had taken decisive action and emigrated. They had had a hard enough time at first, not least coping with the severe North American climate. But just recently they had moved south from Canada to New York State, where Jim had found a post as a gamekeeper on a large estate near Southampton on Long Island. The news from America was terrible now, as the Depression bit and thousands were jobless, but Winnie and Jim, and their two sons – another had been born shortly after they moved to New York – seemed insulated from it in their rural retreat.

Lily, on the other hand, was stuck in Ballymena in a period of intense economic gloom. She had neither the education nor experience to find a better job. She was skilful with her fingers, and could dressmake, but not well enough to earn money by it. She loved reading, and had read far more books than any of her workmates. She knew she was cleverer than average, and could recite from memory poems that her friends had never even read. But none of this made her any more employable.

Like every other working-class girl of her age in Ballymena in 1930, there was only one job for which she was at all qualified. That was housewife and mother. Most girls of her age, 25, who were not already married, had no other ambition. Some still clung to romantic ideas of falling in love with handsome young men, but the majority were more interested in a reliable and presentable partner who would have a steady job and provide a home. The idea of a home of their own was a powerful one for those who longed to escape from the overcrowding and drudgery that was the lot of unmarried daughters in large families.

Moreover, the prospect of being a wife, and a mother, was an attractive one – they were occupations of much greater prestige than being a millie, a doffer, or even a machinist. Not that marriage guaranteed withdrawal from the industrial workforce, for in many houses the wife was the one with the steady job and the husband the one out of work.

Until now the big difference between Lily and her friends and workmates as regards marriage, was that while they saw it as both greatly to be desired and inevitable, she saw it as simply impossible. For years she could not have thought of leaving her stepmother to bring up the three brothers and bring in the money to do so while she went off and got married. Since Lizzie's death, she could not think of anything so selfish as marriage – she simply had to take over sole responsibility for the family.

Then, early in 1931, this argument was suddenly reversed. Jack Kennedy found both the courage and sufficient fluency of tongue to propose marriage. His friendship with Lily had, despite her initial reluctance, developed into something like a courtship. His long absences at work away from Ballymena meant they were not going out regularly in the accepted pattern, and it meant too that Lily had plenty of other young men ready to flirt with her, and offer her a protective arm on an outing to the coast or on a country ramble.

But when he was at home he made Number 19 his priority port of call. He usually had some small present for Hugh, and a bottle of scent or the like from the chemist's shop for Lily. He and Lily took to sitting alone on the couch in the front room when Hugh and Alec had gone to bed or were out. They held hands, and the time came when they parted with a discreet kiss.

On the couch one night, shortly after Bobby had taken the job in Lisburn, Jack nervously asked Lily what she thought she might do in the years ahead.

"You're going to have your hands full trying to raise Alec and Hughie, and keep your own job going. Are you not more than a wee bit worried about the future?"

"Of course I am, but what can be done? So long as we can pay the rent here we will be all right, though what would happen if we couldn't I just do not know."

"You could always marry me, and when I get a proper job we would have enough to get by on."

Lily assumed he was joking. She had no intention of marrying anyone, she said. And how could she? She was not going to be parted from her brothers, and what man in his right mind would want to marry two teenage boys as well as a wife.

Jack suddenly became serious, and somehow blurted out a proper proposal of marriage. He told Lily he loved her, and he loved her brothers, and as soon as he had a job he would marry all three or even four of them. He begged her to say yes, or at least not to say no. Lily was genuinely moved. She told Jack she was very fond of him, and she knew her brothers, particularly Hugh, liked him a lot, and were very grateful for all he did for them.

But she did not know what to say, and anyway, as he himself had said, he would have to find a job first. So she did not say yes, but she did not say no. Jack went home that night blissfully happy. He had fully dreaded a sharp and even scornful no.

Lily told no one. Jack was back in Sligo immediately afterwards, and she did not see him for more than a month. The idea was growing in her mind, not just of becoming Mrs Jack Kennedy, but of having a home provided for herself and at least the two younger boys. Already they all got on fine together. Jack could make them all laugh, and she had seen how kind and generous he had been to his own brothers and to his mother during the loss of Willy.

Crucially, he was saved, and not just that, but was a regular attender at Elim and a stalwart of the Elim Crusaders. Lily was now so immersed in Elim that she could not have contemplated marriage with anyone who did not belong, and she certainly could not marry anyone who was not saved. She remembered how she had laughed at the idea of Jack when he had first asked her out and felt rather guilty when she recalled how she had ridiculed him behind his back.

Certainly he was no stranger. She knew and liked his family, and could not have wished for any better mother-in-law than Mrs Kennedy. (She could not say the same for his father, but you could not have everything.) His older sister Ena had been a good friend until she too had emigrated to Canada. His younger sister, Lily, and her tall dashing boy friend, another Bobby, were fellow-members of the Elim Crusaders, and his younger brother Alfie had become a pal of Bobby Cuthbert.

It was not something that occurred to either of them, but the world economy was also coming down on the side of matrimony. The aftershock of the Wall Street crash and the slump in America was hitting Europe. In Britain hunger marchers were on the road, factories were closing and the numbers of unemployed rising rapidly and alarmingly.

The linen industry was again being squeezed, perhaps as never before. Lily knew from the talk on the Moat Road, and the gossip at work, that the laundry where she was employed was likely to go under, and that finding another job would be almost impossible. On the other hand, the unemployed were more likely to get sick and need medicine than anyone else, so chemists' shops were not going to go out of business.

So when Jack called at the Moat Road a month or so after the proposal, Lily still did not say yes, but by not saying no she was already well down the road to a yes. It remained a fairly leisurely road for several months, for the lack of a permanent job for Jack meant there was no pressure to settle things definitely, and the fact that he was still working away from Ballymena in temporary jobs ensured that they were rarely together and, perhaps just as important, were rarely seen together.

Then, towards the end of 1931, change was prompted from an unexpected quarter. Bobby had settled into his job in Moody's in Lisburn and was doing well. He had joined the Elim Assembly and got to know the town. He was enthusiastic about it when he came back to Ballymena, which was as often as his weekend duties at the shop permitted. It was on one of these trips that he told Jack about a job going in Lisburn.

Alexander Boyd's, the prestige grocery and medical hall which stood on a corner site in the centre of the town just across from the Cathedral and the Assembly Rooms would soon be looking for a chemist's assistant. The job had not been advertised, and probably would not need to be, but Bobby had heard all about it from a friend on the staff, and he urged Jack to put in an application immediately. He was tempted to apply himself, but he felt it would be better to stay longer at Moody's.

Jack, now more anxious than ever to find a proper job, wrote off to Lisburn immediately. The manager at Boyd's was impressed at the experience Jack had acquired around the northern half of Ireland, and invited him to come to Lisburn for an interview. Dressed in his Sunday suit, Jack was a strikingly handsome young man, and, despite the disadvantage of a Ballymena accent, was deemed as possibly suitable to stand among the mahogany and glass cupboards and shelves of Alexander Boyd and Company's Medical Hall, and dispense advice, assurance and medicine to the better classes of the town.

After exhaustive scrutiny of references, he was, some weeks later, offered the job. He was to stay in it for 25 years. With Bobby's help he found digs in Lisburn, with another employee of Boyd's, McClatchey, who presided over one section of the magnificent grocery hall.

He liked the town, and the town liked him. Boyd's was the leading chemist's, standing at the corner of Railway Street and Castle Street. The three or four principal doctors in the town had their surgeries in these streets. The Police station was in Castle Street, and Railway Street led to the military barracks which was the headquarters for the army in Northern Ireland. Boyd's was ideally situated to cater for all these clients.

Jack was soon on first name terms with the doctors, and with the station sergeant and several of the constables. Some of the soldiers from Thiepval Barracks were regular customers, and he got to know them by sight. He had an invitation to drop into the Sergeants' Mess if he found himself with nothing to do of an evening.

At first he had plenty to do of an evening. He had to work often enough, for the shop remained open late to cater for patients coming for prescriptions after evening surgery. He had tea with Bobby once a week at Bobby's digs, and, if work permitted, went with Bobby to the Crusaders' meeting at the Elim Assembly.

A bit to Bobby's surprise, he did not join Elim. His landlord, McClatchey, was a staunch Presbyterian and supporter of the Railway Street congregation. He assumed that a Kennedy from Ballymena was also a Presbyterian, and invited Jack along with him to Railway Street on his first Sunday in Lisburn. Jack was happy enough to go – Bobby was back in Ballymena that weekend – and under interrogation over Sunday lunch told how he had been brought up in West Church in

Ballymena, where all his family were members. It did not seem worth mentioning that he had lately been attached to Elim.

For most Sundays thereafter Jack was working in the shop, and the matter of church allegiance did not arise. Meanwhile, McClatchey, who took things Presbyterian rather seriously, assumed Jack would want his name transferred from the West Church congregational roll to that of Railway Street, and went ahead and did so. When he told Jack, Jack thought it better just to thank him and say nothing.

Jack's application for the job, his interview, and then his actually getting the job, all brought Lily down to earth with a bump on the question of marriage. On Bobby's first visit home after Jack got the job – the very weekend when Jack was backsliding into Presbyterianism – Lily told the brothers that Jack had asked her to marry him, and that he wanted to provide a home for them as well as for her. She had not said yes, and would not if any of them did not want her to.

It would probably mean moving to Lisburn, of course, but that would bring them very close to Bobby again. Alec could as easily look for a job in Lisburn as in Ballymena, and Hugh could go to the Tech there. A bit to her surprise, they all thought it was a great idea. Lily had been a mother to them, and they all loved her dearly. But they knew how much she had sacrificed for them, and they wanted her to have a proper life of her own. Besides which, all teenage boys and young men can weary of too much mothering, and Lily's had been of a rather intense variety.

Leaving Ballymena would be a wrench, and they would be a fair distance from Kellstown and Slemish, but Ballymena's charms were not limitless. Number 19 was very small, and the Moat Road very poor. Money was scarce, and they still had to do without things they rather wished they could have. Alec and Hugh were clearly delighted at the prospect of being close to Bobby again.

Lily told them to think about it, and to pray about it. She wanted to do the right thing, and they did not have to rush into anything. Jack would not be confirmed in his job until he had done two months' trial, and then they would have to find a suitable house in Lisburn. That would take many more months.

Jack had no doubts whatsoever. On his first trip back to Ballymena he proposed all over again, and swept aside all Lily's reservations. He was getting on great in the job, and there was no question but he would be confirmed in a permanent post. Then he played what was to be his trump card, though he had never thought of it that way. He and Bobby had gone to look at some houses for rent, and he was sure that if they both went in together they could afford a good house, large enough to accommodate not just Lily and the two younger brothers, but the whole family.

Lily could hardly believe it – the whole family together again, away from the penny pinching of the Moat Road, with the chance to make a real home for them all, and for herself to escape from the laundry. She said yes, and she felt Jack Kennedy was the kindest man she had ever met, and would make a good husband.

13   TROUBLE AND STRIFE

The wedding was set for June, and Jack and Bobby redoubled their house-hunting in Lisburn. Walterville, on a quiet road on the outskirts of the town, was found. It was a semi-detached villa, with a good garden at the front and another at the back. It had a vast bay-windowed sitting room, with a balcony above it, and it looked out across the road to the town's public playing fields. It had two very large bedrooms, a bathroom and a rather inadequate kitchen or scullery. But it would certainly accommodate the newly weds and their readymade family.

It would be vacant early in the summer, and they could move into it after the honeymoon, if they agreed to rent it. Lily came down from Ballymena by train one Saturday to see it, and was captivated. She had always longed for a garden, particularly a garden with a lawn, and Walterville had not just one lawn, but two. Compared to Number 19, the front door of which opened straight onto the dusty and dirty Moat Road, and which had only a dingy yard at the back, it was a palace set in its own estate. They decided that Jack should see the landlord immediately and try to rent it from the first of June.

The thought of Walterville put other less positive thoughts out of Lily's mind. Some nights she woke up in something approaching terror; had she really agreed to marry Jack Kennedy? Was she really going to marry him in June? She remembered how scornful she had been when people had first begun teasing her about him, how she had then thought he was the last man she would ever want to marry. On nights like that she reassured herself by thinking how kind he had been to her brothers, and to his own mother, how generous.

She knew he had a quick temper, like his father, for she had seen him rounding on his younger sisters. But he had never displayed it towards her or her brothers. She had been disappointed when he told her he had been to Elim only once or twice since moving to Lisburn, and she was surprised that he seemed to be seeing very little of Bobby. She had hoped, and assumed, that they would be the closest of friends.

Time flew. With Jack now working in Lisburn and home only occasional weekends, Lily had to do most of the arranging, not just for the wedding itself, but for the whole transformation of her life which meant giving up her job at the laundry – her only source of income – planning for the move to Lisburn, ensuring that Hugh would be able to get into the Tech there, worrying that Alec would be able to find a job, and, every so often, hoping that she was doing the right thing.

Pastor Cole, the young Englishman who had come to Ballymena as the new Elim Pastor, was the rock she clung to. She would dearly loved to have clung to him in the literal sense, for she had rather fallen for him at first sight, or perhaps first sound. She loved his polite English accent, particularly the way he said Lily, accenting both syllables equally and making it sound like the name of the most beautiful flower in the valley; so different from the Ballymena rendering which rhymed it with valley.

In truth, Lily was more than a little susceptible to young English pastors, and tended to fall in love with most of them. But she had no real hope of becoming a pastor's wife. She was, after all, a stitcher in a laundry, with little education. She had no solo voice for singing, nor was she an accomplished musician, two shortcomings which more or less ruled her out of the pastoral marriage stakes. Hope glowed for a time, for Ted Cole showed early signs of being smitten, and was rather more solicitous of the needs of young Lily and her orphan brothers than the demands of pastoral care actually required. But Jack's proposal and Lily's acceptance meant he could be as solicitous as he wanted, without any real danger.

Meanwhile the rather beautiful and somewhat more socially elevated Mary Kennedy, distant cousin of Jack and enthusiastic convert to Elim, also attracted his attention. She was already a close friend of Lily's and the budding romance between her and Pastor Cole drew them even closer together. Lily knew she could not marry Pastor Cole, so she was delighted that her friend Mary seemed very likely to. In a vague way it made her look more warmly at Jack; already his family, father apart, had helped endear him to her, and now that family was going to include Pastor Cole.

It was Pastor Cole who officiated at the wedding in June 1932, in Ballymena's Elim Tabernacle, with Kate Wallace as Lily's bridesmaid, and Bertie, the oldest of the Kennedy sons, as best man. The wedding was as grand an affair as the little Elim Tabernacle had seen. The dresses and flowers were the best that could be found, and Pastor Cole conducted the ceremony with the utmost dignity. A telegram from Winnie and Jim in Southampton, Long Island, New York, was the icing on the cake. (There was, actually, no cake, for hard times and too much spent on dresses and flowers meant there was no formal reception, just a family spread at Waveney Avenue.)

When she left the small house on the Moat Road on the morning of the wedding, it was Lily's farewell to the home she had loved for almost a decade. In Lisburn, *Walterville* had been rented and Bobby and Jack had already started to make it habitable with some pieces of furniture. The rest would be moved from Number 19 by the brothers during the short honeymoon in Portrush. The Kennedys would begin their married life in Lisburn.

The Moat Road had had its moments, but there had also been times of worry and, though Lily would never have used the word, of poverty. It would be a wrench leaving good friends and neighbours in the Moat Road, and it would be even harder to move so far away from Kellstown and Slemish. A week before the wedding she and Kate Wallace had climbed to the top, and sat in the Wishing Chair, Kate unashamedly wishing out loud for a handsome husband and a thousand a year, while Lily sat tight-lipped and wished silently that she was doing the right thing.

But the early days in *Walterville* eclipsed the Moat Road, Slemish and all such thoughts. Lily vowed she would not be like Lot's wife; she would not look back. *Walterville* began with a delicious surprise for Lily. When she and Jack arrived at the house after the honeymoon to a boisterous welcome from the three brothers, Jack took her first into the great front room – the parlour as it was known – and presented the surprise to her.

It was a piano, a good German over-strung, iron-framed upright, which he and Bobby had managed to buy and have installed, without Lily having any inkling of it. She could not believe it: her own beautiful piano, in her own parlour, in a house with gardens front and back, two lawns, several flower-beds, a balcony and her own family around her. That first day she kept escaping from the endless round of moving furniture and hanging curtains to slip into the parlour and look at the piano, and then, ecstasy itself, to sit down and play her own piano. She was still little more than a learner, and a learner without a teacher or proper lessons, but she had picked up enough to be able to play a few hymns and some popular songs reasonably well.

The piano was part of a whole new life. Lisburn in some ways resembled Ballymena; it too had linen mills and factories – even more than Ballymena – and was surrounded by rich farmland. Its weekly Tuesday market saw a trade in cattle, pigs, poultry and farm produce as lively as in Ballymena. Like Ballymena it had a river running through it, though the Lagan would have been mortally offended at any comparison with the humble Braid water. And *Walterville*, like Number 19, was on the other side of the river from the town centre. *Walterville*, in local terminology, was 'over the County Down' – that is it was on the County Down side of the Lagan, which formed the boundary with Antrim.

But Lisburn was also very different. The accent of the people was harsher, and had nothing of the distinct Scots flavour of the Ballymena tongue. Many Lisburn people worked in Belfast ('the city'), in the shipyards and the engineering works, or in linen. Belfast was close, and could be reached very easily by train or bus. Lisburn was also a more divided town than Ballymena, less Presbyterian. There was lingering bitterness between the sizeable Catholic minority and the Protestant majority. Only a dozen years earlier serious rioting had followed the murder of an RUC District Inspector in the town, and many Catholic businesses and homes had been burned.

For Lily the great difference was that she knew no one in Lisburn. In Ballymena there had been the Kellstown connection, including Kate Wallace as well as the McMasters. In Ballymena itself there was Minnie Currie, just around the corner from the Moat Road, and there was the large Kennedy family with numerous cousins. And there was the band of friends and constant companions in Elim.

There was none of this in Lisburn. In her excitement at the reuniting of the family, and the escape from the precarious situation at Number 19, never mind the upheaval of getting married, Lily had thought very little about what she was giving up leaving Ballymena. She had always been critical of it since she went to live there, mainly on the grounds that it was not Crayford, and was not in England.

She took refuge in letter-writing. She had always been a good correspondent, but now the letters flew between Lisburn and Crayford, between Lisburn and Kellstown, between Lisburn and Ballymena, and between Lisburn and somewhere entirely new – Millbrook, New York. Letters from Winnie now gave a first-hand account of the Depression and the real poverty many in America were facing. Fortunately Jim had found a new job as a gamekeeper on an estate in the Hudson Valley, and with it had come a large and comfortable house in the grounds. Winnie's dream had come true in almost every particular, and to add to her happiness that autumn, she gave birth to a baby daughter.

After some months in Lisburn, Lily found herself thinking of Ballymena as home, and began to make unfavourable comparisons in her mind between it and Lisburn. But they were half-formed and never-expressed doubts. By the autumn of 1932 life at *Walterville* had taken on its own shape and could hardly have been better. Alec had found a job as an assistant in Stewart's Cash Stores grocery shop, and Hugh was enrolled in the local Technical School. Every morning Walterville disgorged four intrepid cyclists to tackle the steep face of Bridge Street, Hugh perched on a new bicycle Jack had bought him to mark his entry into further education. At dinner time all four descended the Bridge Street hill, and with any luck, could free-wheel the whole way from the bridge to *Walterville*. Then it was back up the hill again until six o'clock, and down again for tea.

Jack brought home with him, in the saddle-bag of his bike, a crisp new copy of the *Daily Express*. He had begun buying it shortly after he started work in Boyd's, mainly because all the other employees bought the *Express*, but also because he felt completely out of it when customers, particularly soldiers from the barracks, asked him what he thought of Roosevelt, or this new man Hitler in Germany, or something to do with football or cricket in England.

The *Daily Express* was something of a hit in *Walterville*. It was the first time a daily newspaper had come into either a Cuthbert or a Kennedy household, and it opened a window to a wider world that had been tightly shuttered up to then. Bobby in particular could scarcely wait until Jack had finished reading it, and young Hugh was almost as eager.

Lily had no time for it. She regarded it as 'worldy', almost as bad as a penny dreadful. Most of all she hated the way Jack propped it up in front of him as he ate his midday meal, and read it solidly, ignoring everyone else at the table. That was just bad manners. She told him so, and kept telling him to 'put that old paper away' until she realised he was paying no attention to her at all.

Cooking three meals a day for five, and cleaning and housekeeping, constituted a full-time job for Lily, and there was no question of mill or factory work. The faithful Singer had migrated from Ballymena, and was still in use for repairs and some dressmaking, and Lily was sure she could make some extra money this way when things had settled down.

The scarcity of friends and relatives in Lisburn was soon remedied. It was close to both Belfast and Lurgan, and the Culberts from Roden Street and the Campbells from Lurgan were invited to *Walterville* and became regular visitors. The large front lawn was trimmed and empty soup tins sunk into it to form a putting green. Putting was another of Lily's passions, dating back to the public park in Bexleyheath near Crayford, and practised since on every outing to Portrush. Putters and balls were acquired, and every visitor to *Walterville* was challenged to a game.

The Elim Assembly soon provided a group of ready-made kindred spirits who were already friends of Bobby. By chance, one dedicated Elim family, the Hamiltons, lived almost across from Walterville on the Saintfield Road, and the parents, plus one son and three daughters, dispelled any chance of loneliness or isolation for the inhabitants of *Walterville*.

Lily could hardly believe it when she found out that one daughter was not just a brilliant pianist, but also a qualified music teacher. From then on lessons may not have been formal, but they were frequent and free. Lily, in turn, tried to teach Hugh to play. Jack's mandolin was produced, and on Sunday nights the parlour of *Walterville* was filled with harmonious discord.

A friend at the church produced an old violin and gave it to Lily to see if she could learn to play it. The discord increased, and with it came a degree of gentle teasing, particularly from Jack, who had cheerfully borne incessant criticism of his own strumming efforts. Lily did not like being teased about her music, and for the first time Jack began to wonder if he had married a wife with a highly selective sense of humour. The violin was soon abandoned.

The first real friction arose over Elim. The Jack Kennedy she had agreed to marry had been an enthusiastic attender at Ballymena Elim, and a regular at every Crusader outing. He had been saved, a born-again believer, and as good living as that status demanded.

From her arrival in Lisburn, Lily immersed herself in Elim, and, along with Bobby, was ever present at Crusaders on a Wednesday night, and sometimes at other week-night gatherings. Jack's Sunday mid-day shift at the shop meant he rarely accompanied Lily on Sunday mornings, and Sunday evening stand-by duty ruled out regular attendance at the evening services. He sometimes had to work in the evenings during the week. Before getting married he had joined a badminton club attached to one of the Presbyterian churches, and it met on a Wednesday night. As a member of a team, he simply could not let the others down, so Crusaders were out too.

Lily's initial sympathy turned into puzzlement, and from that to disappointment and anger. In a flash of temper Jack responded to her sharp rebukes by telling her he would do what he liked. He worked hard and fed her and her brothers; he was tired when he came home at half past six in the evening, and he wanted to relax on a Sunday. And anyway, he had joined Railway Street Presbyterian Church, and if he wanted to go to church, that was where he would go.

It was their first real row; the following day Jack felt a bit ashamed of himself, and apologised for speaking like that, though he made no promises on the church-going front. Lily shrugged, and said it was no matter. Privately all her pre-wedding doubts rushed back, but she suppressed them. She would help Jack back to the straight and narrow. All things worked together for them that loved the Lord, and she knew that both of them loved the Lord.

She thought again of Jack's great kindness to his own mother. She saw how good he was to Hugh, and how much Hugh had taken to him. The pair of them went together on long walks along the Lagan towpath with Prince, the Red Setter Jack had added to the family when they moved into *Walterville*.

But early in 1933 another setback for the Kennedy family took minds off who went to which, if any, church on Sundays. Bertie Kennedy, who had been Jack's surprising choice as best man at the wedding, fell ill. The eldest son, he had returned from many years service in the armed forces and joined his father as a bread-server. He was a strong young man, on the committee of the YMCA, and a bowls player. Now 31, he was much older than Jack or the Cuthbert boys, who held him in some awe.

Towards the end of the Great War he had enlisted and become a member of the new Royal Flying corps. Though the war ended before he saw any active service, he had been trained as a flyer, and had served in many overseas postings before returning to Ballymena as something of a local hero.

Spending most of his working days in the open-air, delivering bread from his van, he seemed the picture of health, but his mother noticed how quickly he tired, and when he developed a cough the immediate fear was consumption. It was confirmed early in the spring of 1933, and Bertie resigned himself to an extended stay in hospital, probably in the sanatorium in Belfast. The only possible cure for TB was prolonged rest and good food.

Robert Kennedy was poor at showing affection towards his sons and daughters, but was, at the same time, fiercely protective of them. This manifested itself most often in his exaggerated care for their moral and spiritual welfare, involving a close supervision of their activities and friendships not at all appreciated by those so cherished. He was equally protective of their physical welfare, and decided that Bertie would be better cared for at home, where he would be guaranteed full-time nursing from his mother and sisters, and the very best of nourishment.

Having just lost one son, Willy, to TB, Robert and Jane Kennedy were reluctant to send another off to hospital to die. At the same time there was the fearful risk of infection in the crowded house in Waveney

Avenue. There were several children living at home, with the youngest still a schoolgirl. The problem of infection was resolved by the construction of a wooden shed in the long narrow back garden.

Exposure to as much fresh air as possible was one element in the treatment of TB, and Robert Kennedy had seen how the sanatorium where Willy had been a patient had accommodated some of its patients in what were called chalets, little more than small sheds, set in the grounds away from the main hospital. Some local authorities actually provided such chalets for victims of TB from the poorest families. With the help of his youngest son, Alfie, who was finishing at the Tech and was already a skilled woodworker, Robert Kennedy built such a shed, making it watertight under its felt roof, and big enough to accommodate a single bed, a small table and chair, and a washstand.

Bertie was installed in the shed, and apart from periods of remission, spent most of the remaining year of his life there. His mother and a younger sister ministered to him, ensuring that he was fed large quantities of the best food. Consumption was known as the wasting disease because those suffering from it wasted away, and it was still felt that weight gain through good eating was one way to combat it. Visitors, including brothers and sisters, had to chat to him through the open door, or wave through the small window that had been built into one side of the shed.

Bertie was well used to barrack life and Spartan living, and rather liked his own little private barracks. Again, prayers were fervently offered at the Elim Assembly for another miracle in the Kennedy family, and the pastor was a regular visitor to the shed, anointing Bertie with oil and claiming healing in the name of the Lord. Bertie was as grateful for these spiritual ministrations as he was for the nursing and the food, but had no energy left for either hope or fear. He knew than many people died from TB, but that some recovered. He had no idea which was to be his lot.

Lily and her brothers had not known Bertie before his return, and had seen little of him before he became ill. Fearful as ever for her brothers' health, Lily was relieved that they were now in Lisburn, far away from Ballymena and unable to visit Bertie and risk infection. She was also relieved when Mrs Kennedy flatly refused her offer to come to Ballymena as often as possible to help with Bertie's nursing. This was totally out of the question. No unnecessary risks were going to be taken. Jack, however, insisted on travelling home at every possible opportunity. Any Sunday he was not on duty found him on the train to Ballymena.

Bertie's illness made Lily fuss all the more over the health of her three stepbrothers. If TB could attack two healthy young men like Willy and Bertie Kennedy, who could say it would not take off a Cuthbert? The brothers were constantly reminded of the dangers of getting wet, of the need to change immediately out of wet socks and shoes. They were scolded into wearing caps on any day with a suggestion of a cold wind.

But Bertie's misfortune also showed Lily again, at first hand, the generous side of Jack that she had already noticed during Willy's fatal illness. His work in chemist's shops and his numerous contacts with doctors had given him some rudimentary knowledge of the disease and its treatment, and he assured his mother that he was taking every precaution against infection. He was constantly finding new tonics and special food supplements that were meant to be of great value to the consumptive.

By the middle of 1933 Lily had one other thing to worry about – she was pregnant. Jack was delighted at the prospect of being a father, and showered her with everything the chemist's shop could offer for pregnant mothers and brand new infants. The baby, a son, was born in January 1934, and Jack insisted that he be named Robert, after his own father. Lily refused and they had a row. Jack pointed out that her father, too, had been Robert, and her favourite half-brother was Robert. The boy had to be Robert.

Without too much grace, Lily relented but only to the extent that Robert would be one of two names. He became Ronald Robert, and Lily simply called him Ronald. She had been surprised at Jack's insistence on naming his first son after his own father, for she had never noticed much love between them. Robert Kennedy had been, and still was, a gruff, stern father, who imposed his will on his children and their lives, and on his wife too. With a sinking heart Lily asked herself if Jack was turning into his father. He already had the temper; would he now turn into the tyrant where his own family - and his own wife - were concerned?

It began gradually. Bobby was now into his 20s. He had worked hard at night classes and correspondence courses on pharmacy, and had acquired several diplomas. A much better job came up in a large chemist's in Belfast and Bobby got it, travelling up and down by train. He had become Sunday School superintendent at Elim, and was a constant attender at meetings in Lisburn and Belfast. He was a skilful footballer as well as being a good-looking, likeable if rather quiet young man, and he had a host of friends, including girl-friends.

Jack was only six years his senior. He had long since given up night classes and correspondence courses, and while he liked his job at Boyd's, he was now earning less than Bobby, as Lily pointed out. He could pass himself at badminton, but was no sportsman to compare with Bobby, as Lily pointed out. He was a father, now responsible for a household of six. Bobby, it seemed to him, was as free as a bird.

Meetings and young ladies, and a combination of both, occupied more and more of Bobby's evenings, and his returns to *Walterville* became later and later. With a full household and someone always at home, none of the boys had ever been given, or asked for, a key to the door. There was almost always someone up, even if it was half-past-ten – though once or twice Bobby had had to throw pebbles at the bedroom window to get Alec or Hugh to come down and let him in.

Lily suggested they should give Bobby a key of his own. Jack refused. He then said Bobby would have to be home by eleven o'clock, or he would not get in. Alec and Hugh were warned not to let him in, as was Lily. Lily listened in amazement. Only a few years earlier she had heard Jack and his sisters rile against their father's curfew on them, and say what nonsense it was.

She thought Jack must be joking, and laughed, saying he was getting more like his father every day, and did he not realise it was 1934, Mafeking had been relieved and the Boer War was over. And Queen Victoria was dead. Jack's face flushed deep red and he snapped that she would soon see who was joking. He was tartly told to catch himself on.

Bobby had no wish to cause friction between his sister and her husband, and he was careful to keep the eleven o'clock curfew. But trains were missible, and inevitably one was missed. Alec and Hugh were already in bed, and Jack had just gone up, when eleven o'clock arrived, but no Bobby. Lily had been finishing off some ironing in the kitchen. She had never stopped worrying about the boys, even though they were now young men, and once their normal homecoming time had passed, she immediately imagined all sorts of disasters.

It was this deeply ingrained fear that seized her now, not the nonsense of Jack's curfew. It was almost midnight when she heard Bobby's footsteps on the gravel drive. She had the front door open before he had time to knock, and was demanding what time he thought this was to be coming home, had he no thought for others, did he know she was almost out of her mind with worry?

He had been about to apologise, and explain how the tram he was on had broken down and he had had to run to the station and just missed the train, and had then had to wait for the last one. But Lily's anger was now in full spate, and she cut off his protests and ordered him straight to bed. Bobby thought of reminding his sister that she was not his mother, that he was 21 years of age, and that being out after eleven was not, as far as he knew, actually specified as a misdemeanour in the Ten Commandments. But instead he went quietly up to bed.

Lily soon followed. In the large front bedroom Jack was already asleep, the paperback Western he had been reading lying on the pillow beside him. (Penny dreadfuls Lily called them, and she had been shocked to find that Jack had started reading them.) Lily climbed into bed and relaxed; she was glad Jack was asleep, for the last thing she wanted was a row with him too.

The next morning, as he was getting dressed, Jack asked casually what time Bobby had got home last night. "Oh he was a minute or two late. He missed the train. But don't worry, I gave him the sharp edge of my tongue. There's no need for you to say anything," Lily assured him.

"You're a liar, Lily." It was like a slap across the face, and Lily froze. "'You're a liar," Jack repeated. "For all your Holy Joe nonsense and butter wouldn't melt in your mouth, you're a liar. It was near midnight before he got home, and you defied me; you let him in anyway. We'll see about this."

"Don't be so silly. Did you expect me to leave him on the doorstep all night? It was an accident. He missed the train. Grow up."

Lily's extensive reading of Scripture had not yet made her familiar with *Proverbs* 15 and 1, and she had no notion of turning away Jack's wrath with a soft answer. In fact, the more she saw of Jack's temper the more determined she was to challenge it. He would just have to learn to control it.

Jack knew he had a temper; he had seen his father's temper in full cry, vented on his children and frequently on his wife. Jack's gentleness towards his mother, and his obvious concern for her were, in part, his own response to his father's treatment of her. He knew he had inherited his father's temper, and he tried to control it. He had learned to do so at work, where troublesome customers and difficult bosses had often provoked a rising tide of anger in him that made him want to strike out verbally if not physically.

Now that tide was in full flow against Bobby. He resented Bobby's success with the correspondence courses and night classes, he resented his new job, he resented his ability at sport, and he resented his popularity. But most of all he resented the devotion Lily lavished on Bobby, and the frequency with which she held up Bobby as an example he should be following. He would never have admitted it to himself, but he was now bitterly jealous of Bobby.

It would not do, he told himself. He was head of this household. It was his house, and Lily was his wife. Bobby would do as he was told, for in this house he counted for little – he was there on tolerance, he was there because Jack said he could be, and he would be in at whatever time Jack said he should be. He could not hit Bobby, for he was no longer a child, though he often felt the impulse to do so. But he had to show his authority, and the eleven o'clock curfew had been his way of doing so. Now Lily had dismissed it as nonsense at the first test.

It was in a blind, spluttering rage that he confronted Bobby at the breakfast table. He shouted at him, he told him never, ever, to be out after eleven; he choked on his anger and on his words, and ended by sweeping his plate of bacon and eggs onto the floor and stomping out of the house.

The baby started howling, and Lily and the three brothers looked at each other in dismay. Hugh cleared up the wreckage of the breakfast from the floor and Lily attended to the baby. None of them knew what to say, but they all knew that something much more important than a breakfast plate had been broken. Bobby apologised again for causing all the trouble and rushed off to catch his train to Belfast.

Hugh went out to see where Jack had gone, for it was far too early for him to have set off for work, but his bicycle was gone from the shed. Alec comforted his now weeping sister, and said it was too bad, just too bad, and he did not know what had got into Jack.

Routine is a powerful thing, and it was routine that put the household back on an even keel. Just before half-past-one Jack's bicycle crunched up the gravel path, as it did every day, and, just as it was every day, his dinner was put in front of him as he sat down at the kitchen table. Hugh and Alec arrived in at almost the same time and all four began their meal, with the baby asleep in his cot beside the window.

Nothing was said about the morning's explosion. Bobby was not there of course, as he could not travel home from Belfast for his midday meal, and Jack, it seemed, had no quarrel with anyone else. He asked Hugh about a football match involving the Tech that was to be held the coming Saturday, and he mentioned something about the shop where Alec worked. He asked Lily how the baby was.

As half past one approached, he went over to the circular Morphy Richards wireless and tuned it into Athlone. It was a habit he had picked up while working in Sligo and in Cavan, and anyway he was never home in time to catch the one o'clock news from the BBC. Athlone suited him fine with its half one news. Twenty minutes more and it was time to mount the bicycle and head back up Bridge Street hill and don his white coat for another afternoon at Alexander Boyd & Co.

By six in the evening he had cooled off sufficiently to apologise to Lily for throwing his breakfast on the floor. He had just lost his temper, he said, and if she wanted he would say he was sorry to Bobby for shouting at him. That night in bed he tried to explain why he had been so angry. With the new baby, he said, there really wasn't room for four men in the house. And they were men, for Hugh would soon be leaving the Tech and getting a job.

He had been very happy to give a home to the three brothers when they had been left motherless, but it was almost two years since they had all moved in together into *Walterville*, and Bobby was old enough to be fending for himself. Jack said he did not like to see Lily waiting hand and foot on her brothers, especially now that they had a baby of their own to care for. And it was not right for Bobby to be treating *Walterville* like a boarding house and coming home at whatever time he liked. Jack said he knew how much Lily worked herself up into a state if he was out late, and it was simply not fair. He would not have Bobby treating his sister like that.

The upshot was a reconciliation of sorts. In the coming weeks Jack was his charming best, Bobby was a model of rectitude in his comings and goings, and Lily grudgingly admitted to herself that it was not easy for Jack, taking on her three brothers and providing them with a home. She thought again how generous it had been of him, and how much he must have loved her to do it. But imprinted on her mind's eye were the broken plate on the kitchen floor and the contorted rage on her husband's face – rage directed towards her.

That summer Bertie Kennedy's health had taken a turn for the worse, and Jack spent as many weekends as he could back in Ballymena. Lily was happy to go with him when she could, and take the baby to see his grandparents, and sometimes go on to Kellstown to stay at the McMaster farm. These trips took some of the pressure off communal life in *Walterville*.

Bertie died at the end of September, and again Lily could see how much her mother-in-law looked to Jack for comfort and support, and how readily he gave it. She saw, once more, the better side of his nature. Following the death, her father-in-law surprised everyone by exhibiting something similar. He announced that they were leaving Waveney Avenue; two of his sons, he said, had died of consumption, and he was going to make sure no more of his children suffered the same fate. They were going to live in a good modern house outside the town with a large garden, plenty of fresh air, and away from risk of infection.

He had, it turned out, bought a plot of land on the Circular Road, a new road to the north of the town, linking the Cushendall line to the Ballymoney one, and he had engaged a builder to put a bungalow on it. Within six months the handsome bungalow had been built, and Mrs Kennedy had a vast back garden to cultivate to her heart's content. There was also more room for visitors, and Lily took to bringing her baby son to visit his grandparents on weekend trips, leaving Jack to fend for himself in Lisburn.

Lily's friendship with her mother-in-law had, if anything, become closer as a result of her difficulties with Jack, and she now found great comfort and reassurance as she shared her sorrows and doubts. There were other trips to Ballymena; Jack's younger sister – another Lily – married her long-time Elim boyfriend Bobby Service – another Bobby – in yet another fine ceremony at the Elim Church. Then Bobby Cuthbert was best man at the marriage of Alfie, Jack's younger brother. Their friendship had survived Bobby's exile to Lisburn, and Alfie's resolute loyalty to Presbyterianism.

The links between the Kennedys and the Cuthberts were multiplying on all fronts but one; the weakest link was the central one, between Jack and Lily.

At *Walterville*, the eleven o'clock curfew was still in force. Bobby's careful observance of it meant no further trouble on that front, but relations between Jack and Bobby were never full restored. On Jack's side the lingering resentment and jealousy festered, while Bobby could never forget the bullying side of Jack's nature which had been so frighteningly displayed, and which he feared would inevitably turn against his sister.

Bobby also had other worries. His close circle of friends were all within Elim, but he had a much wider circle of acquaintances, made up of the men he travelled with daily in the train to and from Belfast, and also those with whom he played football. He was a bit surprised to hear Jack's name cropping up from time to time in the train or in the changing rooms.

Jack, it seemed, was a bit of a man about town, with lots of friends that Bobby had never seen at *Walterville*. Jack had kept up contact with one or two of his pals from his pre-married days in Lisburn, but they were frequent visitors at *Walterville*. He knew Jack went out for the occasional evening with these men, and was doing so more often now that he was left at home on Saturdays when Lily and the baby were off visiting in Ballymena or Lurgan.

But these others Bobby had not heard of. From the gossip it seemed they were not averse to visiting public houses, and had been known to flirt with members of the opposite sex. Bobby had never been inside a pub, and the very idea of it genuinely shocked him. The possibility that Lily's husband was going into pubs, and presumably drinking, and possibly even flirting with girls when he was a newly married man and a new father, and was supposed to be a born-again Christian, was almost too much to contemplate.

Bobby thought of confronting Jack, but rapidly thought again. He had no desire to provoke another storm of abuse and temper from Jack, and he knew that the only outcome would be that he would have to leave *Walterville*, and leave Lily without whatever protection he might be able to offer her. He thought of talking to Lily about what he had heard, but then, what had he heard? Nothing but gossip, and she probably knew all about these other friends of Jack's anyway. And if he did say something she would almost certainly fly straight at Jack and throw all Bobby's accusations in his face, which would almost certainly mean Bobby being thrown out anyway. So he said nothing.

Despite these undercurrents, the summer of 1935 was a great success. Jack and Lily and the baby went off to Portrush for a full week in July, and were joined for the last weekend by Jack's two younger sisters. Staying nearby was the third sister, Lily, with her husband Bobby, an athletic swimmer and no mean performer off the diving board.

The week was crowned by a gala diving display at the Blue Pool at

Ramore Head, a dramatic narrow sea inlet framed by precipitous rocks, and equipped with a springboard and a high platform. The display was put on by a group of locals and holiday-makers including Bobby Service. Lily and Jack sat hand in hand on a rocky ledge, spellbound as the daredevils plunged from the top platform or dived gracefully from the springboard.

Some were in fancy dress – one in top hat and tails who earned a mighty cheer when he surfaced from the dark depths with the top hat still in place, and another in elaborate Victorian ladies bathing attire.

The climax, as night was beginning to fall, was the fire-diver – a hooded figure who appeared suddenly on the high platform, burst into flames and plunged down into the depths. The cheer that went up as he surfaced and clambered out onto the rocks was accompanied by gasps from some of the ladies as they saw that he was not wearing the customary one-piece swim suit, but only swimming trunks, something unheard of until then in Portrush. What was more, the chest that was so unexpectedly revealed was one of the hairiest imaginable.

Jack roared and laughed and cheered, and clapping Lily on the back pointed out that the daring young man was none other than his own cousin, Matt McWhirter.

15   GATHERING STORMS

The holiday put new heart into the marriage. Holidays suited Jack; he was ever ready to organise a boat trip, or a game of putting or tennis, even though he was no athletic ace. He took much pleasure in having such a strikingly attractive young lady as Lily on his arm as they strolled by the Arcadia in the evening or down by the harbour. And he enjoyed playing with his toddler son on west strand and introducing him to the Arctic delights of immersion in the freezing waters of the Atlantic.

The feeling of well-being survived the return to *Walterville* and the renewed daily routine. Hugh left the Tech that autumn and after weeks of searching eventually found a job as a trainee assistant in Hardy's, the ladies and gentlemen's outfitters in Bow Street. At seven shillings and sixpence a week it was very poorly paid, but as Jack pointed out Hardy's was the poshest shop in the town and a great place to get a start.

It was, however, not all sunshine. The clouds were gathering over *Walterville* just as they were over Europe. It was obvious, by now, that Jack had finished with Elim, and though he assured Lily that he would certainly go with her whenever he could, he made it clear that he was much happier with the Presbyterianism in which he had grown up. He never did find much time to go there either.

He still had time to go out with his men friends, particularly on Saturday nights, and Bobby heard his name mentioned more often than ever by his carriage companions. Relations between Bobby and Jack were delicately balanced. Bobby kept out of his brother-in-law's way as much as possible, and never broke the curfew, leaving Jack no occasion to vent the anger he still harboured. He talked of going to London, where chemists were looking for trainee pharmacists, and that eased the tension, though it greatly alarmed Lily.

The comparative peace of *Walterville* was disrupted towards the end of 1935 by a warning from the landlord, Mr. Duggan, that he would have to raise the rent from the beginning of 1936. Jack had taken the house in 1932 when times were at their worst, and the linen industry was laying off workers, and Mr. Duggan had been glad to get a family installed, even if the rent was extremely modest.

But things had picked up, and every morning as the immaculately dressed Mr. Duggan – bowler hat, carnation buttonhole and black suit – strode past Walterville on his way to open his public house on Bridge Street, he reflected how easily he could let the house to another tenant at a much higher rate. So one morning he turned into *Walterville* and announced to Lily that the rent would be going up from one pound to one pound ten shillings, and would she please ask her husband to let him know immediately if he wished to continue the tenancy.

Jack knew he could ill afford the new rent, and that it would severely strain even the combined resources of himself and the brothers. Besides, more than three years of living in *Walterville* had revealed some of its shortcomings. It had only two bedrooms, and with the baby that was awkward. Its small scullery was a problem. And it was a devil to heat, particularly the large parlour and the bedrooms. It would make sense to look for a more modern house, even if it was a bit smaller, at a lower rent, particularly if Bobby was serious about going to London.

So house-hunting became a preoccupation, and left little time for worrying about Mussolini invading Ethiopia, Hitler persecuting the Jews and rearming Germany, or the growing talk of war in Europe. The real priority was finding somewhere else to live.

A regular customer in Boyd's was Tommy Cregan, a go-getting good-living builder who was making a name, and a lot of money, for himself erecting houses around Lisburn. He told Jack he was putting up two semis for a young man called Bailie who was going to move into one himself, but would be looking for a tenant for the other.

Jack and Hugh reconnoitred the site on their bicycles one Sunday afternoon, and reported that it was on a quiet country road with farm land at its back, and not much further from the town centre than *Walterville*, though on the other side of Lisburn. A week later Jack and Lily walked the two miles from *Walterville*, through the town centre, up Chapel Hill and Longstone Street to the Causeway End.

The Causeway End, or the Causey End as it was called, had been a narrow country lane that ran off the Ballinderry Road into farmland heavily dotted with cottages. It was, for most of its length, a causeway, a narrow ridge formed millions of years earlier between two glaciers. Those who knew about these things said it was a lateral moraine. Numerous cottages and one or two farmhouses clung to the edges of the ridge.

Since the coming of the railway in the 19th century the Causeway End had been divided between 'below the bridge' and 'above the bridge', for the Great Northern Railway line to the west and south (and to

Dublin) passed under the road in a deep cutting. The short stretch below the bridge was already suburbia, with some bungalows and 'semi-detached villas' joining one or two grander houses. A signpost indicated that the Causeway End was now the Causeway End Road. The roadway was as yet an untarred track, but it was undoubtedly on the way up.

The house Jack and Lily wanted to see was Number Ten, the second of two semi-detached villas, set between rather fine bungalows on the right hand side of the road near to its junction with the Ballinderry Road. The building work was almost finished, at least on the outside. They were able to wander around the site, and Lily was happy to see that it had a good garden at the front, and a large one at the back. Cattle were browsing the winter grazing just over the wire fence at the bottom of the garden.

The house was certainly smaller than *Walterville*, but they knew there was nothing they could do about that. Anyway, as they could see, it had two good-sized bedrooms and one box-room. The three brothers could share the larger front bedroom, the baby could go in the box room, and the back bedroom would be fine for themselves. Downstairs there was a large hallway with two rooms off it, and a kitchen or scullery with a door out to the back garden, and a small brick shed attached to the end of the house.

Moving from the County Down side to the Antrim side of the town was no small thing, for it was generally acknowledged that very different people occupied the different areas. Lily was not at all happy about moving away from the Hamiltons, and none of her new friends in Lisburn lived near Causeway End. But she reckoned Causeway End and *Walterville* were about equidistant from the Elim Tabernacle, which was the centre of her particular universe, so there was no disadvantage there. Causeway End was certainly on higher ground, and more in the countryside, and that end of the town was more fashionable than 'over the County Down'

It was, at first, a great success. The piano was installed in the front room, the parlour, sitting on a plush royal blue carpet. The large overmantle that had started life in the Moat Road adorned the fireplace in the back room which was immediately designated the kitchen, though no cooking was done in it. It was, more accurately, the living room, or even the dining room, but to all it was the kitchen. The kitchen, long, narrow and rather dark, was the scullery.

At the front, a two-bar iron railing formed the boundary with the road. Mr. Bailie had put matching ornamental iron gates on numbers 8 and 10, with a name plate, *Rockcorry*, on his own. Lily immediately ordered a matching one for her gate, and Number 10 became *Earlsfield*. If she could not yet get to Crayford, she could bring Crayford to her.

The early summer was spent settling in, starting work on the garden, and preparing for the arrival of a second child sometime in August. It was not the easiest of times. The house was indeed smaller than *Walterville*. The three brothers were now grown men and fitted uneasily, if at all, into the one bedroom. The bathroom was small and, in terms of supply and demand, highly inadequate between seven and eight thirty in the morning. In short, the house was crowded.

There was some bickering over access to the bathroom; there were some complaints about noise at night. Jack said he could not get to sleep for the three brothers chatting away until all hours. Tempers were sometimes lost in the morning when the bikes in the back shed refused to disentangle themselves. There was simply not room, Jack said, for four bikes.

Universal happiness, however, reigned briefly in early August with the birth of the second child – another son. This time a tiny, premature, boy. Lily, while still in hospital, announced that he would be Dennis Campbell. Campbell had been her own mother's maiden name, and she was determined that this child would be named after her side of the family. Dennis she picked out of a list of names in a magazine, and never did learn that it was derived from *Dionysius*, the Greek God of Wine.

Mother and baby were ferried home from the hospital in style in Billy Bailie's Baby Austin. Mrs Bailie herself was in the advanced stages of pregnancy, and her husband was delighted both to show off his new – first ever – motor car, and to gain some experience in the matters of maternity wards and newborn babies. Tragically, Mrs Bailie's infant son died at birth a month or two later.

Number 10 – no one ever did call it *Earlsfield* - was more crowded than ever. Two children under three can make any residence crowded, no matter how spacious, but add in three adult males, the parents, and a lolloping Irish Setter named Prince, and the situation is serious.

Jack and Bobby quarrelled again. Causeway End was just a bit further from the station than *Walterville*, and Bobby's timekeeping began to slip. Hugh hated his job in Hardy's and was not the relaxed company he usually was. He felt he was going nowhere just when he was ready to go anywhere. Alec, as usual, sailed rather serenely above the tensions around him, and spent as much time as he could out of the house. Jack's temper was in a constantly raised state as he felt more and more submerged in a household over which he was meant to preside. So he escaped for nights out with his men friends, accepted the odd invitation to the Sergeants' Mess at Thiepval Barracks, and took the occasional trip to Dublin.

Lily took delight in her two young sons. The elder, Ronnie, was already a blonde-haired little angel, though number two was disappointingly somewhat darker. The two infants and housekeeping kept her at home more than previously, but she had lost none of her enthusiasm for Elim and for matters spiritual. She read more and more books on deepening spiritual life, on the miraculous ministry of George Jeffreys, on the baptism in the Holy Spirit.

She prayed constantly for Jack, and for their married life together. She was aware, deep within herself, that something was seriously wrong. The life she had envisaged was to have been entirely within Elim, and intensely devotional. The Jack she now wanted was the Jack who had been the life and soul of Crusader outings in Ballymena, and the smiling face of evangelical holiness. But he was nowhere to be seen.

She was worried, too, about the brothers. Alec was wonderfully steady, but he was also stubbornly Presbyterian; Lily could not understand how someone who had come to saving grace through the glorious liberating force of Elim could settle for the dull formalism of Presbyterianism. She gave thanks for his steadfastness, but felt betrayed by his resolute adherence to First Lisburn Presbyterian Church.

Hugh was growing up. She knew the job in Hardy's was not what he wanted. She also knew that he had recently acquired a girl-friend, Dolly, even though both he and she were far too young. Nor was she too happy that the girl was a factory worker from the Low Road who had gone straight from public elementary school to the Island Mill.

She gave thanks for Bobby; he was everything she prayed for – a pillar of Elim, making good progress in his pharmacy courses, a steady influence on his younger brothers. But Bobby, she instinctively knew, was also her greatest concern, for he seemed to have become the key point of contention between herself and Jack. It was wrong and grossly unfair, but she could not help feeling that her whole life was falling apart – her marriage, her family built around her brothers – and that Bobby was somehow central to the impending disaster.

In a sense her life was indeed coming apart, just as all lives do from time to time. Time changes everything, and the family unit is at best a temporary arrangement. So, in the 1930s when Hitler, Stalin, Mussolini and others were rearranging the world to suit themselves and no one else, the little world of 10 Causeway End Road was showing similar fissures.

Take Bobby. In 1936 he was 23. Much as he loved his sister, and felt enormous gratitude to her, he was somewhat tired of being mothered. He was even more tired of living under Jack's constant disapproval and anger. He knew things about Jack that Lily did not, and he agonised over whether or not he should tell her. If he did, it might cause an enormous row and the ruination of the marriage. If he did not, it might mean a chance to save the marriage was lost. Either way he knew he had to move out, he had to leave Lily.

Now, more than ever before, he wanted to make his own life. Travelling home from Belfast every Thursday night, somewhat later than other nights as he had to work a late turn, he began to notice, as he stepped down from the train at Lisburn station, an attractive young lady seeing an elderly couple onto the same train, which went on to Portadown. Once or twice they boarded the carriage from which he was descending, and he politely raised his hat to them.

The young lady always waited on the platform until the train had departed, so Bobby had no chance to see where she went when she left the station. After several weeks he found he was looking forward intensely to Thursday evenings, and the fleeting glance of the young lady. Then he could think of little else.

He simply had to meet her. But no polite young man could simply accost a young lady and express his admiration, let alone his undying love. He had to be introduced. In desperation one evening, while passing the time of day with George the ticket-collector with whom he had a nodding acquaintanceship, Bobby inquired as casually as he could if George knew who that young lady was who saw the older couple onto the Portadown train every Thursday.

George smiled and said of course he knew her, had known her since she was a child. What about her? Bobby flushed deed red and stammered that he thought she was a very nice looking girl and he would love to meet her. George put him out of his misery by telling him she was Ethel Jamison, who lived with her aunts in Bachelors' Walk just beside the station, and those were her parents who lived in Portadown and who came to Lisburn every Thursday to visit. If Bobby held back for a few minutes next Thursday, he would introduce her to him.

And he did. Ethel flushed a red to match Bobby, but was not offended, for she had noticed the handsome young man who always travelled on that train on a Thursday and wondered who he was. He walked her home the few yards to her aunts' house, by which time she had had a potted version of his life, and he had learnt she was just 21, was working as a secretary in Belfast, was a member of Railway Street

Presbyterian Church, sang in the choir and did not seem to have a steady boyfriend.

A week or so later Bobby took her to a concert in Belfast given by the Glasgow Orpheus Choir, and the romance took immediate root and blossomed. But the choir gave too many encores, and the blissful couple ended up on the last train to Lisburn, and it was midnight by the time Bobby, still walking on rose-scented air, reached the Causeway End. There was a fearful row; Lily had come down to let Bobby in, but Jack rushed after her and physically threw Bobby out and slammed the front door.

Soon everyone was up. Alec tried to reason with Jack and was told to mind his own business. Lily told him he was an ignorant bully, and she would call the police if he did not let Bobby in. After five minutes of shouting Jack stumped back up to bed telling them they could do what they damn well liked, but he wanted Bobby out of his house. Bobby was readmitted and the shattered family crept back to bed.

On his next free day Bobby took Hugh to look at houses for rent; he did not tell Lily what he was doing, but he was determined to move out, and he thought the only hope for the marriage was if the three brothers left. The prospects were not good. The few houses they could find were costly, and Alec, with whom he had secretly discussed the situation, was not at all keen. He was sure the storm would blow over, and they should all sit tight.

The Causeway End curfew became a source of both merriment and anger with Ethel. She laughed as Bobby, like Cinderella, sprinted off home as the clock moved towards eleven. But she was also furious at the Hitler who imposed the curfew and treated both his wife and his brother-in-law like dirt. Bobby's thoughts turned more and more to London.

Hugh loathed Hardy's. For a start it meant no more football, for Saturday was the busiest day, and Hardy's did not close until ten at night, and not even then if a customer was still in danger of making a purchase. It was bad enough to have to work a full week, Saturday afternoon's included, for seven shillings and sixpence, but to have to do it in a shop, and to have to bow and scrape to his employers and the customers, was too much. The idea that he was being trained as a shop assistant was a joke in itself. He was rarely allowed to serve, and spent most of his time delivering goods to the homes of customers who were too grand to carry parcels around the town.

Each week he handed his seven shillings and sixpence to his sister, and she gave him back a half-crown. It was not much to get by on, and

Hugh had to seek out the most economical forms of diversion. A poster advertising a magic lantern show at the Salvation Army hall on the Dublin Road caught his attention: *Ten rounds and a knock-out. Admission Free.* Expecting an evening in the company of Jack Dempsey, or the new star, Joe Louis, Hugh headed for the hall, with the bright half crown in his pocket, alongside a solitary penny which had survived from the previous week.

But the ten rounds turned out to be the ten plagues of Egypt, and the knock-out Pharaoh's final come-uppance. Admission was indeed free, but before the end the collection basket was passed around, and Hugh, caught unawares, dived into his pocket for the penny. In his haste his fingers closed around the half-crown – the same size as a penny – and it was in the basket before he realised the error of his ways. Too timid to try to reclaim his weekly income, he slunk home thinking black thoughts about people trapped in slavery in a foreign land, and about the sort of plagues he would like to see visited on Hardy's, Ladies and Gents Outfitters.

Customers of a certain class were treated like royalty in Hardy's; chairs had to be produced, and tea served, and Hugh was usually ordered to get the chairs. For some reason he took a particular dislike to one Quaker family from Hillsborough. Mrs Davis would, once or twice a month, sail like a stately galleon into Hardy's flanked by two or three of her daughters. They all spoke with highly polished accents, not a trace of the harsh tones of Lisburn. After tea, Mrs Davis and the daughters would select their purchases, which would then be wrapped and set aside for delivery, not to Hillsborough, but to the Hillsborough train.

Hugh was usually the chosen messenger. Under the strictest instructions to be at the station exactly five minutes before the Hillsborough train was due to depart, he would turn up burdened with parcels, and hand them up to Mrs Davis after she boarded the train. There was no small talk, no exchange of pleasantries, in fact Hugh was totally ignored until the parcels were safely stowed on the rack. Then, without a word, Mrs Davis would discreetly slip a sixpence into his hand.

The sixpence was fine, but it was small compensation for being treated as if he did not exist. More than ever, he resolved to get out of Hardy's and out of Lisburn. He had been a good pupil at the Tech, and wanted to do something mechanical, not be a shop assistant. He was going as soon as he could.

Jack knew he was wrong to behave as he did towards Bobby, though his temper always got the better of him. But it was even more wrong of Lily to defy him, and to shout at him the way she did. That was totally wrong. He was her husband, he was the head of the house and he could not put up with that sort of treatment. How could she pretend to be so holy and then talk to him like that?

He liked his job, he had made good friends in Lisburn, he had two sons and had moved into a new house in a pleasant area, yet something was wrong. Deep thinking and soul-searching were not part of his nature; he lived more by instinct and feeling – happy as Larry one moment for the simplest of reasons, and in a towering rage the next for something almost as simple. But more and more now the normality between these two extremes was a vague sense of disquiet and resentment.

The resentment was focused on his wife and her treatment of him. He had worshipped her for years, and had entertained little enough hope that she would ever take him seriously. His happiness had been genuine and absolute when they at last became close and she had agreed to marry him. He knew she had a sharp tongue – many of the scathing things she had said about him over the years of his distant pursuit had filtered back to him. He knew he could never share her almost frightening enthusiasm for the spiritual life she found in Elim. And he knew providing a home for her three brothers was not going to be easy.

But none of this had mattered alongside the entrancing prospect of making Lily his wife. Then, suddenly, the miracle happened, and she was Mrs Jack Kennedy. He had won the gold medal, taken the top prize. Perhaps that was the problem. The man who has a long and arduous climb to reach the highest mountain peak takes delight in the achievement and glories in the panoramic view before him. But almost immediately his thoughts turn to the descent, and to telling others he had made it. Residing permanently on the summit is out of the question; that was never the point.

Being married to Lily was not quite the same as marrying Lily. She was a nervous bride. She had come to like Jack and to enjoy his company, and his offer to provide a home for the three boys had been so generous it could only be a measure of his love for her. She wanted to return that love, and she did so by saying yes.

She looked forward to happiness and, for the first time in her life, some security. She saw Jack and herself coming ever closer together, united in their faith, and in the embracing friendship of his family. She was aware that her heart did not, in Biblical fashion, leap within her at his approach, and she was sure he was not the chiefest among ten thousand, but marriage could be built on foundations other than poetic flights of fancy, even Biblical ones.

The prospect was clouded, but not shattered, from the earliest days by Jack's attitude towards Elim. Since her conversion in 1928, Lily's whole existence had been focused on Elim. It was not a strict denomination like the Plymouth Brethren, where rules and discipline were paramount, and could be enforced by the Assembly on the wayward individual. In Elim the strictness was self-imposed, or self-embraced to be more accurate.

The individual's life was transformed, not by any set or rules or prohibitions, but by a total refocusing of the self on the figure of Christ. The state of grace, the knowledge that all one's sins were forgiven, induced enormous happiness in the individual, and a desire to be good. The term 'good-living' was applied to born-again Christians in mild derision, but it reflected something of the inner desire of the convert to be better, to live in harmony with others rather than in bitterness and strife, to seek goodness and shun evil.

For a generation that had known the horrors of the Great War and the deprivation, injustice and poverty of working class life, the Christian experience offered real hope of transfiguration. Poorly dressed people, often hungry, could stand in dingy mission halls with eyes shining and broad smiles on their faces and sing that they were '...living on the mountain, underneath a cloudless sky' and 'drinking at the fountain that never will run dry', for they were dwelling in Beulah Land.

In considerable part, the happiness came from sharing such certainty and hope with others. Ordinary pleasures, like picnics or rambles in the country were made immeasurably more joyful when shared with others of like mind. For Lily, life was lived within the Assembly and every outing, meeting or convention was eagerly looked forward to.

This intensely personal and joyful religious experience had its highest manifestation in the Baptism in the Holy Spirit. Elim was a Pentecostal church, and believed that this spiritual baptism brought the individual into a personal and physical relationship with the divine, usually through 'speaking in tongues' when the baptised began speaking involuntarily, and ecstatically, in an unknown tongue, presumably praising God.

New converts and adherents were encouraged to 'seek the baptism', and pastors and elders often prayed for those seeking, sometimes laying hands on their heads, or anointing them with oil. From time to time one or more of those seeking would burst into tongues, and there would be rejoicing at confirmation of another baptism. Not everyone had this experience. Some members had sought the baptism for years, but had never spoken in tongues. Some spoke in tongues once, but never again. But no one questioned the doctrine, and it was central to the beliefs of Elim.

Lily had been seeking the baptism for some time. Those who sought and didn't find were encouraged to examine their lives, to see if there was some blemish or fault that was keeping the Holy Spirit at bay, some link of weakness in their faith. Lily began to worry that her marriage was an impediment. If she and Jack were now one flesh, one being, then could she also have totally surrendered herself and her life to the Lord? What sort of marriage could it be if what was of supreme and all encompassing importance to her was of little consequence to him?

Lily's life consisted of three elements – her faith, her family and her marriage. Almost without her realising it, the marriage had been relegated to the rank of least important. She had not come to her husband 'forsaking all others' but had brought along the others, including the readymade family, and the others were now more important.

Nor had Jack forsaken all others. In his days away from Ballymena and particularly in his six months or so as an unmarried lodger in Lisburn he had made new friends who were his friends only – not mutual acquaintances with Lily, not part of any church or assembly. And they remained his friends after marriage. Even before serious arguments began, Lily and Jack, far from being everything to each other, were just parts of each other's lives.

Jack had grown up in a family of nine. He had never been very close to his father, nor had he admired or even liked him over much. But he had grown up in a family where the father was head of the household, and commanded respect, or at least obedience, from all. Jack, like his brothers and sisters, had misbehaved and broken the rules, but he had never openly defied his father; he had never challenged him.

One reason why he had been so ready to offer a home to Lily's brothers was that the idea of being instantly head of a family appealed to him. As a younger brother in a large family, who was not brilliantly successful at anything, he had never been taken too seriously. Rather, he was taken for granted by family and friends. But as a married man with his own house, pretty young wife and three young men under his charge, he could see himself as a man of substance, of some importance.

Even at *Walterville* it had begun to dawn on him that no one saw him as head of a family. The stepbrothers treated him like a brother, not a father, and Lily treated him as if she had taken him into her family, not the other way round. As the tensions grew, Lily asked herself if Jack had promised to take in the brothers just to trick her into marriage, and Jack wondered if Lily had agreed to marry him just to guarantee a home for the brothers.

The break-up began in earnest in 1936. Before the end of the following year three things had happened; Bobby had left home and gone to a job in London. Hugh had left home, joined the RAF, got married and produced a son. And Lily had left the marital bed for good.

Bobby's departure was the least unexpected. Life in Causeway End had become more and more uncomfortable, and the rows with Jack ever more frequent. His romance with Ethel had flourished to the point where they had decided to get married as soon as was practicable. She encouraged the idea of moving to London, and had no doubt she would be able to find a job there with her secretarial qualifications.

Just after New Year, Timothy White's provided the job, and Bobby found lodgings in the residential Elim Bible College in Clapham. The choice of lodgings was one small comfort to Lily, but she had no doubt that Bobby had been driven from home by Jack's tyrannical behaviour. And she told him so.

Hugh's deliverance from the land of Hardy's was the result of an unlikely combination of the activities of Adolf Hitler in Berlin, and Winston Churchill in London. Hitler's rearming of Germany, and Churchill's repeated attacks on Britain's unpreparedness for war eventually produced a major recruiting campaign for the RAF.

Hugh could think of no more complete, or more desirable change from Hardy's than being trained as an armourer in the RAF, or failing that, an aerial gunner. So he wrote off offering his services. He was told no vacancies were available for those particular lines of business, but there could be room for trainee wireless operators. So he said yes, and was called to Belfast for a written test in English and Mathematics, which he took one Saturday morning, risking disapproval if not dismissal from Mr. Hardy.

He was told he had passed the test, and would be called when a vacancy arose. Lily was furious, though more with Jack than with Hugh. He was driving Hugh out of the house, just as he had driven out Bobby, she said. Within a month the call came, and in February Hugh went off with a group of other recruits by boat and train to Ruislip, where after a further month's induction, and a great deal of marching and drilling, they were invited either to take the King's shilling, or a last chance to opt out and go home to civvy street.

Hugh took the shilling. A real shilling was formally presented to him by a senior officer at a parade in Uxbridge, and he was henceforth an aircraftman, training as a wireless operator. Knowing that an early overseas posting was likely, he returned home briefly in March to marry Dolly, and, sure enough, found himself in Hong Kong a few months later. It was to be another four years before he was back and had a chance to meet his infant son.

The change in Causeway End was dramatic. Instead of three grown men in the front bedroom, there was now only Alec. He was quiet and shy, and there was rarely any trouble between himself and Jack. In a way they were brought closer when Alec got a job in Alexander Boyd and Co's grocery department, which immediately adjoined the chemists'. His days of pushing an iron-wheeled delivery cart around the town were over, and he now spent them slicing, packing and serving butter and handling other dairy goods, immaculately dressed in a spotless white coat, and drawing admiring glances from the younger female customers, including the Misses Davis from Hillsborough.

Some of the time Lily had spent looking after and fussing over Bobby and Hugh she now spent worrying about them. Bobby had written to tell her he had been off work ill. It seemed he had some sort of blood poisoning, the result of a cut to his hand which had not healed as well as it ought. She also had two young sons to tend, and the round of cooking, washing and housekeeping to occupy her. The thought of Hugh in the RAF was bad enough, but the idea of him on the other side of the world, on the rim of China, prey to oriental diseases and cut-throats, drove her frantic with worry.

It also alerted her to what was happening in the world outside Causeway End, and she began reading the *Daily Express* and listening to the news on the wireless. The constant talk of war in Europe alarmed her even more, though she drew some comfort from the fact that Hugh was about as far from Europe as he could possibly get. She said a prayer of thanks when Mr. Chamberlain came back from Munich with his scrap of paper.

Jack followed the news bulletins more eagerly than ever. He even tried to read *Mein Kampf*, an English translation of which had been issued free, in weekly sections, with the *Express*, and which Jack had carefully collected. But it was heavy going, and the *Fuhrer's* philosophy was consigned to the bottom of Jack's wardrobe.

The departure of two of the brothers should have removed some of Jack's irritations and eased relations between husband and wife. But Lily's repeated accusations that they had been driven from home by Jack's bad temper and selfishness made their absence just as much of an irritant as their presence had been.

Even before Hugh's flight to the RAF, things were becoming much worse. Jack was spending more time away from Causeway End, mostly at the Sergeants' Mess at Thiepval Barracks. He would arrive home between eleven and midnight, often smelling heavily of drink. Once or twice he had been brought home in an army car, having had far too much to drink and been sick. Lily had had to clean him up and put him to bed. The next morning a repentant Jack would mutter an apology.

Saturday evenings were almost always passed in the Mess, and once a month there was a dance there. Gossip began to filter back to Lily that her husband was a regular attender, and had become particularly friendly with the matron of a nursing home who never missed the dances, and who was also a customer at Boyd's.

Confronting Jack with these rumours provoked a ferocious row, and Lily fled with her two sons to the only refuge she could think of – the Kennedy family home in Ballymena. Jane Kennedy received Lily with warmth and, when she heard Lily's tale of woe, floods of tears. They decided they would not tell Jack's father. Lily would stay in Ballymena for a few days, and when she went back, Jack's young sister, Annie, would go with her.

Just what Annie, who was barely 20, was meant to do was not clear, but she and Jack had always got on well, and it was felt that she might be able to talk sense to him, and even if that did not work, her presence should calm him down and shame him into treating his wife with some respect.

To some extent, it did. Jack, already incensed at his wife's abrupt disappearance with the two children, was absolutely furious when he discovered she had gone running off to his own mother to complain about him. Annie was sure he was going to beat Lily in front of her, but all his blows were verbal. Even so, she was horrified at the anger and contempt in his voice. She stayed for the rest of the week in Causeway End, and things subsided. Jack offered an apology of sorts to Lily, and assured her that whatever she had heard, it was all nonsense.

A month later, Annie was back for a few days; then it was Jean, the youngest sister who came from her nursing job in Belfast for an overnight visit. Then Mr. and Mrs Kennedy themselves turned up for two days. It was clear that Jane Kennedy was overseeing a concerted

campaign to save the marriage by the only strategy she could devise –
making Jack behave with restraint in the presence of his sisters and
parents, and offering as much support to Lily as possible.

It seemed to work, but in fact was making things worse. Jack knew
exactly what his mother was doing, and greatly resented what he saw as
intrusion into his affairs. Even more he resented Lily's sharp tongue,
and her readiness to complain openly about his behaviour when his
mother or sisters were present. He also resented Lily's determination to
have as many visits from her friends or relatives as they had from his.

Her cousin Dinah Culbert, Bobby's girl-friend Ethel, and Hugh's
wife Dolly, were the most regular, but friends from Elim were often
asked for tea. Jack went out of his way to embarrass Lily in front of
these visitors, sometimes by his brusqueness of manner, sometimes by
making sharp, even threatening remarks as if they were jokes, and once
or twice by displays of temper. The more often he did this, the more
Lily insisted on inviting people to come. It was as if she wanted to show
to the whole world what a bad-tempered bully her husband was, and to
show to him that he could bully all he wanted, but he would not crush
her.

At the same time she worried more and more about Bobby. His
illness seemed to be recurring, and though he repeatedly assured her in
his letters that it was nothing serious, Lily was not reassured. Nor did
Bobby's illness endear her to Jack; as she repeatedly told him he had
driven Bobby away from home with his bad temper.

A final breach was inevitable, and it came early in 1939. It was a
Wednesday and Jack was relaxing after his dinner and looking forward
to his half-day off from Boyd's. On his own in the kitchen, warming his
backside at the fire, he unthinkingly put his hand in his pocket, took out
a packet of Craven A cigarettes and lit one. He had begun smoking
occasionally earlier that year, mainly to pass himself at the Sergeants'
Mess, but had only very recently started buying and smoking his own.
He had never done it at home.

The door from the hall opened, and Lily walked in. She stared at
Jack, open mouthed. He flushed with embarrassment, and was on the
point of stubbing out the cigarette and apologising, when he reminded
himself it was his house, and he could do what he liked. So he took
another drag at the cigarette and said nothing.

Neither did Lily. She stepped up to him, snatched the cigarette
from his mouth, threw it in the fire, smacked him across the face with
all the force she could muster, then turned on her heel and walked out of
the room. Jack was dumbfounded; his first instinct was to rush after her

and strike back, but something warned him that he might go too far. Instead he took another cigarette out of the packet and lit it.

Lily bundled the two children into their winter clothes, and strapping the younger one into his tan-sad, rushed out of the house. She walked up the Causeway End, over the bridge and along the country road to its very end, before turning and coming back towards the town by way of the Ballinderry Road. This brought her back again to the bottom of the Causeway End, close to Number 10. She could not go in, so she walked on.

Her mind was in turmoil. She knew for certain that the marriage was ruined. It was not that smoking was among the front rank of sins; it was not mentioned in the Ten Commandments, and in 1939 almost everyone did it, and very few thought it in any way harmful. But among born-again Christians it had become a sin of enormous symbolic importance.

The born-again Christian was not perfect, and knew he never could be in this life. Sometimes a born-again Christian might, under pressure, take to drink, or he might covet his neighbour's house, wife, manservant, maidservant or ox. He might even yield to temptation and commit adultery. All these were terrible sins, but man was fallible and if he repented, could be forgiven.

It was hard to say what was morally wrong in the act of smoking, even if it was a bit silly and dirty. But smoking was different. A born-again Christian did not smoke; to smoke was an outward and visible sign of not being born-again. It was a public declaration of unbelief.

For Lily it was the final straw. Her husband was not a Christian. He had just pretended to be saved to get her to marry him. She had been deceived and cheated, and was now unequally yoked together with an unbeliever. At the same time Bobby and Hugh had both been driven away from her. It was a disaster, a catastrophe. Her anger left no room for tender thoughts of leading Jack back to the paths of righteousness, or concern about his now certain eternal damnation.

It was now mid-afternoon, but she could not go home. She turned off towards the small house that Hugh had rented for Dolly and her infant son. Since the birth of the child they had seen a lot of each other, and Lily had begun to see something of what Hugh had seen in Dolly. She may have been a mill-worker, going straight – in one afternoon – from public elementary school to the work-floor of the Island Spinning Mill, but she was sharp-witted and a voracious reader.

Dolly already knew, from Hugh and from her own eyes, that things were not going well between Lily and Jack, and when a tearful Lily, accompanied by her two children, appeared on her doorstep she sensed immediately that a crisis had come. She asked no questions, but listened sympathetically while Lily lifted a small corner of the veil of privacy she characteristically used to shroud her own affairs.

The quiet chat helped her calm down, and after an hour she was ready to retrace her steps to Causeway End. When she came round the back of the house and in through the scullery door she found Alec, on his own, making his tea. Jack, he said, had gone out a while ago and had said he would not be in for his tea.

Lily attended to the children, fed them and prepared them for bed. She then asked Alec to help her move some furniture. Together they moved the baby's cot from the small box room where it had stood alongside the single bed used by the older boy. The cot was put in the back bedroom, alongside the double bed. One wardrobe was taken out of the back bedroom and put into the box-room. Lily transferred all Jack's clothes into it.

That night she was in bed with the older boy beside her and the baby in the cot when Jack arrived home. When he came upstairs to go to bed he found the door to the back bedroom locked. He shook it roughly and called on Lily to open it. She told him to go away, that his bed was made up in the front room.

He rapped sharply on the door and was shouting at Lily to open it when Alec appeared on the landing from his bedroom and urged Jack to quieten down and not frighten the children. In a whisper, he told Jack that Lily had been very upset, and that it was better that they try to sort things out in the morning. Jack, as bewildered as he was angry, stumped into the box-room.

Who knows what might have happened in the morning had not a letter from Bobby arrived by the first post, telling Lily he was in hospital, that his illness had turned out to be more serious than he had thought, and that if he did not make a recovery fairly quickly he would come back to Lisburn. Lily was distraught, and talked immediately of travelling over to London to be with Bobby, but as both Alec and Jack pointed out, with a five-year old and a two-year old, that was just not possible.

Alec said he would talk to Boyd's about getting time off, and should be able to go over very shortly. Concern over Bobby dominated Number 10. Other quarrels were not forgotten, but set aside. Jack was solicitous, and though Lily gave no indication that she would reconsider her revised sleeping arrangements, he did not make an issue of it. Alec crossed to Liverpool at the end of the week, and they waited for news from him.

Then the bombshell arrived; a telegram from Alec announced that Bobby had died in St Mary's hospital. Lily was stunned; as Jack set about arranging the funeral and his own journey over to bring the body home, she sat for most of the day in front of the fire in the kitchen, with her two-year old son on her knee. She spoke to no one, and refused any food, simply sitting and staring into the fire, occasionally lifting the poker and prodding the mixture of coal and slack in the grate. When the children came near, she grasped them both to her and hugged them silently.

That night, when the boys were asleep, she cried for what seemed hours. The next day she resumed her silent vigil in front of the fire. Jack crossed to Liverpool that night en route to London to organise the return of the body. The funeral was to be from Causeway End to Ballymena, where Bobby would be buried alongside his mother. Mr. Bailie took charge of the arrangements and sent off telegrams to relatives and friends. Funeral cars were booked.

It took three days to bring the body back. Lily spent most of them crouched in front of the fire, drinking cups of tea with sympathisers who came to sit with her, but saying almost nothing. In her mind she went over and over her encounters with death – her own mother, then her father, then Mary Wallace, Willy and Bertie Kennedy, Lizzie and, most recently, Mary Kennedy, or Mary Cole as she had been when she had died so tragically in childbirth only sixteen months after marrying Pastor Cole. And now, unthinkably, Bobby.

She could not bear to read most of the letters of sympathy that the postman delivered twice a day in their black-bordered envelopes. But two of them she read over and over again. One was from the matron of the Elim Bible College, who had been Bobby's landlady when he first went to London. It explained that Bobby had died of leukaemia, and that he had been ill for most of two years, indeed from shortly after he had moved to London. He had, she wrote, made little of his illness, and had been the life and soul of the little band of young men who lodged in the college.

He had organised football matches, had sung in the choir, and had been an enthusiastic member of the Elim church in Clapham. At the same time, she said, he had been pursuing his pharmacy studies. He had been very popular, and they all shared in Lily's sense of loss and prayed that she might find comfort in her faith.

The letter upset Lily even more, for it made Bobby's death seem still more unjust, more unfair. Why should such a good person be taken, when others who were selfish and untruthful were left to flourish? She asked the question not to seek an answer, but to make her burden of grief even heavier.

The second letter had no black border; it was from Winnie. It had been written before Bobby's death, and was full of happiness. Winnie had saved enough money to pay for her first trip home, and to bring her nine-year old daughter, Sylvia. She would be in Ireland by the end of July and would be staying for six weeks. Most of that time she would be at Kellstown, but she wanted to keep a week for Lily. Could they put her and Sylvia up? If Lily came up to Kellstown for a few days they could go and climb Slemish.

Lily could scarcely bear to read the letter. It brimmed over with happiness and hope for the future, and was like a bludgeon, hammering home to her her own unhappiness and her total lack of hope.

Her trance-like grief was interrupted by the funeral itself. Bobby lay for one night in his coffin in the parlour at Number 10 before the funeral left for Ballymena. Because of the long distance involved, motor cars had been hired, instead of the usual horse-drawn hearses and carriages. The two children were left in the care of the next-door neighbour, Mrs Bailie, and they watched the cortege leaving from her upstairs window.

17   WAR CLOUDS

Jack was good at sympathy. He had been his mother's main support when first Willy and then Bertie had died. He was genuinely and deeply distressed by Lily's heartbreak and longed to console her. He had unhesitatingly taken on himself the mournful task of bringing Bobby home, and had not spared himself over the complicated, and costly, arrangements.

He had not made much progress in his part-time pharmacy studies, but almost every day he met and tried to help people faced with diseases they knew nothing about. He tried to explain to Lily what leukaemia was, that it was an incurable disease, a cancer of the blood which made the white corpuscles increase in number so that they overwhelmed the red. There was nothing that could have been done to help Bobby. Lily listened, but all she took in was that Bobby had died of a disorder of the blood, and she knew that disorder had started with the cut in his hand which had not been properly looked after. If he had been at home in Lisburn, the cut would have been carefully treated and he would still be alive.

Why had he left home? Because her husband had driven him away. Even in the depths of her grief, Lily did not actually accuse Jack of killing Bobby, but in her own mind she had no doubt he was responsible for his death. It was this conviction which made the breach in the marriage absolute, beyond repair.

In the weeks following the funeral, Lily slowly emerged from the near total silence and isolation of her grief. She talked to Alec, and to Ethel who had been a daily visitor since the tragedy, about Bobby. She put her children to bed every night with tales of Crayford, and what Bobby, Alec and Hugh had done as children, playing in the clay pits and beside the railway. But she did not talk to Jack.

She answered his questions with as few words as possible, and she put questions to him as to whether he would be home for tea, or had he paid the rent. But there was no conversation. She also began to avoid sitting down for meals at the same table with Jack. When he and Alec came home on their bicycles for their mid-day dinner and for their tea at six, she served it up to them, but ate by herself in the scullery, or seated by the fire, away from the table.

Visitors had to be entertained, and often on a Sunday there would be Ethel and Dolly and her baby son, and sometimes a bachelor pal of Alec, so that there would be as many as six adults and three children for the one o'clock meal. The dining table would be opened out and extra chairs brought in from the scullery. Even the piano stool would be pressed into service.

Lily now always made the excuse that the table was far too crowded, and once she had served everyone else, she herself would perch on the arm of a fireside chair, or on a stool by the fire. From there she could still play the hostess, making sure everyone had all that was needed, and taking full part in the conversation around the table. If Jack was away, as he was increasingly often on Sundays, she took her place at the table without comment, squeezing in if she had to.

In the month after Bobby's death, Jack made several fumbling efforts at reconciliation which were met initially by silence, and then by bitter recriminations. Why had he married her? Why had he pretended to be saved when he was not? What about his lady friends? And why had he driven Bobby out of the house? Lily was not seeking answers to these questions – in asking them she was listing the reasons why there could never be a reconciliation.

Her feelings towards Jack were a mixture of anger and something approaching hatred. She had made a bad marriage, but she was still married. She had two young sons to bring up, and she still had a house to run. It never occurred to her to leave her husband. She did not believe in divorce – it was totally unthinkable in Elim circles – and she knew just how impossible it would have been for her to bring up her sons on her own. It was her husband's duty to provide a home and support for her and her sons, and he would have to do so.

The marriage had never been perfect, but gradually she had found her own life inside the marriage, even if it was one that scarcely involved her husband. Her life had been her brothers and her church, then her children too. Jack's backsliding from Elim, and from all church-going, had cut him off from much that was central to his wife's existence – her faith, and, in practical terms, her attendance at all sorts of Elim functions and her close circle of friends. Her regular visits to his parents in Ballymena, and their and their daughters' return visits to Lisburn, in a perverse way emphasised the gulf, for they involved Jack not at all, or at best only marginally when his parents came to Lisburn.

Far from being the head of a household, Jack found himself an isolated and unwanted lodger in his own house. He did not think he was entirely in the wrong, though he knew he had a terrible temper and had behaved badly at times. He could not fully understand what was happening, but he felt he was being treated unfairly, that he had no respect in his own household, and he sensed every day the waves of contempt and resentment that flowed from his wife towards him.

So he lost his temper; he caused scenes, he threw his food back at his wife, he cut down her weekly housekeeping allowance, he was rude to her friends when they came to the house, and he spent almost every evening in the Sergeants' Mess, or with his friends elsewhere. His friends sympathised with him, and told him his wife was being unreasonable, and that he ought to take a firm hand with her.

One night in the Mess, over several glasses of beer, his army friends told him he should join the army. Energetic recruiting was under way, and there might well be a war. In the army he would have his own life back – he would almost certainly be posted to a base in England, and after that who knows where? He would not be deserting his wife, nor would he be running away, but he would be free of her, free as he had never been since his marriage.

It struck Jack as a brilliant idea. His brother Bertie, he knew, had loved life in the services, and, from his letters Hugh was having the time of his life in Hong Kong, playing football, waited on hand and foot by Chinese orderlies, and at the same time regarded at home as something of a hero.

So he volunteered. A few days later he was called for a medical examination, at which point he told Lily what he had done. He said he thought it was his duty, that many men of his age in Lisburn had already enlisted, and that he felt it might be good for both of them if he was away from home for a while. She told him he could do what he liked, and as far as she was concerned it was good riddance to bad rubbish.

He failed the medical; he was turned down on the most unheroic of grounds - that he had flat feet. In 1939 the British Army still marched on its feet, and a serviceable pair was essential. He could not face telling Lily, so he told Alec in her presence. With a snort, that could have been of laughter or contempt, she left the room.

The Auxiliary Fire Service had lower standards as regards feet, and soon Jack was one of the many thousands who joined the various strands of civil defence. Training occupied his time, and he took to fire-fighting as happily as he took to the egalitarian camaraderie of the AFS which placed the unqualified chemist's assistant on first name terms with the local gentry, the mill owner, and everyone in between.

Training occupied all day Sunday, every Sunday, and Lily took some comfort from this enforced absence. Hugh's wife Dolly, and her baby son, came round for dinner almost every Sunday and the opened-up table with several visitors round it made these meals memorable occasions for Lily's two young sons. They were already aware of the different atmosphere when their father was absent, and of their mother's obvious delight in having her friends around her without his menacing presence.

The impending arrival of Winnie and her daughter also helped Lily emerge from her obsessive mourning for Bobby. She was determined they would stay for at least a week in Number 10, and it was arranged that Alec would give up his room to them, and either go and stay with one of his friends, or, if he had to, sleep on a borrowed camp-bed in the parlour.

Winnie wrote in early July giving all the details of her visit. She and Sylvia would be sailing from New York to Glasgow, and staying a few days in Scotland with Kate Wallace, who was married and living there. They would then cross to Belfast. Because of all the rumours of war in Europe, they had decided to go home on an earlier sailing than originally intended, and would be leaving at the beginning of September. Winnie suggested it would be convenient if they could spend the last few days of the holiday at Causeway End, as it would be easy to travel from there to Donegall Quay in Belfast.

Winnie's visit lifted the pall of mourning that had settled over Lily. She arranged to go to Ballymena early in August with the two boys and stay with Jack's parents so that she could spend as much time as possible with Winnie. With a regular bus service to Buckna it was possible to travel out to Kellstown with little difficulty, and the boys loved going to the farm.

So it was on an August afternoon at the foot of the Ballygelly Road, where the bus stopped, that the two old friends met again for the first time for more than a dozen years. Lily had been sure she would never see Winnie again and, though many photos had been exchanged, she could not help looking in amazement at this smart, very American-looking lady with light-rimmed spectacles, her curly hair tightly bobbed, and with her very American nine-year old daughter at her side.

They walked together the mile or so from the bus stop up the

Ballygelly Road and down the loanin. There, another surprise awaited Lily, for Kate, who had been her bridesmaid, had come over from Scotland with Winnie and was staying at Kellstown. At the farm, Robert Hugh's wife Jane had prepared a tea of freshly-baked soda farls and home-made raspberry jam, the speciality of the house. The two boys were sent off to explore the hay-shed and renew acquaintance with the latest pigeon-chasing Bruce.

All three had lots to tell, and lots to hear, about the years since they had last met. Winnie's news was all good – her family of two boys and Sylvia was doing well, Jim was happy in his gamekeeper's job, and they had a fine big house, with central heating, set in beautiful countryside. Its only defect, it transpired, was that it did not have a view of Slemish. They had survived the depression, though some of their friends had lost everything, and Winnie was now working part-time in private nursing, and making some money for herself.

She had no intention of ever coming back to Ireland, though she was still a British citizen with a British passport. She had nothing but praise for President Roosevelt and his New Deal, and said the only time she regretted not taking American citizenship was when the elections came round and she could not vote for him.

Kate was more interested in hearing Winnie's and Lily's news than she was in telling them about life in Scotland. Things were grand there, and she was glad to have a good stretch of sea-water between her and her drunken father. Lily was happy to share in the good fortune of her two friends, though she could not but reflect that all she had to report was the tragic death of a brother and the failure of a marriage. Instead she talked about her two young sons, and about how well Alec and Hugh were doing, and how relieved she was that Hugh had been posted to the Far East, well away from the war that seemed certain to come to Europe.

Both Winnie and Kate knew from Lily's letters that things had gone badly wrong with Jack, and they were deeply shocked at Bobby's death. But Lily looked so well, and her pride and delight in her two sons was so plain to see, that, after sympathising over Bobby, and saying what a wonderful young man he had been, they were discreetly silent about Jack.

The two returned exiles insisted that an expedition to Slemish had to be arranged. So two days later Lily and the boys were back on the morning Buckna bus. The boys were too young for the long trek and the climb, so they stayed happily at the farm, while the three friends, with Sylvia, set off up the lane and along the water-loanin, pausing briefly at the Currie farmhouse to say hello to Winnie's Aunt Annie, now Annie Currie and the mother of a son and three daughters.

Lily had never quite shared the other two's mystic regard for Slemish. She thought it was a beautiful-looking mountain, and she liked climbing it. But she had to admit that she did not find living without a view of it a matter of serious concern. It had been years since the others had climbed it and she was soon infected by their sheer delight in doing so once more. They recalled previous trips with old boy friends, and as they rose to higher ground they paused repeatedly to pick out the different farms.

Soon they were on the top, sitting on a rock and eating their sandwiches and drinking lemonade. Then they raced along the ridge and down to the Wishing Chair at its northern end. Winnie was first into the seat, followed by Kate, and both, in keeping with the rules, refused to say what they had wished for. Lily said she would not bother, she did not think it was right to go along with an old superstition like that, and anyway, what had she to wish for.

The others would hear nothing of such talk, and Lily was told to stop her nonsense and get into the seat. She sat there for ages, smiling at her friends, and wondering what, if she believed in such nonsense, she really would wish for. In her heart she knew it would have been to have a daughter; she loved her sons, but from her own girlhood in Crayford, looking after the three brothers, she had always looked forward to having her own little girl. Now she knew it could never be. So she wished instead, fervently, that her two sons would not grow up to be like their father.

The month of August passed rapidly for Winnie and for Lily, and for any remaining hope of peace in Europe. Jack took a week's annual holiday in the middle of the month, and simply announced he was going to the Isle of Man with two of his friends. Hitler and Stalin signed their non-aggression pact, and ever-more warlike sounds emanated from Berlin, but Lily was too busy cleaning and tidying Number 10 to notice. Much more menacing was the news of increased IRA activity. On August 25th an IRA bomb in Coventry, in the English midlands, killed five and injured 60.

Winnie, however, was forced to take notice. The threat of war was prompting much public discussion of the menace which had been posed by the new German U-Boats in the Atlantic at the end of the Great War, just 20 years earlier. The local papers reported a debate in Parliament during which the First Lord of the Admiralty boasted that British advances in submarine counter-measures had been extraordinary.

There were renewed calls for an international agreement to ban submarines, to outlaw them as weapons of war. The Government announced the addition of 180 ships to its anti-submarine patrols.

The House of Lords was assured that all nations agreed that civilian liners should not be attacked by submarines. Herr Hitler, the House of Lords was told early in August, was himself of this mind. Even so, all cruises out of Britain were cancelled, as were some scheduled services. Winnie, already alarmed at the talk of war, and anxious to return to America as quickly as possible, was thrown into near panic when the passage she had booked for herself and Sylvia back to New York was abruptly cancelled two days before she was due to come to Lisburn. With war now thought inevitable, the ship had been requisitioned for military purposes. A frantic search began with the shipping agents to find an alternative, and she was told she would have to take the first passage available to any North American port.

Winnie and Sylvia had just arrived in Causeway End when a telegram came telling them they were booked on the *SS Athenia*, sailing on September 1st from Liverpool to Montreal, and picking up passengers at Belfast. They would board the tender in Belfast on Friday evening, and transfer at sea, at the mouth of Belfast Lough, to the *Athenia*. This meant chopping some days off the end of their holiday, but Winnie was just glad to have secured a passage, and to be heading home to America before war broke out.

Despite being overshadowed by the seeming inevitability of war and the daily announcement of new preparations – arrangements were put in place to evacuate 70,000 schoolchildren from Belfast if necessary, and black-out regulations were published - the last days in Lisburn went well. Jack returned home from holiday and was politeness itself, and Winnie wondered if Lily had not exaggerated her difficulties just a little bit. Sylvia loved the company of the two boys younger than herself. It made a welcome change from being pushed around by her two older brothers.

Friday came all too quickly. Winnie and Sylvia were due to board the tender at Donegall Quay at six that evening. Their trunks had already been collected by the shipping agent's men, and they only had one small suitcase each to carry as they, along with Lily and the boys, took the train to Belfast and the tram to the quayside. The grandly named Transatlantic Shed was just that - a large shed crammed with all manner of packing cases, trunks, bundles and assorted cargo. At two points, narrow gaps between large doors allowed gangplanks to lead out from the floor of the shed to the ship, which could just be glimpsed through the opening.

The boys were dismayed when they were told they had to stay in the shed; no one was allowed onto the quayside. At first they had thought they would be seeing the visitors off onto an ocean-going liner, something like the recently launched *Queen Elizabeth*, the biggest passenger ship in the world. But Winnie had assured them it was only a small tender that docked in Belfast, and took them out to the *Athenia*. A tender, they knew, was something that went on the back of a railway engine, and they wondered what odd sort of boat it was going to be.

But the glimpse they got through the nearly closed doors was exciting enough – the tender looked very like a proper ship, and a big one at that. Winnie and Sylvia disappeared into the small office at one end of the shed, and then came back to say they would be boarding almost immediately. The farewells were scarcely completed when all passengers were called, and Winnie and Sylvia were swallowed up in the gap between the doors.

Their mother said it was time to go, and was shepherding them towards the tram when the great doors were pulled back and friends and relatives were allowed to stream through onto the quayside to wave goodbye to those on board. Held well back from the edge, they waved like mad at the crowded rails of the tender, though no one was sure who was waving at whom. The tender slipped its moorings, and with several blasts on its ship's siren, it eased away from the quayside and moved down the Lough towards the open sea.

Lily and the boys walked back to the tram and then the train. The boys chatted away about the ship, as they called the tender, and wondered how Winnie and Sylvia would manage to jump from it onto the big liner out at sea. Lily was very quiet, and said little. It had been wonderful to see Winnie again, and she envied her sailing off again to America, to that wonderful new life she had always said she would have. What a lucky thing she was. By the time they reached Lisburn it was becoming dark. It was the first night of the black-out, cars and buses had paper pasted across their headlamps, and the shops that were still open had blinds drawn, and curtains over their doors. As the gas street-lighting was still blazing brightly, this seemed rather odd. But it was the beginning of wartime.

Sunday, September 3rd 1939 was a momentous day for 10 Causeway End Road. Jack left early, just after breakfast, for a day's training with the AFS. Alec went out to church before eleven, leaving Lily with the two children, who were too young to leave on their own, and not old enough to take to church with her. Just after 11 she switched on the wireless to hear the Prime Minister's broadcast, and to learn that war with Germany had started. She said a silent prayer of thanks that Winnie and Sylvia were already on their way home.

Less than half an hour later, the thunder storm began. It had been threatening since mid-morning, and when it broke, it was dramatic; the sky darkened and after the first peals of thunder the rain began to fall. Lily was terrified of thunder, as was Prince the dog. He may have been a gundog, but any loud report remotely resembling a gunshot set him quivering and whimpering. Thunder always pushed him over the edge, and he would rush madly around the house, knocking over chairs, smashing ornaments, in a demented panic. They had hit on the idea of putting him in the cupboard under the stairs and shutting the door on him when there was thunder in the area.

The two boys had caught some of their mother's fear of thunder, and were more than happy to retreat with Prince and a flashlamp to the snug, dark, safety of the cupboard. Lily joined them, in case they were afraid, she explained. The thunder was the loudest they had ever heard, and seemed directly overhead. Even in the blackness of the cupboard they could see the lightning flashes through the crack under the door. There was very little room on the cupboard and the two boys were happy to snuggle up close to their mother.

It was God's anger at the war, she said. He was showing the world how disobedient it had been, and how displeased he was with it. The thought that God was in such a temper was not too comforting for the boys. They had always been told that thunder was the noise of God moving the furniture about in heaven, and they rather liked that idea. Thunder sounded just like someone pulling a table or a heavy chair across a wooden floor, but today it was much more violent. God was throwing the furniture all over the place.

One particularly brilliant flash under the door was followed by the loudest peal of thunder yet, and by a sharp cracking noise from very close by. They all wondered what it was, but Lily would not let them leave the cupboard. It was only when Alec arrived home from church that the refugees emerged and saw what had happened.

Lightning had struck the tall wooden pole Jack had erected at the foot of the garden to carry an aerial back to the wireless set in the kitchen. The top of the pole had snapped off and was lying in the flooded cabbage patch. The wire that ran to the chimney pot, and from there down to the kitchen window and into the wireless, trailed the length of the garden. Before going out, Jack had disconnected the wireless from the mains electricity, and had thrown the breaker switch behind the set which isolated it from the aerial. So the wireless had survived, and no harm was done to the house.

Alec got a ladder and reattached the aerial to the remaining portion of the pole, which to two very excited young boys still seemed incredibly high. They longed to run round to Mr. and Mrs Bailie with the exciting news that their pole had been struck by lightning, and then to every house in the Causeway End where there were children of their own age, but that was out of the question on a Sunday. Instead they were told to help lay the table for dinner.

For Corporal Hugh Cuthbert, six thousand miles away in Hong Kong and seven hours ahead of London, the day was almost over. His shift as operator in the wireless cabin at the end of the runway at Kai Tak airport would be finished in another two hours, and he would be glad to get out of the stifling heat of the small room and back to his billet at the base. He was still aching from a great game of football the previous day against a team from a visiting French flotilla, and he looked forward to a long relaxing bath and a leisurely dinner.

Just after seven in the evening the set crackled into life and Hugh adjusted his earphones and grasped his pencil to transcribe the morse code message. *Admiralty calling China Station; Naval Message* was the heading, which was standard enough, but what followed made Hugh sit up and listen with greater attention than usual.

To all concerned at home and abroad. Most immediate. Commence hostilities at once with Germany.

He typed up the message and pasted in onto the forms provided, one copy for the base commander, and one for the file. Then he typed a third which he kept for himself, for he was already an inveterate collector. A flurry of messages followed, including another collectible: *A state of war exists between France and Germany from 1700 today, September 3rd.* It was one to show his French footballing opponents if they were still around.

Back in Lisburn, the table had been opened out, the tablecloth spread and places laid for eight – full capacity. Just before the meal Alec said they should put on the wireless to hear the news, and see if there was anything more about Poland. The set was still working, and they sat in silence to the voice of Neville Chamberlain telling them they were at war with Germany.

No one knew what it would mean for them. Dolly said she was glad Hugh was in Hong Kong and well away from it. They had a war there too, but it had been going on for years between Japan and China, and had nothing to do with Hong Kong. Lily said thank goodness Winnie and Sylvia had got away before the war started. They would be well on their way in the Atlantic by now. It was lucky they had managed to get the berths on the *Athenia* at such short notice. To the two boys, Mr. Chamberlain and his war were far less important, and certainly far less exciting, than the aerial pole being hit by lightning.

On the *Athenia*, some two hundred miles west of the Hebrides, Winnie, on her way to the Third Class Dining Room for lunch with Sylvia, read the notices posted by Captain James Cook announcing that war had been declared between Germany and Britain. In the dining room they were assured that this posed no threat to them; Hitler had given specific orders that his much feared U-boats were not, under any circumstances, to attack passenger liners. The *Athenia*, the captain assured some passengers sharing his luncheon table, would make good time to Montreal, though they would be altering course from time to time as a precaution. There was no need to be alarmed. Reassured, Winne and Sylvia spent the afternoon quietly in their cabin.

Winnie was not a good sailor. She had been nine when the *Titanic* had gone down with a loss of 1,500 souls, tearing the heart out of Ulster. Around Kellstown the talk for months had been of local families who had lost relatives in the tragedy, and the disaster had rapidly become a parable beloved of every preacher eager to denounce the folly of pride and the worship of progress. Almost thirty years on Winnie still thought of the *Titanic* every time she boarded a ship, and she had done so more vividly than ever when they had been transferred from the tender to the *Athenia*.

There were three sittings for dinner in the Third Class Dining Room, but Winnie was not sure she wanted to go to any of them. Sylvia was feeling seasick, so they decided they would stay in their cabin and have an early night. It was already their third night on board the *Athenia*. They changed into their nightgowns, and sat gazing out of the porthole at the calm North Atlantic stretching away to the horizon in the clear evening light. It was just after half past seven.

What they could not see was the periscope of U-30 through which Oberleutenant Fritz-Julien Lemp was appraising the *Athenia* and deciding it was a possible target. Oberleutenant Lemp was one of the more zealous U-boat commanders patrolling the North Atlantic off the west coast of Ireland. He had, some hours earlier, received the coded message telling him that Germany was at war with Great Britain and that attacks on enemy shipping – but not passenger liners - should commence immediately.

He had already identified the ship as British by its flag. He had noted how it had been following a zigzag course, a well-known device to avoid attack by torpedo. He had been warned that armoured cruisers could be disguised as merchantmen. If he attacked now, he could probably claim the first U-boat prize of the war.

The first torpedo hit the *Athenia* amidships, crippling the engine-room. The second misfired, careering off course, and, in accordance with standard practice, Lemp ordered an immediate dive to avert the possibility of being hit by his own rogue torpedo. Some forty minutes later he resurfaced to periscope level, and to his surprise saw the target still afloat and showing no immediate signs of sinking, though lifeboats had been launched. So he fired a third torpedo.

It missed, and as he looked again at the target, and at the life boats pulling away from it, he realised that he had been wrong – it was no disguised cruiser, but a liner, and judging from the crowded lifeboats had been full of passengers. As he looked, the U-boat's wireless operator passed on a distress call he had intercepted from the target, identifying itself as the British liner *Athenia*, with 1,418 souls on board, severely damaged by presumed torpedo attack and in need of urgent assistance.

Oberleutenant Lemp again ordered his U-boat to dive. His dream of claiming the first U-boat kill of the war had evaporated, to be replaced by a determination to make no claim at all, to report no firing of torpedoes, to make no mention of the *Athenia*. To make sure no one else on board did, he ordered complete radio silence for the next eleven days.

Winnie and Sylvia did not see the first two torpedoes, but they had a close-up view of the third as it passed underneath their crowded lifeboat, rocking it violently in its wake. They had been looking out the cabin porthole when the first torpedo struck. They heard the explosion and felt the shudder going through the ship. The lights went out, but as it was still broad daylight they were more puzzled than frightened.

Still in their nightdresses, they went out into the dark passageway to find out what had happened. People were coming out of their cabins, and others were rushing back from the dining room. The word torpedo was on everyone's lips, and though no one was panicking, crew members were telling passengers to make their way to the assembly point on the upper-deck. Grasping Sylvia's hand Winnie pushed her way up one companionway until they were halted by the press of people being marshalled into some sort of orderly queue by stewards from the dining room.

Sylvia noticed that everyone else was wearing a lifejacket and said they should go back and get theirs from the cabin. Winnie asked a steward if they had time to do this, and he said they had, if they were quick. He assured them there was no immediate danger. The ship was not sinking, and they might not have to take to the lifeboats at all, but as a precaution the captain had given the order to follow the emergency lifeboat drill they had already practised the previous afternoon. Winnie was more frightened by the thought of going back down below than she was reassured by this news.

She was even less reassured when reaching the lower level they found it deserted and awash with water. The sight of the water drove out all thoughts of getting dressed or rescuing some of their possessions, and they grabbed the lifejackets and splashed back to the stairs. At the top the crowd was as dense as ever, but the steward was still there and he cleared a way for them to get through to the upper deck. Another crew member rushed them to a lifeboat, but it was already full, and they had to move along the deck to the next one.

As they waited for it to be made ready they could see other lifeboats, already carrying sixty or more people, being lowered down the side of the ship. As they watched, one suddenly lurched down, throwing its occupants into the sea. But it was quickly righted and lowered, and people scrambled back on board or were hauled out of the mercifully calm sea by crewmen and fellow passengers.

It was only when they were in the lifeboat and it had moved out of the shadow of the ship that Winnie realised with embarrassment that she was still in her nightdress, and that she was wet and shivering. Blankets were quickly distributed, and Winnie and Sylvia were soon warmly wrapped up, and sheltered from the night air by the crush of people around them.

They could now see the *Athenia*, and something of the damage done by the torpedo. A fire was burning amidships, though the ship was still sitting well up in the water and not listing. It was this same sight that prompted Oberleutenant Lemp to fire his third torpedo, to finish off the target, just as it was the sight of this and the other lifeboats which helped convince him he had better waste no more time on the *Athenia.*

The close passage of that third torpedo, and the sudden impact of its wash on the lifeboat, reawakened feelings of terror in Winnie. Up to that point she had been so determined to get herself and Sylvia into a lifeboat and away from the stricken ship that she had been almost unaware of fear. From the moment of the first impact the word *Titanic* and all it stood for had been in the back of her mind. At one point in the crowd waiting for the lifeboat, the mournful strains of *Nearer My God to Thee* had surfaced from her subconscious.

Now, in the lifeboat, she could think of nothing but the *Titanic,* and the 1,500 souls that had been lost. Someone close by was thanking God that they had been saved, and that they would soon be picked up; they were very lucky. Winnie was not so sure. She had prayed every night over the past week for her and her daughter's safe return home. The cancellation of their original passage and the imminent threat of war had really worried her. All she had wanted was to be back in good old America, safe with Jim in their rural retreat.

God moved in mysterious ways, she knew, but did he have to allow the *Athenia,* of all possible marine targets, to be torpedoed on the very first day of the war? Did she and her nine-year old daughter have to end up in a lifeboat in their nightdresses in the middle of the Atlantic? She thanked God they were on the surface of the Atlantic, not at the bottom of it, but surely things could have been better arranged than this.

In fact they were in the lifeboat all night. The crewman in charge said their surest bet was to remain more or less where they were, as the rescue ships would all be heading for the last position of the *Athenia.* Several of the lifeboats were able to link together in a semicircle, awaiting rescue. As darkness fell, they could see the abandoned *Athenia* settling in the water. During the night the wind rose and the sea became quite choppy, and many of the survivors had seasickness added to the misery of cold and fear.

To their surprise the *Athenia* was still there as dawn broke after the short northern night. And so were they, for although rescue ships had arrived, the task of locating lifeboats and recovering their passengers in darkness was not easy. Once or twice, searchlights from the ships had passed over their boat, but it was daylight before the Royal Navy destroyer *Electra* picked them up. They clambered up rope-ladders on the destroyer's side and were grasped by the sailors and helped onto the deck.

On board, in warm clothing and with hot food inside then, Winnie felt she could thank God without reservation. As they were being picked up they saw the last of the *Athenia*, as she slipped beneath the rising waves. Winnie's last thoughts were for her clothes and money, all the presents she had bought, not least the dartboard for the two boys. She and Sylvia had nothing but their nightdresses, two blankets and borrowed sweaters and trousers several sizes too large for them.

News of the attack on the *Athenia* was broadcast on Monday morning. Jack heard it first on the BBC, and told Lily. A statement from the Admiralty said simply that the ship had been hit and the latest information was that it was sinking rapidly. There was no news of casualties – or of survivors. That evening another bulletin said survivors had been picked up and were being brought back to Galway and to Glasgow, but there was no estimate of how many of the 1,400 or so on board had been lost.

Lily immediately assumed the worst - that Winnie and Sylvia had drowned. She could not imagine anyone surviving on a ship torpedoed far out in the Atlantic, and she had come to expect nothing but disappointment and disaster from life. She sat listening to the wireless all evening, but no list of survivors was given. It was midday on Tuesday before a telegram boy knocked at the door of Number 10, and Lily grasped the small yellow envelope fully expecting the worst possible news.

There were only three words in the message. 'Both safe; Winnie' it said, telling all, and with characteristic economy wasting no expenditure on superfluous detail. It was as well the telegram arrived when it did, for when Jack pedalled home shortly afterwards for his dinner, he brought the *Newsletter* with the first list of survivors. Among those who had been landed at Greenock on the Clyde was 'Mrs Wilhelmina Greer, 10 Causeway End Road, Lisburn'. But there was no mention of Sylvia, sending Lily into fresh despair. But her name, and 10 Causeway End Road, appeared the next day in a supplementary list. In all 128 lives had been lost, almost all of them killed in the explosion when the torpedo struck.

Ronnie asked if Hitler would have seen the newspaper and would now have their address. He was worried that Number 10 might be a target for the bombers.

It was four weeks later that a letter arrived from Winnie giving a full account of their ordeal. She was full of praise for the crew of the *Athenia*, who had got the passengers into lifeboats and away from the liner remarkably quickly. Winnie reckoned they had been off the ship before nine o'clock, and were at that time confident they would be picked up very quickly. After the fright of the torpedo passing close to their boat, there was no sign of the U-Boat. They sat and waited.

Hours passed and the sea roughened; despite trying to stay in a tight circle the lifeboats began to drift apart. She reckoned it must have been midnight before they saw the lights of the first rescue ship, which she later learned had been a Norwegian cargo vessel, but by that time the lifeboats were widely scattered over the ocean. It was another six hours before they were picked up by the destroyer.

Back in Scotland they had to wait two weeks before they could embark again on an American ship which had been sent to pick them up. Even then it was not plain sailing for Winnie. The US Ambassador in London, Joe Kennedy, had sent his younger son up to Glasgow to help organise the repatriation of the American survivors. He had, Winnie reported, allocated a place for Sylvia, who was an American citizen, on the *Orizaba*, due to sail in a week's time from Glasgow, but none for her, as she was not an American citizen.

This, it seems, had led to a sharp public altercation, as Winnie, surrounded by her fellow survivors, told the young John F Kennedy he had no business trying to separate a mother from her daughter, and that he had better find a place for her on the *Orizaba*, that it was a scandal that he could even think of sending a nine-year old American girl, who had only just survived one sinking at sea, unaccompanied on another voyage. The intensity of the tirade, delivered in a Braid accent only slightly modified by a decade in North America, unnerved the brash young man, and Winnie's name was promptly added to the *Orizaba* passenger list.

Lily read and re-read the letter, laughing with relief and smiling at Winnie's droll account of everything that had happened to her. It brought some light into what had become a dark world.

The imposition of black-out meant everyone, even in the Causeway End, was at war. Two round storage drums now sat in the scullery, one filled with sugar, the other with flour, for it was rumoured that food-rationing would start in the new year, and Alec had been bringing home extra supplies from work. Lily now listened to all the news bulletins on the wireless. She worried about Hugh in Hong Kong, and thanked God that the Japanese, while very friendly with Germany, had not entered the war on her side. She thanked God her two sons were far too young to have to fight in this war, and that Causeway End Road was away beyond the reach of the German bombers everyone was now talking about.

The outbreak of war, and the drama of the *Athenia*, had given her much more to think about than her failed marriage. Jack's involvement in the AFS meant he was away from home more than ever – every weekend and several evenings a week. At Boyd's, the staff now had to share in air-raid precautions and Jack did one night fire-watching each week, sleeping on the premises.

At home, there had been no reconciliation. Jack still slept in the small front room, and Lily shared the double bed in the back with her two sons. The routine of the house went on; they spoke to each other when information had to be exchanged or messages conveyed, but there was no real conversation. Jack's occasional attempts to joke Lily out of her hostility were met with icy silence.

In truth, Lily had no interest in reconciliation; she did not want it. Jack had married her under false pretences, and had shown himself a bully. He was still her husband, and it was his duty to provide a home for her and the two boys, just as it was hers to run the home, prepare meals, clean the house and do his washing. She had been doing this from her young days as a girl in Crayford, and had survived the deaths of her father and her stepmother.

Now she would survive the death of her marriage, and just as she had devoted herself to her three brothers, she would now devote herself to her two sons. She would do everything for them; they would be educated, and they would, when the time came, be saved. One of them might even become an Elim pastor. But above all else, they would not grow up to be like their father.

PART TWO

'Before the war' is history, nothing to do with me. I think I can remember the day the war broke out, and certainly that Sunday was a memorable one for 10 Causeway End. It is not every day your wireless mast is struck by lightening, war is declared, your relatives are torpedoed by a U-Boat, and your own address is published in the newspaper. I was three years and one month old, and it is just possible I can remember it.

I might even be able to go back a bit further. I have a picture in my mind of going to the front hall to collect the post that had just fallen through the letterbox, and my mother asking me if there were any with black borders. That must have been some months earlier, just after Bobby's death,

For a long time I claimed my earliest memory had been watching Bobby's funeral from Mrs Bailie's upstairs' window, but years later, recounting this to Mrs Bailie and giving her a full description of the great black horses pulling the hearse, I was abashed to be told that there were no horses, that because the funeral was going to Ballymena, it was a motorised hearse, in fact it was one of the first funerals in Lisburn to use motor cars.

So maybe I was only remembering what other people remembered. But whether my memories were first or second-hand, the beginning of the war was also the beginning of everything.

The war, at first, was terrible. My mother worried all the time about someone called Hugh, who, I was told, was my uncle and was in the Air Force somewhere on the other side of the world. She listened to all the news bulletins on the wireless, and exclaimed "Dreadful, terrible" and kept saying it was going to be just like the Great War. Someone called Hitler was gobbling up just about everywhere – places called Poland, Holland, Belgium, France – and was expected any day in Lisburn.

The wireless so upset my mother that I begged her to switch it off and not to listen to it. But it was on for every bulletin, and I began to run out of the kitchen as soon as the news started, so I would not have to hear it, or see my mother's worried face. All the war news was bad. Every bulletin brought reports of more victories for Hitler, of more

British ships being torpedoed, and then of the blitz, this new word that meant the bombing of London and other cities.

Another new word was siren, the wailing klaxon in the centre of the town that told us an air raid was expected, and the different tone that announced the all-clear. These sounds were practised regularly and became very familiar, though there was, of course, no chance of a real air raid as we were much too far from Germany. Then, after one such alert, the news leaked out that it had been triggered off by a German reconnaissance (another new word) plane high over Belfast. Perhaps Germany was not so far away.

Proof that it was much nearer than we thought came on the night of April 7th, 1941, when a small number of German planes diverted from raids in England to hit Belfast, bombing the docks and Harland and Wolff's shipyard. We slept through it all, and only heard about it the next morning, when our mother told us what had happened, and mentioned in passing that our father, as a member of the AFS, had been called out and was still in Belfast.

When he came home later that day his face was black and his uniform smeared with mud and ash. His account of the fires that had raged in Belfast gave us our first taste of the excitement of war.

A week later the excitement was multiplied a hundred fold. It was Easter Tuesday; the siren went off early in the afternoon, and an hour later came the all-clear. We were in bed, as usual, by eight o'clock, and fast asleep before our mother slipped in beside us. Then towards eleven we were wakened by the sirens again. Before we could be persuaded to go back to sleep we heard the sound of aeroplanes. The noise became louder and louder, and soon was directly overhead.

Our bedroom window at the back of the house looked east and north towards Belfast. From it we could see fields stretching away towards the Antrim Hills, the ridge of mountains that closed in the north side of the city, and though we could not see it, the heart of the city was no more than six or seven miles away as the crow flies.

By now our mother was up and dressed, and my brother and I, with an eiderdown wrapped around us, were glued to the window and peering up at the stream of German bombers passing overhead. To our right the sky was pierced by some searchlight beams, and then suddenly illuminated by hundreds of magnesium flares, dropped from the bombers. We could hear the distant crump of explosions, and see some fires.

How long we sat there I have no idea, but by five the next morning the raid was over, the all-clear had sounded and almost a thousand people had been killed, though no one admitted that at the time. Around the Causeway End, the older boys talked knowledgeably about Heinkels and Junkers, about landmines and incendiary bombs. We were rather proud that our father, again called out for AFS duties, had not yet returned.

When he did, we had more reports from the Belfast front line. He had gone into one bomb-damaged house off York Street to make sure there were no casualties in it, but there was no sign of anyone. Just to make sure, he opened the cupboard under the stairs – the accepted place of refuge in an emergency. There, sitting tightly crowded together, was the entire family of five – the parents and three children.

There was not a mark on them, but they were all dead. The blast, he said, had killed them. It was an image that was to stay with me; I was familiar with our cupboard under the stairs. It was a place of refuge for us from thunder and lightning, and I had begun to find it a useful bolt-hole when my mother lost her temper with my brother and me and came after us with a cane. In the deep recesses of the cupboard, beyond the reach of my mother and of her cane, I was safe. My brother preferred to scamper up the stairs and into the bathroom where he could lock the door and weather the storm.

The Easter Tuesday raid on Belfast was one of the worst of the early years of the blitz. More people had been killed in Belfast that night than in any other single raid outside London, up to that date. But Hitler was not quite finished with us yet. Three weeks later he was back with a spectacular fire raid on Belfast.

Much to our disappointment, we missed it. My brother and I had gone to bed as usual on Sunday, May the Third, only to be awakened towards ten o'clock and told to wrap up warm as we were being evacuated. Before we had time to think about it, we had been bundled into Mr. Bradbury's car – Mr. Bradbury lived opposite and was something senior in the ARP – and, with our mother crushed in too, we were driven a few miles outside Lisburn to a cottage at Church Lane in Broomhedge.

There we were taken in by Mrs Kidd, who was no stranger to us, as she kept Brown's shoe shop in Lisburn which was one of our mother's regular ports of call on shopping trips. The shop had a small back room with a tower paraffin heater, and we were frequent guests sitting round the heater and sipping tea. That night we had something much superior to an Aladdin.

Mrs Kidd's cottage had a large open turf fire in its kitchen, to which was attached the most marvellous piece of machinery – a wheel bellows.

As we – my brother and I – were to sleep in the kitchen, squeezed into a reclining chair, Mrs Kidd obligingly instructed us in use of the bellows, in case we felt cold during the night. After my mother had gone back to Lisburn with Mr. Bradbury, and Mrs Kidd had gone to bed, we made full use of it.

A modest twirl of the wheel set the turf glowing nicely; a more rapid spinning sent showers of sparks up the chimney, and taking turns, my brother and I soon had the kitchen glowing bright red, and the year's supply of turf much depleted. Perhaps that was why we were never evacuated again.

Back in Lisburn the following afternoon, our mother told us there had been a big raid the night before, and that thousands of incendiary bombs had started fires all over Belfast. She had heard nothing from our father and had no idea where he was. We waited up for him that night, but there was no sign of him. The next morning we heard on the wireless than the Germans had been back during the night, and that two air-raid shelters had been hit. But it had been a very small raid, with few planes involved. We were not too disappointed we had missed it.

At mid-day on Wednesday our father turned up after almost three days continuous duty. He had a bath and slept for almost another day, but not before he had presented us with our greatest trophy, which was to have pride of place in our back shed for the rest of the war. It was the remains of a German incendiary bomb which he himself had put out. Part of the metal canister was intact, and spreading out from it was a flattened, black blob of congealed matter, bearing the imprint of the sandbag with which it had been extinguished.

The bomb gave us considerable status, and all our friends came round to see it and hold it. We were taken aback six months later when Trevor Sherman somehow acquired an intact, but defused, incendiary bomb which was installed in his back shed. It looked much more menacing than our trophy, but then, as we pointed out, it had never actually exploded. Ours was the real thing.

Almost ranking with it was the Sears Roebuck mail order catalogue which Winnie sent to our mother ever autumn along with a parcel of packaged and tinned foods unobtainable in wartime Europe. The box always had American candy bars for us. The bars were too precious to share with our friends, but we did let them look at the catalogue, with its pages of toys we could only dream of – Red Indian costumes, cowboy outfits with six-shooters, sledges for the snow, tents for camping.

The weekend after the fire raid, our mother took us by train to Belfast to see the damage. Holding tightly to her hands we walked around the centre of the city and as far as York Street. Enormous piles of rubble, some still smouldering, showed where the *Luftwaffe* had destroyed whole buildings.

No one knew it at the time, but that was the last of the air-raids on Belfast, and it also marked a turning point in our attitudes towards the war. Excitement had replaced fear, and most of our worries were dispelled a month later when we heard on the wireless that Hitler had invaded Russia, and Russia was now our ally against him.

We discussed the news with the Colhouns, sitting in the gravel with our backs against the side of the house. Ronnie went in to get his school atlas to see just where Russia was. When we found it, and compared the size of it, stretching from Poland to the far end of Siberia, with the size of Germany, even if you included those countries Hitler had occupied, there was clearly no contest. Hitler had no chance. Now I wanted to hear the news, not flee from it.

Later, our mother took us to queue up at Belfast's City Hall to file past the jewelled Sword of Stalingrad, which King George was giving to 'the steel-hearted citizens of Stalingrad...as a token of the homage of the British people', after the great battle. By now, Uncle Joe was one of our heroes.

Of more immediate concern to us, the war meant no sweets and no ice-cream. But it had its compensations; we all got gas masks, and when you put them on for practice, and blew very hard, you could make a rude noise as the air squeezed out at the edges.

The blackout was great too. In winter, it turned the Causeway End into a mysterious wonderland, where you could rush in pitch darkness from one house to another, and slip in as quickly as you could once the door was opened a sliver, and only for a second. I was still too young to be allowed out much after tea, so I missed the endless chasing games with the older boys and girls that my brother boasted about.

My father went out every night after tea. Sometimes it was to AFS practice nights, and I was allowed to shine the bright buttons on his dark tunic, slipping the brass template round each button to protect the cloth, and polishing like mad. I loved it when he put on his tin helmet, adjusted his hatchet in its holster on his belt, and hung his gas mask – a really special gas mask for firemen – around his neck.

My mother still went out to church two nights a week, to the Prayer Meeting on Tuesday night and to Bible Study on Thursdays. Then she started going to dressmaking classes – the Haslem System with all its mysteries – and to art classes. And every night she went out, my brother and I raced round to the Bailies' for hide-and-seek in the blackout. The

Bailies were childless, having lost a baby shortly after I was born, and they showered us with the love they would have given their own.

Mrs Bailie went out one or two nights a week, but Mr. Bailie was almost always at home, and always ready to plunge the house into total inky blackness for hide-and-seek. The Bailie house was the same size as our own, a three-bedroomed semi, but nowhere was off limits in the hide and seek - the cupboard below the stairs, inside wardrobes, under the beds, under tables, behind curtains. Mr. Bailie took his hide-and-seek seriously – he did nearly all the seeking and we did the hiding - and he made a very sinister pursuer. He could move with total silence in the dark, and just when you were beginning to get frightened of being so long alone in the dark and wondering if a burglar might have broken in, he would pounce.

We never tired of hide-and-seek; Mr. Bailie was very skilled at not finding us in the first place he looked, and at coming very close in the dark, but just missing us. After an hour or so of terror mixed with hilarity, Mrs Bailie would come home and some treats would be produced, before we two were dispatched home. Another thing I really liked about the Bailies was that they never shouted at each other, were never cross.

Our mother and father never talked normally to each other, or joked the way the Bailies did; if they spoke at all, it was only to ask or answer questions. For the most part this did not worry me overmuch, for I had never known things to be any other way. But I did not like it when they were really cross with each other, when my father shouted at my mother, and sometimes threw things at her. I hated it especially when, in the early morning or at night, I was in bed and the row would break out down below. Then I buried my head under the pillow and tried not to hear.

Very early in the war I provided the family, and myself, with a piece of excitement we could well have done without. Further up the Causeway End, on the other side, lived the Colhouns. There were two boys in the family, roughly the same ages as my brother and myself. Their father, Sergeant Colhoun of the RUC, was an expert carpenter, and kept a garage full of lethally sharp tools. At the start of the war he built an air-raid shelter in his back garden, totally underground, with a ridged cover over the main entrance down from the garden, and an escape hatch that led up into the garage.

He then added another attraction at the bottom of the garden, a large wooden hen house with wire cages in it to hold the hens that kept the Colhouns supplied with eggs, no matter how many countries Hitler occupied. With hens, an air-raid shelter and a garage full of tools, the Colhouns' garden was an interesting place, and we spent almost as much time in it as we did in our own garden. Touching, let alone playing with the tools, was totally forbidden for the younger children. But hens were harmless, and the younger Colhoun and myself often amused ourselves by poking bits of grass through the wire of the cages, making sure we got our fingers out of the way of the sharp beaks of the Rhode Island Reds.

Enjoying this particular game, young Colhoun looked around for a good supply of grass. His father had left the lawnmower out, intending to finish cutting the lawn when he came off shift, and Ian decided he could push it easily enough to cut some supplies for the hens. This was hard work, a bit boring and not too productive.

The lawnmower, like all Sergeant Colhoun's tools, was razor sharp, and oiled in every particular. It whirred and clicked efficiency. Just why the two of us decided to experiment with its grass-cutting mechanism was never explained. The idea was for me to get long blades of grass, pulled from the uncut verge at the bottom of the garden, and hold them just in front of the flashing blades, as Ian pushed the mower to activate the drum. Whether the pace of retreat dropped, or the push accelerated, was similarly never explained, but in a trice the top of the index finger on my right hand disappeared, having been neatly sliced off just above the joint, and was never seen again, despite a subsequent and extensive search of the lawn by our older brothers.

Streaming blood and howling in terror, I dashed down the Causeway End to confront my mother with the severed digit. Fortunately it was Saturday afternoon, and Mr. Bailie was at home. The injured party, with a towel wrapped around the finger, was rushed to the Infirmary in the back of Mr. Bailie's Austin. There I was perched on a high stool and the finger plunged into icy water. Eventually we went home with a large dressing on my finger, and my arm strapped to my chest to hold the finger upright.

I had some difficulty explaining the loss of the top of a finger. There could, of course, be no question of involving a lawnmower. Lawnmowers of any type were explicitly off-limits, and a lawnmower owned and sharpened by Sergeant Colhoun doubly so. So I tried to blame the hens. I had, I said quite truthfully, been poking my finger through the wire at the hens, but under cross-examination could not be sure whether a hen had pecked off the finger, or the finger had been caught in the wire and somehow dropped off. I need not have bothered, for within a few hours the story of the missing finger and Colhouns' lawnmower was all over the Causeway End.

My mother's fury at such behaviour was soon swallowed up by a mixture of love and sorrow. It was little over a year since Bobby had died from leukaemia, and she was still convinced that that had started with an infection from a cut hand. How could a child so badly injured in an accident with a lawnmower escape the same infection? Even if he did, her little boy had been irreparably damaged, and in a way that could never be repaired. The perfect had been made permanently imperfect.

Her instinctive anger at such wilful misbehaviour gave way to an overwhelming desire to help and protect, and this found a daily outlet in walking the mile and an half from Causeway End to the Infirmary, pushing me in my tan-sad, to have the wound dressed. The doctors assured her there was no infection, but they feared they might have to amputate the finger below the joint. This provoked a whole range of new fears. Would he be able to write properly? Would he be able to play the piano?

When, after two weeks, the hospital told her the finger was healing satisfactorily and they would not have to amputate, she accepted this as a wonderful answer to her prayers, and those of the Elim Assembly which had been mobilised in the cause. It never occurred to my mother to question why God had allowed such a frightful accident to happen to her child – she knew and understood that the accident had resulted entirely from disobedience, and disobedience was part of the nature of man. Instead, she genuinely rejoiced in the goodness of a God who was now limiting the damage and healing the wound.

As for the injured party, I was surprised and relieved that my mother's anger had evaporated so quickly. I had her daily undivided and devoted attention, and I enjoyed the walk through the town, my mother pushing me in my tan-sad past Alexander Boyd & Co where both my father and my uncle worked, past the police barracks and the Castle Gardens, and down Seymour Street to the Infirmary. There I was warmly welcomed by the nurses, and placed on the high stool to have the finger dressed, and be told how brave I was.

Every day a large and rather strange woman came into the treatment room to see how I was doing. She smiled at me, and pointed, and nodded to my mother, but never said a word. When I asked, my mother told me she was a dummy, which meant she could not speak. She had a cleaning job at the hospital, and had been working on the afternoon when I had been brought in by Mr. Bailie, and ever since had taken a particular interest in the poor little lad. Meeting a dummy for the first time was exciting, besides which, I rather liked her.

The finger healed well, for which I was much praised by the nurses, and the bulky dressing was replaced by a smaller one protected by a leather fingerstall, which covered the entire finger, came down the back of the hand, and was secured by a cord around the wrist. I became very fond of the fingerstall. I wore it for months, and when it had to be thrown away because it was dirty, and because I had chewed through the end of it, I got a new one.

I was still wearing it when I started school at the end of that summer. Uncle Alec took me that first morning on the bar of his bike to the gates of the Central Public Elementary School - the name Lisburn had been chiselled off the plaque on the gates, and off the façade of the school so that Hitler would not know where he was when he invaded - and my brother marched me up the hill and deposited me in the infants' class.

I hated school, mainly because of the noise and the roughness of the boys. It was a new school, built around a large concrete yard. Before classes, and at break and midday, the yard was crowded with shouting boys and girls playing tig, skipping, sliding and other games, all of which involved making the greatest possible noise which was amplified by the enclosed nature of the yard, and by its concrete floor.

Sliding was particularly noisy. In one corner of the yard the concrete had been honed down to a slick smoothness by the steel studs, cleats and sparables embedded in the soles of countless boots. Pushing, shoving and shouting the boys lined up to take their turn – a race to get up speed, then one foot thrust out in front and the other lined up behind, both arms extended to get balance, hunkering down to reduce wind resistance, and a hurtling slide to the wall. The very best sliders could guarantee a shower of sparks from their studs as they flew down. All this was accompanied by whoops of delight, roars of encouragement, screams of anguish from the fallers, and the deafening thunder of steel on concrete.

It was all too much for a small boy – and I was very small for my age. On that first morning when my brother, under orders from the teachers, led me by the hand into the yard at play time, I begged to be taken home. No such luck, I had to stay.

The fingerstall was my salvation. It was visible evidence of a spectacular injury, and it spared me the terror of having a go on the slide. Other small boys wanted to have a look at it, and some begged me, in vain, to take it off so that they could see the full horror of the mutilated finger. The teacher made a fuss of me, and, unlike my fellow infants, I never had my knuckles rapped for failure to emulate the copper-plate examples in my Vere Foster copybook.

Soon, school was not so bad after all. Learning came easy, and in a year or so I was coming top in the examinations in reading and sums, though never in writing. But there my missing finger-top stood by me; though the fingerstall had been discarded, the shortened index finger on my right hand was a permanent and perfect excuse for less than perfect handwriting. After three years I was suddenly promoted two classes, not one, and the following year was again promoted halfway through the year. New subjects were no problem; geometry held no mysteries, and geography was a pleasure.

By my last year I was in Seventh class, the highest in the school, and I was the youngest, and the smallest boy in the class. My teacher, Mr. Thompson, was delighted to have such a bright pupil to offset the dullards, but never showed favouritism. Indeed he took some pleasure in criticising loudly his star pupil's handwriting, saying the missing finger-top was no excuse. At the end of that final year I came top in the examinations in every subject, including, for the first time, handwriting. That particular exam had been given to a part-time visiting teacher to mark, and to Mr. Thompson's outrage and mystification, she had given my spindly effort nine out of ten.

No pupil had ever come top in all subjects in Mr. Thompson's class. Though prizes were unheard of in public elementary schools, he went out and bought a copy of *Masterman Ready* and presented it to me, suitably inscribed, on my last day. But I left Lisburn Central still protesting that I hated school.

21 THE CAUSEWAY END GANG

School was little more than an incidental part of life in the Causeway End. All the gang went to Central, or almost all of them. It was only five days a week, with holidays at Christmas and Easter and for ages in the summer. It ended at three o'clock and by half past all the Causeway End gang were back home, changed out of their school clothes, and out in the street or into each other's gardens, garages or back sheds.

The Kennedys and the Shermans had back sheds, the Mulhollands, who shared their house with the Minnises during the war, had a garage and an air-raid shelter, the Colhouns the same, and the Gallaghers, who lived next door to us in a rather large bungalow, had a garage and big washroom or laundry. The Allens had a garage and an air-raid shelter, but both were off-limits to children, and anyway the Allen brothers were a shade younger than the rest. The Hatricks, just over the railway bridge, had neither garage nor shed, nor even a garden, but they lived, not in a semi or a bungalow, but in an old railway carriage, erected on blocks just inside a cornfield, hidden behind a great hawthorn hedge. Everyone envied the Hatricks.

The Minnises were a bonus from the blitz; their home had been in north Belfast, where some of the worst damage had been caused, and they had fled to Lisburn to live with their relatives, the Mulhollands. Their son Robert was almost the same age as myself.

Back sheds, garages and air-raid shelters provided places to meet and play, or just sit and talk without parental intrusion. Girls could be excluded by force, something which was often necessary, as the Shermans, the Mulhollands and the Minnises all had sisters. The Crawfords, two brothers who lived right at the top of the road near the bridge, were part-time members of the gang, but they had a fierce bulldog called Caesar whose slavering jaws and teeth meant no one ever entered their garden.

Houses, gardens, garages, shelters, fields and the road itself – almost totally devoid of traffic – were our playground. We played Cowboys and Indians, hiding, chasing, hut-building, walking the railway bridge, marbles, rounders, football, and cricket. These last were played in

Welch's field, which ran behind the houses on the left hand side of the Causeway End. It was easily reached via the fence at the bottom of the gardens of the Colhouns, the Mulhollands or the Allens, and, more importantly, the same fences meant that a rapid exodus could be made on the appearance of an irate Mr. Welch. These were quite frequent, as the Welch farmhouse sat in an orchard at the corner of the field, and Mr. Welch took serious and permanent exception to anyone trespassing in his field.

But age and rheumatism were on the side of the gang, and Old Welch, as he was known, lost enthusiasm for the chase, and was almost forgotten. Towards the end of the war when the gang had taken to cricket and the older Colhoun boy shaped a superb set of stumps on his father's lathe, we were bold enough to manhandle a lawnmower over the fence and cut something resembling a wicket. Look-outs were posted, but there was no sign of Welch, and the pitch proved quite a success.

It was not a proper wicket, and only one end was used for batting. That was the end nearest the fence, which was handy for stopping balls that eluded the wicketkeeper, and meant balls were rarely lost that end. But a lusty swipe of the bat could send the ball soaring away in the other direction into Welch's orchard. As we had only one cricket ball – composite, not real leather – whoever hit it had to go and get it back. This involved climbing the barbed-wire fence and entering the orchard, going almost up to the farmyard itself if the blow had been a mighty one.

Rheumatism or not, this was too much for Old Welch, and he resumed his counter-attacks with a zeal that alarmed the gang. Now the stumps, bails, bats and the ball all had to be secured and rushed over the fence in face of the advancing enemy. Welch also took to standing at the fence and shouting into the garden, but as the gardens were all reasonably long, and the gang well experienced in hiding in sheds, behind bushes or down air-raid shelters, this only added to the excitement.

After a time Welch again seemed to give up, and the cricket went well. But the pitch was on the bumpy side. What it needed was a roller. We were the only house on the road which had a roller, our father having purchased one in his first enthusiasm for gardening when he came to Causeway End. To my horror Ronnie volunteered our roller. One afternoon when no one was at home, he and the other older boys trundled it as quietly as possible out of our back garden, up the road and through Colhouns' garden.

It took all the older boys working together to manhandle the roller on to the top of the fence and drop it over into the field. Even though they had waited for a spell of rain to soften the ground, the roller had little effect. They were trying it with added weight, in the shape of two smaller boys standing on the handle where it spread out to grip the drum, clinging on to the two older boys pushing it, when Welch suddenly appeared.

In the panic each member of the gang dashed for whatever part of the fence he thought would be easiest to climb. But the roller was the problem; Ronnie and the older Colhoun boy were still clasping the handle when Welch was roaring and shouting half way across the field. Their first instinct was to flee, to head for the fence, but their second was concern for property. The roller had, of course, been borrowed without parental permission or knowledge, and its loss would mean retribution of the highest order.

Pulling as hard as they could, they raced for Mullhollands' garden in the far corner of the field, with the roller bouncing behind them. The others were tumbling over other parts of the fence into various gardens, with Welch waving his stick and closing quickly on them. Safely behind his own fence, the younger Colhoun, instead of disappearing, stuck his face over the fence and did the rudest thing he knew – he put the his right thumb on his nose, and with his hand spread out towards Welch, waggled the other four fingers. Welch went apoplectic and rushed to the fence, hammering it with his stick, while young Colhoun retreated behind the hen house. Fifty yards away in the corner of the field, his older brother and Ronnie were desperately trying to heave the roller on to the top of the fence.

Twice they almost got it there only for it to defeat them and crash back into the field as they jumped for safety; at the third attempt they again had it almost at the point where they could tip it over when they felt it tilting back towards them. At the same moment, a roar from Welch told them he had spotted them and was crashing through the thistles towards them. It was an inspiring sight, just enough to give them the strength to tumble the roller into the garden, and to throw themselves after it. It was a famous victory, from which Old Welch never recovered.

Later that year, when the football season began, the gang agreed that putting down jerseys to mark the goals was too childish for them. The tall Kennedy wireless aerial, that part of it which had survived the lightning strike, was now redundant, as a new-fangled metal aerial was attached to the chimney. The pole, still a good height, was due to be felled and used for firewood. Instead it became the new set of goal posts.

174

It was cut in two, and ropes were attached to each post, and a length strung between them. With the help of tent pegs the two posts were secured to the ground in Welch's field, this time at the top end, as far away from the farmhouse as possible. They served as excellent goals, fully portable, easily dismantled in case of a Welch-occasioned emergency. It was a bother erecting and taking them down every time we wanted to play football, but they could be stored in one of the gardens just over the fence. And they were splendid goals.

A sportsman to the end, Old Welch tested their portability on a couple of occasions, but knew when he was beaten.

Welch's field was not the only facility available to the gang. Further up the Causeway End, over the bridge and well into the country was Boomer's farm and adjoining sandpits. The Boomer sons and daughters were always happy to have other children to play with, and even the farmer and his eldest son, who ran the farm, were never bothered by the gang's frequent invasions. The farm, with horses and a terrifying stallion which we called Sultan, was an attraction in itself, but nothing to compare with the sandpits.

One, quite close to the farmyard, was still being worked occasionally, which meant that it was not overgrown, and the sand in it was deliciously soft. It was a great hole in the ground, of quarry dimensions, with a way in and out for lorries at one end, where the ground level sloped down. Elsewhere around the rim it was possible, indeed it was impossible not to, to race along the turf to the rim and launch oneself out into the void and then drop and tumble into the welcoming sand, and roll over and over down to the bottom. There were no rocks, and no machinery permanently in the pit, and no one was ever hurt.

Less exciting but still interesting was watching the sand martins. These birds had made their homes in holes bored into the steeper faces of the pit. The gang had been warned not to interfere with the birds or their nests, but one of the Boomer boys had pulled out a nest and shown us the eggs in it. The gang were big into huts, and someone had the idea of tunnelling into the face of the pit, like the sand martins, and building a hut. For several days we tunnelled away, and were about six feet in when the farmer discovered the tunnel and promptly demolished it, telling us how dangerous it was, and how a young boy had been killed when a tunnel just like that had collapsed and buried him.

After that the working pit was more or less out of bounds. But the second sandpit was not. It lay further into the fields, across the Dummy's Lane which ran from the Causeway End across to the Antrim

Road, and had long been abandoned. It was not one large hole, but a series of workings which were now a jumble of grassy hillocks and interconnecting paths, covered in places with whin bushes.

My first visit to the sandpits happened one day when the word went round the Causeway End that they were burning the winds at Boomers. Or at least that was what I thought they said. Just how you made wind burn I did not know, but it sounded exciting. The gang raced up to the second pit to find it ablaze – the farmer had been making his annual attempt to control the spread of the whins by setting fire to them, only thanks to a very dry spell and an unexpected breeze, things had got out of hand and the fire-brigade had been sent for. All in all, it was a splendid day.

Round the corner on the Ballinderry Road, the Chestnut Field, or cheeser field as we called it, came into its own twice a year. It was one half of a deep valley, with a long line of horse chestnut trees along the bottom where a stream would be if there had been one. It was owned by a rather posh family, the Alexanders, whose large house sat at the top of the hill, and who, unlike Old Welch, had no objections at all to the gang descending upon their property. Mrs Alexander was the writer, Janet MacNeill.

The first descent occurred when the chestnuts were ripe and ready for harvesting. This involved much throwing of sticks up into the trees, some adventurous climbing of the trees, and a lot of noise, and invariably resulted in an enviable harvest of beautiful, glossy and very large chestnuts – great ammunition for the cheeser season. The second descent depended upon the weather, specifically on a snowfall, for the Chestnut Field with its long and steep slope was tailor-made for sledges. Sometimes when the snow was really good, the Alexanders would emerge from their grand house and join the gang.

The Chestnut Field had other attributes. Just across the fence at the foot of the hill, the ground rose steeply to a dense grove of trees, mainly conifers, and at one point close to the road these formed a secret glade, very dark and sinister. It was bounded on the far side by an avenue that led up to something even more sinister – a Catholic Retreat House. In fact, it was a retirement home for elderly nuns, but to us it was mysterious and a bit frightening. The only signs of life about it were occasional glimpses of heavily cowled figures.

This dark glade was a useful place for various games, and had within it the Aeroplane Tree. This was a very large sycamore with a long, pendular branch which drooped down over the deepest part of the glade. By climbing out along it and balancing carefully with the help of a grasp on other branches, it was possible for one or two adventurous boys to bounce the branch up and down and set it springing on long upward and downward sweeps.

The glade was also the scene of the gang's annual firework display. With the outbreak of war, fireworks became both unobtainable and illegal. Hallowe'en passed each year without benefit of fireworks, but we had access to a secret supply. It was very limited access, for the supply belonged to the ever-resourceful Sergeant Colhoun, and was very much off-limits to his sons. But they were as resourceful as their father, and every Hallowe'en the elder Colhoun would filch one firework – it had to be a banger, and the favourite was a Boy Scout Rouser – and only one, for any more and the Sergeant would have been on to them.

With the Boy Scout Rouser safely out of the Colhoun house, and matches secured, we would race round the corner and up the Ballinderry Road to the Chestnut Field and over to the glade. There in secrecy and defiance of law and parents, the firework would be lit and the bang awaited. That single detonation was magic; the gang would cheer and live on the memory until the next year.

Down the fields behind our side of the Causeway End was the Fairy Well. This was visited annually by the gang, not for its mystic properties, but for its frog-spawn. A stagnant pool under a large hawthorn, it unfailingly produced masses of spawn which could be scooped out and taken home in jam jars. Weeks later, half a dozen of the gardens on Causeway End would be alive with tiny frogs, who would soon be eaten by dogs and cats, or die for lack of water.

Perhaps the handiest attraction and that most used by the gang, apart from Old Welch's field, was the railway, which general term included the track itself and the trains that ran on it, the steep banks and the lush grassland at their top, and the bridge – particularly the two-foot wide parapet that topped the walls bounding the narrow road on top of the bridge. The grassy banks were excellent for hut-making; halfpennies could be placed on the track and flattened out into pennies by passing trains (at least that was the theory) and pins placed cross-ways could be similarly fused together into decorative crossed swords (again in theory).

In practice, the trains usually scattered the halfpennies and pins among the ballast, never to be found again. The real point of the exercise was the thrill of actually being down on the railway lines – totally forbidden – and once there, of staying as long as one dared, preferably until the train was in sight. The older boys swore that if you lay on the rail with your ear pressed down onto it, you could hear the train a mile away. The only trouble with that was in that position you had very little chance of seeing the approaching train. I never tried it.

For the really bold and totally disobedient, the ultimate challenge was walking the bridge. This meant mounting the parapet at one end, and crossing the entire length of the bridge on it. The drop to the lines in the centre would have been forty feet or more, and could well have been fatal. In fact the parapet was wide enough to make the passage reasonably easy, though still highly dangerous. Some of the older boys had done it so often that they could run across.

For the rest it was a standing challenge; the young ones were not expected to, and were never encouraged to, but there came a time when an eleven-year-old's manhood would be in doubt until he had done it. (None of this applied to girls, and indeed no one wanted to walk the bridge in their presence, as they were notorious for telling on anyone who did.) Ronnie did it one day when I was not there, but I soon heard about it, and used it to blackmail him into all sorts of favours for months to come.

22 TO HELL WITH THE CLB

The gang was our world, and we were suspicious of anything outside it. But people were growing up, and discovering there was life away from the Causeway End. The first real trouble was over the Boy Scouts.

Perhaps it was because Godfrey Colhoun was involved. He was one of the gang, of course, but very prickly, and we felt it was just like him to slip off and join the Boy Scouts without a word to anyone. He was a couple of years older than me, he could run faster than any of us, and he was a good fighter. I think three things were against him - his name, his glasses and his temper. To be called Godfrey was tough enough, and to have to wear glasses on top of it was even tougher. We might have forgiven this, as we did in my elder brother who was not too well off for a name either, and also wore glasses, if it had not been for the temper. When a row began, Godfrey's glasses would come off, his eyes would narrow, and he would slaughter anyone within range.

More often than not this was Big Trevor. Trevor, also the son of a policeman, was a year older than Godfrey, and a fair bit taller, but was no match for the smarting fists and the slit eyes. It was Trevor got word of the Scouts.

'Wait till he gets his uniform, there'll be no standing him," opined Trevor to the rest of us, as we sat in our stick and grass hut high up on the railway embankment.

It was the uniform that stuck in our throats. We had lived for years with uniforms – soldiers, bandsmen, even prisoners of war – and we knew all about them. Our mother had made army style tunics for my brother and me in khaki, which we loved, but they were not the real thing. The thought of Godfrey going off on his own, and getting a proper uniform before anyone else, was too much to bear.

For the next day or two we thought of nothing else. We sat in our hut, not even bothering to put pins or halfpennies on the railway lines. For three whole summer afternoons no one walked the parapet of the bridge. Godfrey was away visiting an uncle in the country, so we were able to talk about him. At least I sat in the hut and listened to the others; as a younger brother I was not allowed to say much. My brother and Big Trevor took the lead, and Billy Hatrick from over the bridge joined in. He was younger than the other two, but the possession of a small brother gave him senior status.

Mostly it was just a recital of the evil points of Godfrey's nature, with a few slanderous remarks about Boy Scouts in general. There was no hiding the hurt; Godfrey had hit us hard.

On the third day Big Trevor turned up with some information. It appeared the Scouts did not give out uniforms right away; you had to be in for at least six weeks, and then pass some sort of test before you could wear the shorts and bush shirt, and the Baden Powell hat, the scarf and the woggle. This was some comfort, but Godfrey was well on the way to the six weeks, and we knew he would never fail any test. That was another thing we disliked about him. We could, just see him in the uniform, swanking it up the road, ready to murder anyone who looked sideways at him.

It was the next day that Big Trevor came storming over the wire fence and through the long grass, bursting into the hut with some real news;

"Wait till you hear, wait till you hear this. The C.L.B. gives you a uniform as soon as you join, and Duck Hagen says we can all join tonight."

We sat looking at him. I was terrified at the thought of joining the C.L.B. - the Church Lads Brigade, a rival youth organisation to the Scouts, attached to the Church of Ireland – and I think the others were too, for the very idea of joining anything was foreign to us, reared as we had been in the jungle freedom of wartime blackout. We envied Godfrey his uniform, not his membership of anything.

Besides, we had all had experience of some of Big Trevor's schemes before, and were not too happy about rushing after him. The mention of Duck Hagen was not so good, either, as we all knew Duck from school. His real name was Donald, but we called him Duck and he was always good for a laugh. But he was not the sort of fellow we would have quoted as an authority.

"But they haven't got a proper uniform," put in Billy, more to say something than to register a serious objection. "You have to wear your own suit."

"Of course they have a uniform, you idiot. They give you the black belt and white strap thing and the cap as soon as you join."

The C.L.B. had a more modern look than the Scouts, with a military side cap, a white cross strap, and a black belt with a pouch on it.

True you had to wear your own suit under that, but Trevor added the clincher on that score: "And you can wear your long trousers."

Now that indeed was a point, especially to a fellow who had just fought his way out of shorts. As for me, of course, it made no difference, I would be in shorts for years yet. "As soon as you join properly they give you the cap and belt thing," repeated Trevor, "Duck has it already. We'll all go tonight, and wait till you see Godfrey's face when we march home."

The argument over the uniform had pushed aside the daunting thought of actually joining that night. But before anyone could think up a fresh objection, Trevor charged on: "And they have a band, with bugles and drums, and Duck's learning to play the drum."

Well that did it. We all sat there and saw ourselves marching home that night, or better still, slipping home with our uniforms in our pockets, our bugles and drums under our coats. With a bit of luck we would be able to play them by the following week when Godfrey was due back.

"They start at seven, and Duck says he'll meet us outside."

That brought us all back to earth with a bump. We had never joined anything in our lives; we would have opted out of school if that had been possible. But there it was. On the one hand, Godfrey swanking up the road in his Scout togs, on the other, the rest of us in smart C.L.B rig, with bugles and drums, and, best of all, the look on Godfrey's face when he saw us. Mind you I was still hoping I would be too young for the C.L.B. But my brother squashed that hope:

"Well, we'll all go together, so that'll be five of us, counting your young Joe, " said he looking at Billy. At the mention of Joe I knew I was for it, for Joe was a few months younger than me. I was a conscript.

Anyway, we went that Friday evening, five recruits in search of a uniform. The C.L.B. met in a church hall in the middle of the town, a mile from our road. We were in no hurry to get there, so by the time we arrived, there was no Duck outside the hall, and it was obvious the meeting had started. The hall was an old-fashioned building, a little behind the church itself. The porch was in the middle of the side wall, and the inner door opened right onto the meeting room. We hung around for a minute or two, plucking up our reserves of courage.

At last we pushed our way in, Big Trevor managing to come last. Stretched from one end of the room to the other, in a line facing the door where we stood, were about thirty boys, ranging from big seventeen year olds down to some as young as myself. They all wore the side cap and cross-strap uniform. They were standing rigidly to attention, and in front of them with his back to us, stood a smallish, tightly built, young man. He had on the belt and cross-strap, but no hat. His fair wisps of hair crawled about on premature baldness. As we clung to the door he swelled visibly and opened his mouth, roaring "Right Turn". The line swivelled to the right. "Face front" and the line swung back again.

"There's Duck", whispered Trevor, waving at our sole ally near the head of the line. Duck waved back.

"Haaaaaagen". The yell almost blew the line a pace backward, and we could see the crimson spreading backwards over the bald head "Hagen, attennnnnnnnnshun." Duck froze back into position. There was not a sound in the room. The five of us stood to attention behind Baldyhead's back.

"Form fourrrrrrrrs". The roof echoed again, and the boys stepped smartly across and up, to form a marching column, four abreast. We were quite impressed by that manoeuvre, but Baldyhead was not. He yelled a few more names, and several ranks had to do it all again. Then he turned to face us.

"Newcomers ? What are you called ?"

He was still red and angry looking, and we could see the wrinkles running up his forehead and into the bald patch. We told him our names, and before we had time even to say we wanted to join, he had us in a line five abreast at the back of the column. And then he ignored us. It was worse than school. But before we had time to know how we felt, he was at it again.

"Quick march: right wheel........halt"

We followed the column as best we could, self-conscious without our uniforms, awkward because there were five of us in the row. We marched on and on, swinging around the room, halting, wheeling, marking time. Every now and again a boy would provoke Baldyhead and be yelled at. Duck was a favourite target.

" Hagen: don't wave your arms about or with your ears you'll take off."

Now we were all for making fun of Duck - he was always good for a laugh. But this was different. Moreover, Duck was a deal site better at marching than any of us. We marched on. I kept an eye open for the uniforms, but there was no sign of extra supplies of them in the big empty hall, nor of any bugles or drums.

Then he started on us.

"Come on you five infants at the back. What's wrong with you? Three feet apiece or something ?"

We blushed scarlet and stumbled on. I kept my eyes glued to the back of the neck of the boy in front, scared of putting a foot wrong. Big Trevor was on the outside of the row, and had to keep running to catch up after the corners. Baldyhead soon picked him out for special attention.

I was tucked in the middle of the row, with my brother on the inside, nearest Baldyhead, so I escaped any personal abuse. We kept marching. It seemed the CLB did nothing but march. Then, as we drew near the door in the side wall, it happened. Big Trevor made a dive for the handle, pulled it open, and yelling 'Come on' was out, followed by Billy and Joe. My brother gave me a shove, and we were out too, running like blazes down the path from the porch. Big Trevor was waiting for us at the gate, and we stood there, listening for the sounds of pursuit. We were routed, defeated, humiliated by Baldyhead, and we had no uniform to show for it.

Suddenly Big Trevor had a purple moment. He cupped his hands to his mouth and yelled back at the doorway: "To Hell with the C.L.B.". Defeat was transformed into glorious victory. We took to our heels and ran all the way to the Causeway End. Then we laughed our heads off, and when, six weeks later, Godfrey appeared in his B P hat, bush shirt and shorts, we laughed our heads off again.

The only member of the gang who did not go to Lisburn Central was Brian Gallagher. He was the oldest member of the gang by a year, and the youngest of a family of four who lived over the hedge from us, on the other side from the Bailies. Brian went to the Boys School, as it was called. It was the Catholic primary school, a rather forbidding structure right beside the chapel on Chapel Hill, which meants its pupils were on a daily collision course with the Central scholars on their way home.

But religion meant nothing to the Gang, which included First Lisburn Presbyterians, Railway Street Presbyterians, Christ Church Church of Irelanders and Cathedral Church of Irelanders, the two of us from Elim, and Brian, the sole Catholic. The only problem we had with his Catholicism was that it meant he played gaelic football at school, and had the habit, when playing with us, of kicking the ball over whatever passed for the crossbar –the top of a gate or a hedge – and claiming a point, only to be shouted at by the rest of us for missing a sitter.

The Gallaghers were not the only Catholics in our part of the Causeway End. Next door to the Colhouns were the Elmores, but as they had no children, we knew them only by sight, and by repute. Mr. Elmore owned the big fishmonger's in Lisburn, and the family name was immortalised in a rhyme known to every child in the town.

> Paddy Elmore sells fish
> Three ha'pence a dish
> Cut the heads off
> Cut the tails off
> Paddy Elmore sells fish

Some years later the headmaster of the Boys' School moved into the Causeway End, and though he had no children himself, a nephew from Sligo came to live with him, and he added a new dimension to the gang.

Brian's father, a former RIC man now an RUC sergeant, was from Donegal and had the accent to prove it, and his mother from Cavan, and both had country ways. Sergeant Gallagher rode a large push bike with enormous dignity. Of the three, and at one time four policemen who lived on the road, he was the least intimidating, always ready to welcome my brother and me into his house with a cheerful, if largely incomprehensible, shouted greeting.

Mrs Gallagher was as restless as her husband was relaxed. She had a sharp tongue and a shrill Cavan accent, and though she always made us welcome, she was also ready to set us straight as to any shortcomings in our behaviour. After one boisterous game of soldiers, during which a missile struck, but mercifully did not break the window in the gable end of her bungalow, she warned us she would tell our mother if she ever caught us 'pingin stones and cloddin sticks' again.

Dodging down behind the hedge that separated our house from hers we doubled up with laughter, and for months after that constantly told each other to stop 'pinging' this or 'clodding' that, in the process reducing ourselves to helpless mirth, and endless arguments over which missiles you 'pinged' and which you 'clodded'.

The Gallagher house was the liveliest on the road. Mrs Gallagher was permanently busy, often in the laundry at the back of the bungalow with its enormous sink and great head of steam. The two older sisters were old enough to want to mother someone as young as myself, and always had time to talk. We felt very much at home in the Gallaghers', even if they had a large picture of the Sacred Heart on the wall.

Mrs Gallagher was ambitious for her children, and was, with good reason, proud of what the older ones had already achieved. The eldest was training to be a doctor in Dublin, the second had a civil service job at Stormont, and the third eventually went to university. She expected great things of Brian, and fussed over him and his health. To us he was big and tough, but not to his mother. She thought he was delicate.

She had great belief in the efficacy of goats' milk, and insisted that this should constitute a regular supplement to Brian's diet. This meant weekly trips for Brian up over the bridge to the McCormack cottage, equipped with a white enamel milk jug with hinged lid in which to bring home the wonder cure. It was a pleasant walk and I often went with him. Goats' milk was not the only remedy available. Mrs McCormack had the charm for warts, and when Brian developed one or two, he was dispatched by his mother for treatment.

Again, I was with him. The charm could be something simple, but had to be administered by the individual gifted with it. For warts it was, in Mrs McCormack's pharmacopoeia, a slice of white bread and butter, coated with sugar. Even though I was wart-free, Mrs McCormack obligingly gave me a slice as well. It must have worked, for I never did have a wart.

Brian knew the top of the road far better than we did, partly because many of the families living there were Catholic. Through him we got to know the Ferris boys and girls and several others, and we also learned more about some of the eccentrics that roamed the top end of the road.

There was the Harbison family who lived in the Causeway Castle, an unusual cottage built into the slope of the hill at right angles to the road, and reaching two storeys at the back. Probably for that reason the derisory term 'castle' was applied to it. It was ruled over by old Ma Harbison, who, with a ferocious temper and tongue to match, was the terror of the Causeway End. She had three sons, one quite normal, who tolled the bell in the chapel each Sunday, and two others, Tetsy and Patsy, neither of whom was the full shilling.

Patsy was the more seriously unusual, and spent periods in Antrim asylum. His sole talent lay in singing; he had a fine voice and had picked up a repertoire from listening to recordings of Count John McCormack. Walking past the Castle we could sometimes hear Patsy giving full voice from somewhere nearby. It was said he frequently entertained the residents of the hen house – serenading the bemused birds as they sat on the ascending tiers of roosting poles.

We knew Tetsy better, for he was well enough to work as a cobbler in Belfast, and, apart from occasional breaks when he was 'away in Antrim', walked up and down past our house every morning and evening. Tetsy was not a singer but an orator. He never stopped talking, particularly when he was in motion. On the bus he was silent when the bus stopped, but started up again as soon as it did.

He was hot on politics. "British democracy?" he would declaim in an interrogatory tone, "British democracy? Buy it at the Post Office, buy it at the Post Office." And then he would burst into chuckles. Sometimes he had a news items: "Its coming; its coming. The Free State navy's invading. It's coming up the Lagan. They've taken the gasworks," again followed by much private chuckling.

Wayside pulpits were common in Lisburn – texts from Scripture posted onto placards on trees, or more sophisticated notice boards with glass fronts. Tetsey was a connoisseur of these, and often found inspiration in their messages for his morning orations on the bus:

"'Prepare to meet thy God", he would bellow at his fellow-passengers, and then add politely "'Good morning God, what religion are you today?", before bursting into peals of laughter. A few minutes later he would start up again: "Repent; buy repentance at the post-office."

Other Side of the Hedge

Towards the end of one summer, I saw him standing in the road a few yards down from our house gazing up at the telegraph wires, where, as usual at that time of year, a big congregation of swallows had gathered en route to the south. Tetsy was addressing them, and I just heard the end of the sermon as he told the swallows that they neither sowed nor did they reap, but they caught the bus all the same. As he walked away, the serried ranks of swallows stared after him.

We were always careful to keep a few seats away from Tetsy on the bus, and we never tangled with him on the road. He was big and burley and a bit frightening. Jimmy McCormack, on the other hand, held no terrors for us. He was a small man, very simple, who came every day to the upper Causeway End to draw water for the numerous cottages which had no supply. His other mission in life was closing gates, a necessary function on a road that saw herds of cattle passing up and down. So on our suburban part of the road, which he traversed morning and evening, he closed every gate, and if he met any of us, or our parents, he would stop to assure us that he had closed our gate.

With the cheerful cruelty of children everywhere, we teased Jimmy mercilessly. If asked, he would recite his ABCs; "AhBCD aideyaswhy" he would reply with a grin. "Give us a dance, Jimmy?" and he would start hopping from one Wellington boot to the other, delighted to oblige. And then, because we knew what would happen, we would remark "you're very late today Jimmy" and he would fly into a rage, throw his pipe on the ground, and charge at us, as we fled in laughter.

Not all the oddballs in the Causeway End lived in the cottages above the bridge. James Johnston occupied a fine bungalow two doors down from us, but that did not stop him getting drunk regularly and beating his wife. He was a commercial traveller for spectacle frames, and set out every morning for Belfast in his Anthony Eden hat and horn-rimmed glasses, the picture of respectability.

Almost every night he would return home singing and roaring, the hat askew and the coat undone. He had a habit of keeling over when drunk and landing in the nearest hedge. Once or twice he had been found sleeping peacefully in a hedge early the next morning. His poor wife sometimes took refuge in our house, where she had a sympathetic listener in our mother. More than once my brother and I were sent out to search the hedges for the horn-rimmed glasses, which tended to detach themselves from the drunken Mr. Johnston.

We knew Jimmy McCormack and the Harbisons were Catholics, because you knew everyone's religion, but that was not what made them different. We knew Mr. Johnston was Protestant. But we were largely

187

unaware of the great divide between Catholics and Protestants that ran through political life in Northern Ireland, and were blissfully untainted by any feelings of animosity relating to religion.

This was hardly surprising. Our next-door neighbours were Catholics, and we were as friendly with them as with any other people on the road. Our family doctor was a Catholic – his surgery was in Railway Street and our father had become pally with him when he first came to Lisburn. Later our barber was Catholic, largely because his shop was on Chapel Hill which we had to pass on our way home from school.

Elim was evangelically Protestant, but my mother had no difficulty being friendly with the Gallaghers. I came home from school one day to find her having tea with a nun in our kitchen. Overcoming my shock – nuns were certainly different - I recognised the face peeping out from the starched cowl as one of the elderly nuns from the Retreat House on the Ballinderry Road who was a regular visitor to the Gallaghers. My mother had got to know her through chats over our front garden hedge, and had asked her in that day as the Gallaghers were out.

On the other hand we did know about the Irish Republican Army; we knew the IRA was a frightening and sinister organisation which murdered policemen and organised spectacular break-outs from the Crumlin Road prison in Belfast and from Derry jail. We read with horror how it had taken over the Broadway Cinema in Belfast for a celebration and how it had 'collected' money from those inside for IRA funds. The names McAteer and Steele were familiar to us, and struck a note of horror.

But we never thought of them as Catholic, or if we did, we made no connection between them and the Catholics we knew – our neighbours, our doctor, our barber and our friends up over the bridge. Nor do I ever remember anyone using the term 'nationalist' to describe our Catholic neighbours.

There was one incident early in the war that, with hindsight, had some political overtones. The Government decided that all iron gates and railings on private dwellings would be requisitioned and used to make munitions. A gang of workmen arrived in the Causeway End with oxyacetylene burners and proceeded to cut them all away and load them onto carts. No one was too happy about this, as gates and railings were not just for decoration – they were needed to keep out the cattle and sheep. When the workmen came to the Gallaghers', Mrs Gallagher came storming out and ordered them to keep their hands off her gate, and when told it was for the war-effort she responded that it was not her war, the war had nothing to do with her.

We never thought of it at the time, but she was from Cavan, in the neutral Free State, so in a sense it was not her war. We just assumed that she was annoyed because the Gallaghers owned their own house, so the gate and railings were their property. We knew our gate belonged to Mr. Bailie, and he would have to replace it, which he soon did with a wooden one. In the event, the gates and railings were to lie unused for the duration, not being suitable for turning into guns.

Ironically, it was the end of the war in Europe that gave me my first experience of the sectarian antagonisms that lay under the surface, even of the Causeway End. Our mother was bringing us home from a visit to Belfast one evening in May 1945. As we climbed Chapel Hill and made our way towards Causeway End we came upon a crowd of locals blocking the footpath outside one of the small houses in the long terrace that made up one side of Longstone Street.

The crowd was excited, and angry. My mother asked what was going on, and was told that bunting which had just been put up to celebrate VE Day, had been pulled down. A man had appeared at the upstairs window, had given a Nazi salute, and then tore the bunting down from the gutter above the window, yelling that no one was going to put red, white and blue flags on his house. Some younger men had wanted to force their way into the house and put the bunting back up, but older heads had said they should send for the police.

As we were hearing that, the police arrived in the person of Sergeant Colhoun accompanied by a constable. Nothing would tear us away from the scene now. Sergeant Colhoun disappeared into the house for a negotiation with the occupants. Five minutes later he emerged, and with a dramatic gesture towards the guttering, declared "Put up that bunting". The crowd cheered, and our mother rushed us home.

That was not quite the end of the story, for shortly afterwards the *Lisburn Standard* carried a report of the appearance at the Petty Sessions of a Longstone Street resident charged with a breach of the peace. After the bunting had been replaced – this time out of reach of the upstairs window – and the police had departed, the householder had brought out a ladder and climbed up to remove, once more, the offending colours.

Before he could do so, the crowd had rushed forward, grabbed the ladder, and forced it and its occupant through the first-floor window. The householder had subsequently reappeared at the window, according to a witness in court, and had started bombarding the crowd with empty beer bottles. He was bound over to keep the peace for twelve months, appropriately enough.

189

24 GETTING AWAY

No one, except Mr. Bailie, had a car. But that did not mean we stayed at home. Our mother was an inveterate traveller, and apart from a long annual holiday to Ballymena and the Braid, we also stayed at the farm for shorter periods at Easter and around Christmas. We visited Belfast frequently, enduring tea in the gloomy house in Roden Street, and our mother's visiting list also included the Campbell relatives in Lurgan.

She was a great attender at Elim Conventions, and my brother and I were dragged along on day-trips to Bangor, Newtownards, Lurgan, Ballymena and even Annaghanoon, as well as to the great gatherings at Easter and Christmas at Elim's cathedral, the Ulster Temple on the Ravenhill Road in Belfast.

All this travelling was done by bus, train and tram, and often involved much walking. To get to the Braid usually meant taking the GNR to Antrim, waiting there for the LMS from Belfast to take us to Ballymena, and from there by bus to Ballygelly, followed by a mile or so on foot up the Ballygelly Road and down the loanin to Kellstown. Sometimes this route was varied by going by train to Belfast, then by tram across to the York Road terminus of the LMS, and from there to Ballymena.

To my mother, all these trips were 'getting away'; we would hear her telling a neighbour that she hoped to 'get away to Ballymena' for a few days, and we would be delighted. I think it was more than just a turn of speech; she really was 'getting away' – getting away from our father, getting away from her marriage. And we shared that feeling, for we were getting away from the tension of a divided home.

All holidays were spent with relatives, and all without our father. It was through these visits that we knew something of previous generations, and through them that we grew up with some sense of belonging. But we were highly selective.

The briefest and most infrequent visits were to the Campbell relatives in Lurgan, and were sometimes combined with the Lurgan Elim Convention, for the Elim Church in Lurgan was just across Windsor Avenue from the Campbell relations' house. There was only one Campbell cousin anywhere near our age, and she was a girl, so there was no one to play with, no one to get to know. Because our mother's Campbell mother had died not just before the War, but before the Great War, she was ancient history to us. I don't think we ever worked out just how we were related to the people we were visiting. Anyway, we were Lisburn men and had little time for Lurgan.

Roden Street was a bit different, but no more exciting. My memory of it is unrelieved gloom, the street dominated by the vast mill chimney just across from the house, and the interior even darker, with the only light coming in from the back yard through the kitchen window. The two elderly ladies who lived there – they seemed not just elderly but ancient to us – were always happy to see us, and made a great fuss of our mother. Sometimes their niece Dinah was there, a very fat young lady given to sighing a lot, and recounting endless tales of woe.

We knew these were our relatives, but as the older ladies were simply known to us and to our mother as Martha and Sarah. We were given no clue as to the precise relationship, and we assumed they were not aunts, or we would have called them Aunt. They talked a lot about people we did not know, about Sammy and Willy, who were also somehow related to us, but who never appeared. They sometimes mentioned our mother's father – we never thought of him as our grandfather, or indeed any relative at all, for he had died long ago, long before the war.

There was nothing to do at Roden Street, except sit and listen to grown-ups talking. There was no question of going out into the street to play, and the only visits to the back yard were to a smelly outside lavatory. Roden Street was not high on our list of favourite places.

Ballymena was a mixed bag. 'Getting away to Ballymena' could mean various things. It could mean staying at Granda Kennedy's bungalow on the Circular Road, which was not bad, as it had a long back garden with an old car abandoned in it, and two of my father's younger sisters were still living at home and keeping things lively. Sometimes we stayed at our Aunt Lily's house, just two doors away on the same road, and that was good too, as Lily, another sister of my father, could never stop talking and was married to our Uncle Bobby who was everything an uncle should be.

There were four cousins in the house, the older three girls, but good company for all that. Various other houses had to be visited at least once on every trip to Ballymena. Uncle Alfie, our father's younger brother, lived with our Aunt Nanny and their two daughters in a terraced house in Hill Street. As relatives of Aunt Nanny occupied the house next door, and other relatives lived nearby, the house in Hill Street resembled a small railway station at rush hour.

It had, however, a highly desirable large backyard, which it shared with next door. At the back end of the yard was a pigeon loft, tended by Uncle Tosh, an elderly relative of the next door family. We learned a great deal from him about pigeons and pigeon racing, and had the good fortune, once or twice, to be visiting when the birds were returning from a race.

The pride and joy of the yard, however, was a steam engine. Not a steam roller, but a traction engine. We could climb all over it and pretend to drive it. Just how long it had sat in the yard, and whether it was capable of being steamed up ever again, we had no idea, but it was a great refuge from the incessant reminiscing that was going on inside.

Hill Street had other delights. One Sunday afternoon a young man, a relative from next door, turned up in the yard and was chatting to our uncle, discussing with him a gleaming new air rifle he had just acquired. We knew all about air rifles and air pistols, though we had never owned one and would never have been allowed to touch one. This one was very accurate, the young man boasted. "See that bell in the church?" he said to us, pointing to a small cupola high on the roof of the Methodist Church a few doors up Hill Street, and visible across the high yard walls.

The bell could just be seen behind the slats of the simple bell-tower on the roof of the church. The marksman took aim and fired, and we could hear the distant ping of the slug hitting the metal. What excitement. I waited nervously for a Methodist equivalent of Old Welch to come charging down the street and into the house, but instead the young man took aim and fired again. After that our uncle had a go. I was still worried about the consequences, and about what was happening to all those slugs after they hit the bell. Had they fallen down into the church and were now lying there as evidence? Had they fallen on a Methodist head?

There was no such excitement at Ballymarlow, a few miles outside Ballymena where our Aunt Ena lived. She was our father's oldest sister and a fiercely holy Elimite, who lived in a pebble-dashed detached house with her amiable husband Dave, and two daughters and a young son. A third daughter was already working in Belfast. Ena and our mother were the greatest of friends. At least one day of every holiday in Ballymena had to be spent at Ballymarlow.

All these visits were to my father's family, but never once did he come with us. My mother remained on the best of terms with his mother and with his sisters and brother. We were made very welcome, but my brother and I never felt at home in Ballymena; we were Lisburn men and regarded Ballymena as a very inferior spot where people spoke with a decidedly odd accent.

The low point of Ballymena was the mandatory trip to the Moat Road in Harryville. There were no Kennedy relatives there, but our mother still had friends and neighbours who had to be visited, and, scrubbed and brushed, we were dragged along. Just as our mother loved the day spent on the Moat Road, we hated it. The houses were poor, and seemed full of bare-bottomed infants squatting on chamber pots. In an emergency, we ourselves were faced with that icon of poverty, the smelly outside lavatory.

The only relief was usually a short walk up to the Moat, the big earth-work or motte at the top of the road. From there we could look down the steep slope to the Braid river, with its weir, and beyond it to the tower of Ballymena Castle. But we were never allowed to play there on our own. There was too much talking to be done in the Moat Road. Often the agony was extended to include an afternoon visit to Minnie Currie, the severely crippled music teacher who lived nearby.

Escape from Ballymena was on the Buckna bus. It ran from beside the Pentagon to the two Bucknas, Upper and Lower, via the village of Broughshane. If we were in luck the driver might be Matt McWhirter, a distant relative of our father, once famous as a dare-devil high diver in Portrush, but now renowned as the fastest, most reckless driver on the Buckna route. With Matt at the wheel we really could feel we were making a break for freedom from the drabness of Ballymena to the magic of Slemish.

In Broughshane the bus turned sharp right off the main street and straight up as far as Lisnamurrican school before turning left again along a switchback of a road, where Matt, in full cry, made sure we were bodily lifted off the hard wooden slats of the seats. It was at that point that Slemish would appear, rising high and impressive in front and to the right. A few more twists and we would be at the twin white gate posts, with conical tops to keep the fairies from sitting on them, that were the landmark for the Ballygelly Road and our stop.

The war had brought another landmark to this unlikely spot, in the shape of a small blockhouse, built in the corner of the field right at the road junction. Complete with gun slits, it sat there ready to thwart Hitler's *Panzers* should they decide to attack Buckna.

Minnie, the youngest member of the McMaster family, was usually waiting for us. Our first call was into a farm just up the Ballygelly Road, where we would leave our cases, to be collected later by someone from the farm and brought up by cart. Then on up the road, past the Water Loanin and finally into the Kellstown loanin itself and along it to the farm. We were back in the world of stone dikes and the sweet smell of burning turf.

We loved the place. We were instantly at home. Coming down the slope off the loanin, past the dark plantation on the left, with the sound of the burn rushing through it, was like returning to a small, private world where everything was both familiar and exciting. There was the turf shed on our left, with the cart sitting in it with its shafts pointing skywards, and the small boiler house on our right. Then down past the byre, with its half-door open ready to receive the cows back at milking time, and beyond that the farmhouse, where the door was never closed.

Jane would be on the step, wiping her hands on the sack tied round her waist as an apron and smiling a welcome. Bruce the dog – each succeeding dog was called Bruce – would pause momentarily in his pursuit of pigeons to wag a greeting, and Robert Hugh, with grizzled hair, walrus moustache and vast belly, would shout his invariable greeting from the stable; "Boys Lally, you're looking powerful", or some variation on it. A pile of fresh soda bread, still warm from the griddle, would be awaiting us, and, laden with homemade raspberry jam, would be washed down with tea.

Robert Hugh was a remote patriarch to us children; he never had much to say, and what he had was in broad Ulster-Scots filtered through his moustache and lost on us, but he never scolded us or shouted. All his warmth was reserved for our mother, and his face would light up with pleasure when she arrived. We never called him and Jane uncle and aunt, nor did our mother, for they were not our uncle and aunt. In fact, as we eventually worked out, they were no relation at all. Robert Hugh was the older brother of my mother's stepmother, and that was the only connection.

There was always a lot to do at Kellstown. Haymaking meant rides on the ruckshifter, buried in the hay on the way back to the farm, and bouncing perilously on the bare boards on the return out to the field. Flax was grown and pulled during the war – a dirty wet job, but it too meant thrilling rides back to the farm perched high on the top of the pulled flax being taken to the lint dam.

At harvest time, Robert Hugh employed young men from neighbouring farms who were more interested in what they called sport than in good husbandry of horses, or the safety of young fellows. We would find ourselves clinging in terror and delight to any handhold on the ruckshifter as our daredevil driver stood erect, feet wide apart, and lashed the startled carthorse into a gallop, and we careered across the bumpy field to head off a rival to the gate.

For us, too young to be expected to do any real work, it was all sport. Back in the farm yard the hayshed, open along one side, but protected from wind and rain on the other three, offered endless scope for sport. When almost full, secret dens could be made away up under the galvanised roof, admirable hiding places for all sorts of games. There was always the thrill of sliding down a cliff face of hay unto a soft pile at the bottom (bales had not yet been invented, or had not reached Kellstown). In these games we usually had the company of another McMaster, Robert, the grandson of Robert Hugh who lived in Broughshane but spent all his spare time at the farm, and made sure he was always there when we were staying.

About my own age, he shared the McMaster desire for sport and readiness to laugh at anything and anybody. He had a mania for buses; his father was a bus driver with the NIRTB, as was his uncle Tommy who lived in a small bungalow along the loanin from Kellstown. Robert was determined to be a bus driver, and in training for his vocation had already acquired the steering wheel from a real bus. This he drove endlessly around the farmyard, arms wrapped around the top of the wheel in the approved style, turning, reversing, changing gear and supplying a convincing sound track as he manoeuvred.

He was generous in lending his wheel to amateurs like my brother and me, but we never matched his expertise. We had the company, too, of Beth, another grandchild, who lived with her parents along the loanin. She was younger than us, with startlingly long blond curls, the cherished darling of her parents and grandparents. Fortunately this meant she was not allowed to stray far from the farmhouse, nor join in our more adventurous games.

Even the hayshed was put out of bounds for her after an unfortunate accident involving the sharp wheel of a mechanical rake buried in loose hay. Beth had tumbled sideways from the top of a pile of hay, hit the wheel and cut her head. We had to admit that the sight of the crimson blood on the blond hair was pretty gruesome.

The farmhouse had no electricity and no running water. There was no wireless. My brother and I washed each morning at the spout across the yard from the house, splashing happily in summer, and shivering in winter. The only lavatory was a smelly privy behind the stable, almost buried in nettles. We never used it, preferring to brave the brambles between the hayshed and the high thorn hedge of the back field.

Climbing Slemish

Light came from candles and oil lamps, and from a single Tilley in the kitchen. We were never excluded from the conversation and sat around the glowing range listening to accounts of marriages and deaths, of good behaviour and bad behaviour, and to endless reminiscences of our mother's early days visiting the Braid. Most of these involved outings to Slemish, or to socials, and to boys with whom the girls had flirted, and had sometimes clicked. It meant little enough to us, but we loved seeing our mother helpless with laughter, with tears of happiness flowing down her face.

The Tilley had a mantle fed by pressurised paraffin, and was lit only when twilight was turning into stygian gloom. It would then transform the kitchen into a hive of activity and conversation. It was the signal for yet another meal, usually called supper but taken around the table, with lots of bread and jam. I once calculated that six meals a day were served at that table. There was an early breakfast about six, of which we heard rumblings as we burrowed deeper into the blankets. Then there was the main breakfast about nine, for us, and for Robert Hugh and any farm workers who had been out and about since six. Just after eleven in the morning, dinner was the main meal of the day. Then in the afternoon, about four, we had tea, again a proper sit down-meal with eggs or meat. Supper followed at six, and another supper after the lighting of the Tilley.

That second supper was the signal for bed for us. After a final trip to the back of the hayshed we would take our candle and go upstairs, along the corridor above the kitchen – with the knot hole through which we could spy on the adults below – and into the spare bedroom, with its slanted ceiling and ice-cold linoleum. In summer it would be light enough to read in bed, and warm enough to encourage us to slip out to spy and listen at the knot hole, but in winter it was straight under the blankets followed by a scramble to get our feet on the earthenware hot water jar.

Then we would settle down to listen to the mice. (At least we hoped they were mice.) The spare bedroom was at the end of the house, up against the loft above the byre. We were told the cows helped keep our room warm in winter, but we never noticed. Certainly the loft, with its piles of corn and bundles of hay, attracted the mice, and from there they could roam over the roof space above our bed. Each night we went to sleep to a symphony of scurrying and scraping, with the occasional squeal and sometimes the sharp report of a trap snapping closed on the neck of an intruder, for the mice did not feel under any obligation to stay in the roof space.

We were usually fast asleep when our mother would slip in beside us in the dark. We were used to sleeping three in a bed. That was the way we slept at home in Causeway End, usually with our mother in the middle to stop territorial disputes. It was only late in the war, after our Uncle Alec had moved out, that the sleeping arrangements were adjusted and my brother moved into the box room vacated by my father, who transferred to Alec's, leaving my mother and me in the back room.

Our mother's devotion to visiting involved statutory side trips while we were in the Braid. The one we liked best was to Broughshane, where Willy McMaster lived with his wife May and his son, our friend Robert, and a daughter, Hilda, in the main street. The front room of the small terraced house, not far from the village pump, had been turned into a grocery shop run by May. Willy, as well as driving buses, for a time ran a mobile grocery, a tiny van stuffed with every imaginable grocery item, which he drove around the farms of the Braid valley .

The living room of the house was the small back room behind the shop, dominated by a large pot-bellied stove which burned summer and winter and ensured the room was always welcoming and cheerful. Equally so was May, who was built on the same lines as the stove – she was immensely fat, rather short, and irrepressibly jolly. Our arrival would be greeted with an immediate offer of a 'wee scoot o tay', the preparation and serving of which would not interrupt the flow of questions and comments, and much laughter. A ping from the bell on the shop door would send her trundling off, talking away, and she would still be talking when she trundled back.

At the other limit of the enjoyment scale was the obligatory trip down the loanin to the second McMaster farm, to visit Isa and Mary, the two spinster daughters of Samuel Alexander McMaster, Robert Hugh's older brother. We hated it, and often hid in the hayshed hoping our mother would go without us. But go we had to, hands and faces scrubbed, hair brushed and on our best behaviour. We had to sit on hard wooden chairs in the dark farm kitchen, listening to the two sisters and our mother talking soberly about this one and that one until they took pity on us and sent us out to play.

There was little enough to play with. The farm buildings were kept firmly shut, and the only excitement came from a horse-powered grinding machine, operated by a long metal bar on a central pivot in rough ground behind one of the sheds. There was little sign that it had been used in recent years, but with some effort we could get it moving, and if we rotated it hard enough we could hear the rumble of machinery from inside the shed. It was worth doing, but not for too long.

There was some consolation before we left; we would be called in for the tea, but for us there would be a glass of Mary's ginger cordial, fiery hot and sweet. Samuel Alexander would come in from somewhere to say hello to our mother. He was a tall, gaunt, and to us incredibly old man who moved with calculated slowness and spoke little. It was said above at Robert Hugh's that he had never recovered from the death of his only son as a child, years earlier.

There was always at least one visit to the Currie farm at Racavan, reigned over by Annie Currie, a fearsome widow, the sister of Robert Hugh, who had married Jane's now dead brother, Jamsie Currie. My brother and I liked the farm for it had an almost enclosed, diamond shaped, yard with a properly built spout in the middle of it, and just outside the yard an unusually large lint dam. Around the back of the farm buildings there was a disused motor car – long out of action, but still equipped with a steering wheel, pedals and seats.

We gave Annie a wide berth, especially after an incident on an early visit when we had driven her ducks, fattening for market, out of the yard and into the lint dam, to see if they really could swim. She had one daughter living at home with her, May (known as May of Racavan, and after marriage, May of the Mountain, to distinguish her from May of Broughshane) who was a great friend of our mother, and a son Jamsie, who worked the farm and was a motor mechanic with a garage nearby.

To my brother and me, his chief claim to fame was that he was a side-drummer in Teeney's Flute Band, and could, on occasion, be persuaded to beat out a roll for our entertainment. We were disappointed that Teeney's was only a flute band, not a 'kiltie', or pipe, band, which was the only sort of band we really cared for.

A distant cousin side-drummer in Teeney's flute band was about the closest connection any branch of our oddly constructed family had with Orangemen or Loyal Orders. Neither Cuthberts nor Culberts, nor Kennedys nor Campbells nor McMasters had any men in the Orange or Black.

That did not stop us watching the processions or going to the Twelfth Field, which was a major social event, particularly in the Braid. Pipe bands and Lambeg drums were our particular interest, and we could never get enough of either.

One Twelfth sticks in my memory. We were staying at Kellstown, and the Twelfth Field that year was at the Sheddings, on the road from Broughshane to Carnlough. As it happened my mother's old friend, and bridesmaid, Kate Wallace, had come home from Scotland and was staying with relatives at the Sheddings, so it was arranged we would get a lift over to see her on the Twelfth.

So off we went, and, after a while at the Field, Kate suggested we go down and visit more connections at O'Neill's pub, for she was related by marriage to the family that owned it. To our surprise, our mother agreed and, not being at all sure what was happening, my brother and I found ourselves for the first time in our lives entering a public house, on the busiest day of its year, albeit by the side door and into the private living accommodation.

There we had the familiar routine of introductions, reminiscences and tea, but all to the unfamiliar, to us, accompaniment of raucous laughter and the clinking of glasses from just across the hallway. When we left it was late evening, and the heavy smell of drink was in the air. As we walked down the road I noticed Orangemen solemnly removing their sashes, folding them up and putting them in paper bags before entering the pub. Out of respect, I was told. I also saw drunken Orangemen stretched out in the ditch, with their sashes still around their necks.

Every summer there was talk of climbing Slemish. To us it sounded like an enormous adventure, not in the same league as Everest, but a serious undertaking nonetheless. Slemish dominated the farmhouse. It was the first thing we saw in the morning, though we had to get out of the high bed and stoop to peer through the low window in the back wall to see it. We had our favourite views of it; there was the first glimpse of it from the bus, and the spectacular panorama from the foot of the Ballygelly Road where we alighted. That way you saw the full breadth of the front of the mountain – any other view showed a truncated, distorted mound, not the real thing at all.

But most dramatic of all was the view from the gate to the back field, which you came upon as you rounded the corner of the farmhouse. In the morning, with the sun rising behind it, it was sombre, a stark, even menacing, outline. But in the evening it caught, full on, the rays of the setting sun and looked magnificent and inviting, warm and green with a touch of purple. We would spend hours looking at it, picking out the steepest parts with faces of bare rock, imagining just how hard it would be to climb it, and how long it would take.

Then, suddenly, at breakfast one summer day, Minnie announced that we were going to Slemish. May of Racavan was getting married and was moving into an old farmhouse right at the foot of the mountain and Minnie was dying to have a look at it. We could go by it on our way to the top. My brother and I were delighted at the news, but a little taken aback that such a major expedition could be decided upon so casually, with the only apparent preparation being the cutting of some sandwiches and the making of a flask of tea.

Still, at last, I was going to climb Slemish. My mother and Minnie packed sandwiches and the four of us set out up the lane, down the water loanin, stepping on the stones across the burn, and over the fields towards the mountain. It was much further than it looked, and once we had to stop to ask which way to take. Then we lost our way and found ourselves in a cabbage field. But Minnie was determined to see what sort of a house May had landed for herself and eventually, after climbing numerous stone dikes, we found ourselves standing in front of a forlorn two-storied farmhouse, locked and shuttered, and looking as if it had not been lived in for generations.

Far from being at the foot of the mountain, it seemed halfway up it. At the back it was cut right into the rock, and it was clear that heavy rains had been washing down the hill and over the house. Behind it was a field of rough grazing and then the heather, fern and rock of the mountain itself. Minnie declared that it would take a very wealthy, and very good-looking farmer, to tempt her to live in a place like that.

With that we left the farmhouse behind and pushed on over the heather and fern-clad lower slopes. I was surprised. It was all very untidy. Rocks were scattered here and there among the heather as if they had been carelessly dropped; the mountain itself, this close, had lost most of its distinct shape. I hardly recognised it. Minnie led us round the mountain rather than straight up it, and on to a grassy path that sloped upwards.

There was scarcely a rock to be seen; we were able to climb quite comfortably, with just a few scrambles over steep places. In a short time the slope lessened and I realised that we were almost on the top, at the lower end of the great ridge. It was very grassy, and here and there quite boggy. It had been no real climb at all.

But the view was breathtaking; I had never been up this high in my life, and I now saw the world as I had never seen it before. Fields were reduced to tiny squares, and farmhouses to toy building blocks. I could trace the roads the way you could on a map. In one direction I could see the blue of the sea, and the misty mountains of Scotland beyond it. Minnie pointed out the farm and I could just make out the hayshed to one side.

We ate our sandwiches on the top, and went and sat on St Patrick's Wishing Chair. I wished for a bicycle and for a cigarette lighter; the first because everybody had to have one and I desperately wanted one, the second because, while I hated smoking, I loved the silky metallic surface of my father's Ronson, and the efficient clicking of the mechanism as the wheel hit the flint and ignited the beautiful flame.

We all had a wish in the chair, even, after a lot of coaxing, our mother. She sat in the cleft in the rock for a long time, looking very serious, and then refused to tell us what she had been wishing for.

On the way down my brother and I took a shorter, steeper route, descending nearer to the face of the mountain. As we came down I could see the chaos of it all – rocks strewn at random, bits of heather, some scrawny bushes. Nothing had any shape to it, just disorder. Looking back over my shoulder there was nothing but a misshapen heap of ground.

It was getting late, and I was hungry and tired. We hurried back across the fields and lanes to the farm. After a tea of boiled eggs, soda bread and raspberry jam, my brother and I wandered out of the house, round the corner and up to the gate. There was Slemish, put back together again, magnificent as ever. But I knew that it was not what it seemed; it was just a heap of rubble. Or was it? Which was the real mountain – the one everyone could recognise, or the one only those who had gone to climb it knew about? I went to sleep that night thinking about Slemish, and wondering what it was my mother had wished for.

What my mother wished for, I am sure, was that her two sons would not grow up to be like their father. That was the cardinal principle which guided her hand in our upbringing.

It showed itself in bizarre ways, notably in the matter of food. My father loved fresh herrings, and insisted on having them for his tea once a week. My mother did not like fresh herrings – I suspect she thought they were poor, that is, they were the sort of thing poor people ate, but it was my father's taste for them that finished them with my mother.

The result was that my brother and I did not like fresh herrings, so we were informed, and we were never served them. On the other hand we grew up with an abiding love of kippers – one of our mother's favourites. I was in my twenties before I discovered just how tasty the flesh of a good herring could be.

My father loved pork, and during the days of rationing somehow managed to find a steady supply of fillets and chops. My mother did not like pork, perhaps on principle because he did, possibly because of the bad press pork got in the *Old Testament*. She cooked it for my father, but never for us. We did not like pork, or so we grew up to believe. The same went for coffee; during the war there was no real coffee available, but my father had a taste for Camp Coffee, and there was always a bottle of this sticky chicory-based concoction in the cupboard in the scullery. My mother did not like coffee, so neither, we were assured, did we. Even as a teenager I would carefully avoid the coffee creams in chocolate boxes.

Our mother constantly scrutinised us for any signs that we were developing failings she regarded as characteristic of our father. There were two prime faults in this regard – laziness and bad temper, and she was determined that we would grow up with neither, even if she had to beat them out of us. Breakfast in bed, which my father enjoyed every Sunday, was also a sign of great moral weakness, and was denied to us except in case of serious illness.

To combat laziness we were given tasks around the house. It was our duty to keep the fire supplied with shovelfuls of coal from the shed, and to empty the ash out in the morning. We had to lay the table for meals, and clear away after, and there was a rota for dishwashing and drying.

We even learned to iron – at least handkerchiefs and other uncomplicated items. Ironing was one of the standard duties of whoever of us was on home duty on Sunday mornings, while our father lay above in bed and our mother went to church with the son not on duty. The key task was to put the potatoes on to boil at exactly forty minutes before one o'clock, and to take them off the gas and strain them if the worshippers had not returned by one.

There was nothing onerous about these tasks, and we probably did even less to help around the house than most children in those days, certainly less than would have been expected from a daughter. But refusal to do them, or even a show of reluctance, would throw our mother into a temper, and she would produce her short bamboo rod and whack us across the backs of our legs, or she would try to as we fled to our respective sanctuaries – mine below the stairs and Ronnie to the bathroom. This attempted assault would invariably be accompanied by loud accusations that we were just like our father.

Any show of temper towards her, or towards each other, would provoke a similar reaction, and we would flee from the bamboo followed by unflattering references to our father, and in the case of temper, to 'his old father' too. Any tendency to lie in bed in the mornings, and later, to be out late at night, could incur censure on the same grounds; our father, who worked all day Saturday all his life, had taken to staying in bed until midday on Sunday, and never came home much before midnight almost every night of the week. Two more of his habits were smacked out of us at an early stage - reading at the table at meal times was not tolerated, and reading while on the lavatory was both dirty and decadent.

The sharp sting of the bamboo across the calf left no doubt as to our mother's genuine concern for our spiritual welfare. At times she hit hard enough to leave vivid red marks on our legs which we were not slow to exploit, though rather than sympathy and contrition on her part, our complaints usually resulted in the further indignity of having our legs painted with iodine. Iodine was the infallible remedy for all ills from bruises to sore throats; we even had our tonsils painted with iodine. The virtue of iodine was one thing our parents seemed to agree upon.

These dire warnings against growing up to be like our father were always accompanied by references to her three stepbrothers, Bobby, Alec, and Hugh, who were held up as paragons of industry, sweettemperedness and Christian virtue. Alec, of course, we knew, as he lived with us, but the other two were largely fictional characters. Bobby was dead, and almost beatified, while Hugh was off fighting Hitler.

We knew them through the large photograph my mother had of them, all three in their petticoats, taken sometime around the Great War, and through their golden ringlets, carefully preserved in tissue paper and kept in the bottom of our mother's wardrobe. In one sense they fused into one, and the cry of Bobby-Alec-and-Hugh was as much a joke to us as Mrs Gallagher's clodding and pinging.

Our father certainly was a bully where our mother was concerned, and he had a very short temper. He treated her badly, but his violence usually stopped short of actually hitting her. I remember only once having to intervene between them as he tried physically to throw her out of the house, and I must have been eleven or twelve by then. I remember him throwing his laden dinner plate at the wall, and I recall once going out in the rain to rescue the contents of her sewing and knitting box which he had flung out into the backyard when his meal had not been on time.

He insisted on his dinner being on the table at half past one sharp, when he would arrive home on his bicycle from Boyd's. For some reason, this was very important to him, and he would fly into an immediate rage if there was any delay. One day, as he came in through the back door into the scullery our mother was still cooking the dinner, and it was clear it would not be ready for several minutes. He flared up and was about to say something abusive when our mother told him to shut up, he was early, and it was not yet half past.

He stalked through into the kitchen and looked at the clock, which was indeed still a few minutes short of the half-hour. He went over to the mantelpiece, opened the glass face, and pushed the minute hand on to five minutes past the half hour. My brother was in the kitchen and watched this performance, before running into the scullery and loudly announcing that his father had just put the clock on.

My father was on his heels, giving Ronnie a quick clip across the ear, and telling him that clashing on people was not something he should do. It was the only time either of us could remember being hit by him, and he never seemed to lose his temper with us.

But the rows with our mother were frequent and frightening; he shouted abuse and became very angry indeed, while my mother, though not returning the abuse, was never meekly submissive. Between the rows there was sullen silence, except when our mother was complaining about the house.

The back of the house faced north, so the yard and the back door were dark and damp. This serious defect, she managed to imply, was his fault. The fire in the kitchen was the only source of hot water in the house, and worked very inefficiently. It did not draw properly, and every Saturday had to be banked high and kept fed to ensure enough hot water for our weekly bath. She complained constantly about the fire's failure to draw, and laid the blame squarely on our father's shoulders.

To us boys he was almost an absentee father. We saw him at breakfast and tea, we took him up his breakfast in bed on Sunday mornings, and we had Sunday dinner with him, and sometimes tea if he was at home. But he rarely took us out anywhere or even played with us in the garden. He never came on holidays with us, or on any of our frequent away trips to see relatives, including his. He never came to church with us.

Once a year, however, he took us to the circus in Belfast, to Dr Hunter's Christmas Circus at the Hippodrome. We loved it, and looked forward to it each year. Also at Christmas, and before our main holiday every year, he would share equally between us his collection of Free State threepenny pieces. These 'rabbit bits' as we erroneously called them – the beautifully designed silver coin portrayed a hare – were collected throughout the year in a jar kept on his dressing table. The Free State coinage circulated freely in Northern Ireland, on a par with sterling, and he had begun collecting the threepenny, and later also the sixpenny bits, for us. At work he was able to exchange the Free State coins for his own sterling every time a customer proffered one.

So twice a year we had the pleasure of emptying out the jar and counting the proceeds, which, for the time, were surprisingly large. As I recall there was never less than about £5 to share between us, and sometimes in summer it reached £5 each. After the war, the middle class invention of pocket money filtered down to our level, and while our initial half crown a week was modest enough, we never felt he was being mean towards us, as he undoubtedly was towards our mother, giving her the barest minimum on which to run the house, and from time to time cutting it because of some misdemeanour or supposed extravagance on her part.

He did introduce us to photography, and bought us both Box Brownie cameras. He fitted up the back shed as a dark room, which was not difficult given the gloomy aspect of the back yard and the shed's single small window. There he taught us how to make contact prints using the old wood and glass frames with metal clips, which had once belonged to Bobby. He kept us supplied with printing paper and with developer and hypo from Boyd's.

Surprisingly, our mother never criticised our interest in photography; perhaps it reminded her of Bobby, who had been even keener on it than my father.

In one way above all others, our mother was determined we would not follow our father – we would be Christians. In practice this meant that from our earliest days we were enrolled in Sunday School, and went to church at least twice on Sundays. We did not go to the pictures, ever. On Monday mornings I would have to endure the acute boredom of listening to my classmates relating at great length the exploits of the Three Stooges (thus pronounced), Gene Autry and Roy Rogers, as witnessed by all of them, but not by me, at Lisburn Picture House on the previous Saturday morning.

We knelt at our bedside every night, on very cold linoleum, to say our prayers, and we were told Bible stories by our mother. She would also recite poetry to us, at which she was rather good, and our favourite was *Abou Ben Adhem*. She had learnt this Leigh Hunt poem as a girl in Crayford, and as she declaimed it her English accent came through loud and clear.

Her repertoire also included *Mary Call the Cattle Home*, *The Charge of the Light Brigade*, 'Break, break, break at the foot of thy crags, O sea' from Tennyson's *The Sailor Boy*, and Cowper's version of what Alexander Selkirk said about life on a desert island

> I am monarch of all I survey,
> My right there is none to dispute;
> From the centre right round to the sea,
> I am lord of the fowl and the brute....

We knew all about Selkirk being the real Robinson Crusoe, and this was much better than the version in children's books. 'Lord of the fowl and the brute' was strong stuff, and when we in turn spat it out, it was as near to bad language as we dared. 'Better dwell in the midst of alarms, Than reign in this horrible place' was real poetry to us.

But none of these could compare spiritually or in any other way with *Abou Ben Adhem* (may his tribe increase). We loved the image of Abou Ben Adhem awakening from a dream and seeing, within the moonlight in his room, an angel writing in a book of gold. (We saw the angel just between the foot of our bed and the triple-mirrored dressing table.) We shared his sadness when the angel told him his name was not among those who loved the Lord, and we almost cheered when Abou Ben Adhem replied 'I pray thee then, write me as one that loves his fellow men'. The last line of the poem always sent us to sleep comforted by the happiest of endings; when the angel returned the next night and showed the list, 'Lo, Ben Adhem's name led all the rest'.

Sunday was a day of church-going rather than of rest. There was enforced rest from some things – there was no going out to play on Sundays, and anyway we were too well dressed to play. There was no wireless, except for news, and later, for Children's Hour, which we managed to persuade our mother was highly educational, as indeed it was.

On the wider moral front, the limits of Christian behaviour were neatly laid out in easily remembered form in the verse our mother taught us:

> There are three things I must not do
> I must not gamble, smoke or chew,
> And if I dance on the Devil's dance floor,
> I'll dance right through the Devil's front door.

We were not in great danger on any of these counts. Smoking we knew was the greatest sin anyone could commit, and I never even tried it. Chewing had to be explained at first, but our mother conjured up such an alarming picture of Oul Jamie Wallace sitting spitting his cud into the fire at Kellstown that we thought no more of such a disgusting habit. Gambling was beyond our ken, and dancing was away up there in the pantheon of sins reserved for grown-ups. Our father was guilty on all fronts except chewing tobacco. We, of course, knew he smoked, and the arrival of books of ballots from time to time gave the game away on gambling. The dancing we only began to suspect when we found a gleaming pair of patent leather shoes in the bottom of his wardrobe which we learned were dancing shoes.

Sticking to all these guidelines, we knew, would not make us Christians. That would happen only when we got saved, and that would mean putting our hands up in response to an appeal at a gospel meeting; that was how you got saved. Soon our mother was urging us to get saved; she did this in a rather impatient way, telling us it was high time we were saved, adding that Bobby-Alec-and-Hugh had all been saved by our age.

Our Uncle Alec, who lived with us until 1943, was just as much saved as our mother, but did not go to Elim. He took an interest in our spiritual welfare, and one day announced that Sunday afternoon Sunday

School was fine, but we should also go to one in the morning, before church. The Baptist church, not too far from Causeway End, had one, and he volunteered to take us.

We were not too keen. Sunday School at Elim was all right, but enough was enough, and besides we would not know anyone at this new one. But Alec insisted, and one morning he marched us off, bright and early, to the Baptist Church. When we arrived it was locked and barred, and after waiting for ten minutes we were forced to abandon the exercise and go home, two delighted young boys accompanied by a furious uncle.

We later learned that the Sunday School had been cancelled because of a holiday, but our uncle never tried to enlist us again. He may have noticed our reluctance to go and our delight at the last-minute reprieve, or, more likely, decided that a Sunday School which took holidays was probably not worth going to anyway. After that we were somewhat wary of Uncle Alec.

He had one thing in his favour, however. He owned a splendid Hornby train set - clockwork, 0 gauge, with an oval set of rails, branch line and points. To run on these he had a glorious LNER *Flying Scotsman* passenger train, and a goods train with all sorts of wagons. At a time when there were no toys to buy anywhere, and the only ones we had were survivors from the pre-war days, this train set was a treasure. We were allowed to play with it two or three times a year, once at Christmas, and on birthdays.

The rest of the year it lay in Alec's room, neatly boxed. When he got married and left home, we got the train, but we had to buy it. He charged us five pounds, which was a fortune to us in 1943. Years later, when he had children of his own, he bought it back from us. We charged him five pounds. By then it had been totally eclipsed by Mr. Moller's magnificent electric train network in the attic of his large house just round the corner on Longstone Street.

Mr. Moller was a Danish engineer who had come to Ireland as a diesel specialist, and had married and settled here. He had two sons a bit younger than my brother and myself, and this most marvellous 00 Trix (not Hornby) electric network. The attic was reached up a narrow, almost secret, staircase, and the trains ran on broad shelves all around the room. In the centre, to reach which you had to crawl under one of the shelves, was a control point. You could sit at it and marshal all the trains, change the points, work the level crossings. It was a young boy's dream, especially in those days. What was even more wonderful, the Mollers gave us a standing invitation to come and play with the trains anytime we liked, even if their own sons were not there.

We were encouraged not to read comics on Sundays, though I do not recall this rule being enforced too strictly. Comics meant *The Hotspur, The Wizard, The Rover* and *Adventure*. We did not buy them, but got them second-hand from the Colhouns. These were not comic strips, but solid magazines almost without illustration, and crammed with print relaying the exploits of the Great Wilson, the Slugger from the Hills, Alf Tupper, Smith of the Lower Third and Roy of the Rovers himself. If you read every story in each issue, and we did, then each week you got through the equivalent of a medium length novel.

Given our mother's often expressed distaste for any paperback literature, all of which she termed penny-dreadfuls, she was surprisingly tolerant of our addiction to comics. I remember being impressed on holidays one summer by her readiness to defend comics at a Christian guesthouse in Portstewart. We were all gathered in the lounge awaiting the ringing of the gong that would summon us to tea. My brother and I were devouring *The Wizard* and *The Hotspur* under the disapproving eye of Mrs Cregan, the wife of the same muscular Christian builder who had built Number 10. Mrs Cregan, and all the Cregans, were renowned in Lisburn for their piety.

'I'm surprised you let your boys read those things', she remarked to our mother in tones loud enough to get the attention of the entire room. To my amazement our mother, who was chronically shy and timid outside the house, replied in a firm voice. 'I always think of St Paul, who said that when he was a child he thought as a child, but when he became a man he put away childish things. The boys are still children and the comics will do them no harm.' Mrs Cregan, for once, was silenced.

We were encouraged to read 'Christian' books, and struggled through classics like *Pilgrim's Progress*, but rather enjoyed the stream of sturdy novels for young people with a Gospel message which came our way annually at the Sunday School prize-giving. Every Christmas our stockings also included at least one *Biggles* adventure and one *Just William* (we had graduated from *Rupert Bear*).

We were also supposed to read *The Bible*, and our mother repeatedly reminded us that Bobby-Alec-and-Hugh had all read it by our age. Reading *The Bible* meant not just dipping into it, but beginning at Genesis 1.1 and proceeding to the end of Revelation via all 66 books and almost 800,000 words. It was something we knew we had to do, but we felt we could put it off until we were saved.

Of that fundamental requirement we were publicly reminded at least once a week at Elim's Sunday evening Gospel service. The Elim

Tabernacle was a modest hall in a pleasant avenue near the centre of Lisburn. It had a small garden in front and grass all round. Inside, a dozen long benches – not pews –held about a hundred people if packed solid, which they never were. When we first started going, it was still lit by gas lamps hanging down from the ceiling and warmed by a coke-burning stove that sat half-way along one side wall. In winter the seats closest to the stove were taken by the early arrivals.

Starting at half past six and finishing, with luck, by eight o'clock, Sunday evening was a Gospel service, with the plight of the sinner and his need of salvation the theme of every hymn, prayer, testimony, and of a lengthy, thundering, proclamation of the Gospel.

Sometimes the sermon would be followed by an appeal, when, with all heads bowed, the preacher would cajole, beg, persuade and sometimes try to bully the lost sheep into the fold. Someone would start singing *Just as I am, without one plea....*, and the agony for us the unsaved, staring sheepishly at our boots, would be prolonged.

Above the pulpit, neatly fronted with blue velvet, stretched a banner proclaiming *Jesus Christ, the same yesterday today and for ever.* At every service I sat reading that message and wondering why it was there. It was not the sort of text I learned in Sunday School.

Forty minutes, often a full hour, left time enough to ponder these things at some length, for the sermons were almost always intensely boring. Occasionally a preacher would turn up who was funny, or might have an engaging speech defect, or would simply have the gift of oratory, but, for the most part, the resident pastor droned on. Surviving the sermon became a major challenge.

There were occasional light moments. One pastor, a retired policeman who most certainly had no gift for oratory, was particularly hard to bear. He was a fire and brimstone man, who put himself and his congregation through fifty minutes agony every Sunday as he sought to bring sinners to salvation. One winter night, as the congregation of twenty five squirmed or dozed under the hissing gas lamps, his voice dropped and he warned us all that the door was closing, that the day of salvation was ending. We had very little time left. Soon that door would close....

In the back row, Dan the caretaker slept soundly. He had never recovered from shell-shock in Flanders in the Great War, and was reputed to be unable to sleep at night, spending hours walking the streets of Lisburn. He made up for some of this deprivation every Sunday during the pastor's sermons.

Yes, said the pastor in a whisper, the door is closing. "And one day soon...," he paused, and then, in the hushed silence, brought his two massive palms together in a thunderous clap and roared at the top of his voice "... it will be slammed shut".

We all sat up at that. In the back row, Dan, thinking he was back at Ypres, shot bolt upright out of his seat, hit his head on the Free-Will offering box hanging from the partition behind him, sent it flying from its nail, and then dived for cover under the bench in front. It took some time to persuade him that the war was over.

But such diversions were rare, and as a way of passing the time during the sermon, I took to reading the words of the hymns in the *Redemption Hymnal*, the only reading material to hand, apart from *The Bible*. As a very young child I had cheerfully tried to sing along as I stood beside my mother in church, but was soon silenced by a loud shush. I was told I did not have a tune in my head – another serious character defect inherited from my father. Thereafter I stood silently reading the words, which, from the point of view of my spiritual development, was a serious mistake. Most of the hymns made even less sense than the Pastor's sermons.

But many of them did reinforce the stark message that you had to get saved, and if you didn't, you were in for it. 'Life at best is very brief,' the hymn told us, 'like the falling of a leaf, like the binding of a sheaf,' and we had to be in time. 'The die would soon be cast, and the fatal line be pass'd'. If in sin we longer waited, we would find no open gate, and our cry would be just too late. We had to be in time.

To most, the door that might suddenly slam shut was death, but to those of us not yet ten years old that was far enough away not to worry about. Elim, however, was very hot on the Second Coming, that is the return of Christ and the Rapture of the Saints before Armageddon and Lord knows what. Hopes, or fears, that the end of the world was imminent were strong in several Christian denominations at the end of the war, especially those like Elim which were still relatively new and were convinced that world events and their own growth and experience of the supernatural, in the form of miracles of healing and prophesying and speaking in tongues, all indicated that we were living in 'the last times'.

The atomic bombs over Japan had caused 'the elements to melt with fervent heat' exactly as predicted in Second Peter, and that meant that the Day of the Lord was coming, when the heavens would pass away and the earth and the works that were therein should be burned up. But before that would be the Second Coming, when Christ would return to earth to gather all born-again Christians to himself, and remove them from the awful perils that were going to hit the earth.

These impending catastrophes were brought alarmingly close to my brother and me by a book he received as a Sunday School prize. It was called *The Mark of the Beast*, and told the story of the Second Coming as experienced by a family not unlike ourselves. Our mother read it to us in bed and it scared the wits out of us. The family in the book, like ours, had some members who were saved, and some who were not. At the crucial moment, the saved ones suddenly disappeared, leaving the unsaved to their fate, which was first to endure a reign of terror under The Beast, to have his mark '666' put on their foreheads, and after that to settle down to eternal damnation.

We kept a closer eye on our mother and her comings and goings after that. As we got older, she regularly left us alone in the house as she went to church meetings or art classes or visiting. Lying alone in bed in the back room, I would listen eagerly for my mother's footsteps on the gravel at the side of the house to be reassured that the Second Coming had been put off for a while yet.

Sometimes, after the art class, she would go home with one of our neighbours for supper, and could be quite late. This left me extra time to worry about the Second Coming, and I remember one night, as eleven o'clock came and went, having a fit of the terrors, convinced that It had happened, she would not be coming home, and we were lost. I went into Ronnie's room and wakened him up, telling him I was feeling very sick, and would he go over to Mulhollands' and get our mother.

I must have been in a terrible state, for he actually got up and dressed and ran across the road to our neighbour's. I can still remember the relief I felt five minutes later when I heard her voice at the side of the house.

Elim was an interesting church in those days. It was, in the proper sense of the word, very puritan – that is it sought purity in its forms of worship and in its doctrine. It was not dour and restrictive like the Plymouth Brethren, but encouraged lively music and did not expect its members to be 'exclusive', that is did not expect them to cut off all relations with other denominations. When we visited our relatives in Ballymena or elsewhere we often went to Presbyterian churches or even the Church of Ireland.

Elim had a Pastor, who could not be called Reverend, and who could not wear a dog-collar. (Roman collar it was termed in Lisburn.) But the pastor was no authoritarian priest, and had to submit to the rule of the Elders Meeting. Elim's constitution expressly forbade a robed choir (shades of Anglicanism or Catholicism) but allowed a choir without robes. In that case the choir was not permitted to rise before the congregation at the beginning of a hymn, as was usual in other Protestant denominations. Such behaviour would smack of formality, of ritual, and Elim was dead against ritual.

Nor was it, then, rabidly anti-intellectual. Its leaders, who came regularly to speak at conventions, were often educated men who had thought deeply about many of the issues raised by a church founded, in the 20th century on miracles and mystical manifestations which most other Christians felt belonged to the Acts, and the age, of the Apostles. They discussed the role of the emotions in faith, they analysed what one preacher called 'ecstatic religion', and they explored how the individual could be transformed in his thinking and his way of life through the spiritual experience of conversion.

But it was Pentecostal; it was a Holy Roller church, even if no one rolled. It believed in miracles of healing, in prophesying and in speaking in tongues, and was therefore, if not outside the ecclesiastic pale in Lisburn, at least right up against the fence. We never managed a miracle in Lisburn, but we did have people who spoke in tongues. It was eerie, even frightening at first, for a youngster, but was in a way fascinating.

During prayer someone in the congregation would suddenly burst into an unknown language, usually declaiming very fluently and loudly, and continue for several minutes. There would then be a period of silence as everyone waited nervously for the interpretation. This would come from someone else, though very occasionally from the original speaker.

Sometimes there would be no interpretation, and it would be assumed this was because there was no one present with the gift of interpretation. (Just why the Holy Spirit was not aware of this when he gave the original message was never explained.) The interpretation was usually a prayer of praise or exaltation, but could, on rare occasions, imply a direct message, even a warning, to some unspecified recipient.

It was clear that it was the act of speaking in tongues that was important, not the message; it was explained as the Holy Spirit entering into the individual, possessing him or her, and then using his voice to praise God in an ecstatic utterance. Certainly the utterance was, if not supernatural, at least unnatural.

These matters could waver between the mystic and the comic. For several years a very nice and rather wealthy lady attended Elim; she became friendly with our mother and visited our house, and we liked her. She was fiercely spiritual and frequently spoke in tongues on Sunday mornings. Dressed in her fur coat, she usually sat alone at the end of one of the front benches.

During the period of open worship on Sunday mornings – half an hour or more – the congregation turned round and knelt on the floor, leaning on the bench seat. The benches were long, and were supported by three thin metal frames and under-struts. If only one end of a bench was occupied, the other end tended to spring up a fraction of an inch from the floor. The grand lady in the fur coat combined speaking with tongues with animated shaking of her whole body, with the result that, if the other end of her bench was unoccupied, it would vibrate rapidly, beating a resounding tattoo on the wooden floor.

That was excruciatingly embarrassing. Eventually one of the heavier elders would make a point of slipping into the far end of her bench just as the worship period began. In some ways, belonging to Elim was a succession of embarrassments. You had to explain to your friends what funny sort of church it was; you had to sit on Sunday nights and count the numbers coming in wondering just how few would turn up. At Central School, when the clergymen came in once a week to take religious instruction, you were ignominiously lumped in with 'Church of Ireland and Others', as distinct from Presbyterian.

The 'Others' label was largely ignored, and we others – Baptists, Brethren, Salvation Army and myself - also had to learn the Creed and the Church of Ireland catechism from the visiting curate. An eager young man, and close friend of the Bailies, he offered a modest prize to the pupil best at learning the catechism. He was as amused as I was embarrassed when it turned out to be me.

Elim was a highly distinctive and central part of our lives, but it was only a part. We had friends of our own age in Elim, but none of them lived near us, none went to our school, and we saw them only on Sundays and special occasions. For the most part we joined in with the Gang, played football and cricket, and collected cigarette cards – pre-war rarities and highly desirable - all without benefit of Elim.

27   WINNING THE WAR

As the war progressed we lost one uncle and gained another. In 1943, to our mother's surprise, Uncle Alec got married and left home. His wedding, war or no war, was a grand affair, celebrated in the small Quaker Meeting House in Hillsborough and afterwards at his bride's home, a big house in Hillsborough, sitting in its own grounds, and with a large marquee erected for the occasion on the tennis court.

The house even had a 'school room' in which we children had our own boisterous reception. Up to then, private houses having school rooms and tennis courts had existed only in books.

The bride, our new aunt, and the house, belonged to the Davises, the same family, we later learned, which had so annoyed our Uncle Hugh when he was the least of Mr. Hardy's employees. At the time of the wedding he was off in the RAF and his reaction to acquiring one of the Davis girls as a sister-in-law went unrecorded. Our uncle and his bride settled into a detached house, *Park Dale*, in several acres just outside Hillsborough, a gift to them from the bride's parents.

Park Dale was somewhere else to visit. A short train ride from Lisburn, and a long walk up into and through the village got us there, and it was close enough for day trips. Our uncle, swinging a hurricane lamp and accompanied by his sheepdog, would escort us on the long trek back to the station in the darkness. Soon we were staying for short holidays. We found Uncle Alec transformed; he no longer bossed us around but was kindness itself, and we loved our new aunt.

About the same time, to our mother's evident displeasure, Ethel suddenly announced that she, too, was getting married. Although Bobby's tragic death had meant she never actually became our aunt, she had been a constant visitor at Causeway End and was always our Aunt Ethel and addressed as such. She married George, a much older but very amiable ticket collector from the railway station, and their house off the Antrim Road became another place to visit. We liked George, but he never became Uncle George. It was many years later that Ethel, long a widow, told me the story of how George had first introduced her to Bobby at Lisburn station.

I had met our other real uncle, Hugh, a year earlier, when he had come home on leave after four years in Hong Kong and Singapore. He brought lots of interesting things back with him, including a large bunch of bananas from South Africa, where his troop ship had stopped, plus a Zulu shield and spear, and a magnificent model of a Chinese junk.

He had exciting stories about the evacuation of Singapore days before the Japanese arrived, about how brand new motor cars were being pushed off the quayside into the harbour to stop them falling into the hands of the enemy. He seemed very young for an uncle, was never too serious, and we were just getting to like him when he disappeared off to rejoin his unit in England.

The appearance of an uncle in RAF uniform did much to restore our prestige with the Gang. The Mulhollands' Uncle Andy was a Dispatch Rider with the 8th Army, and had routed Rommel in the desert, with some help from Montgomery, and we were more than a little tired of his exploits. But by then, the middle of the war, the only uncles who really counted were Uncle Joe and Uncle Sam.

After the blitz in 1941 we were short of first-hand war experiences. A military transport plane crash-landed in a field off the Ballinderry Road and that gave us a week or so of excitement. We were disappointed that it was not a German plane that had been shot down, but even so, there it was, a large camouflaged aeroplane sitting flat on its belly in one of Boomer's fields.

The Gang rushed to the field hoping to explore the plane and try the pilot's seat. But we found it under guard, and we were rudely chased away at the gate of the field. That was a set-back, but one of the bolder spirits pointed out that the grass in the field was very long, and we could easily crawl through it undetected and get to the plane. So we climbed over the hedge well away from the gate, and made it to within a few yards of the plane before the sentry spotted us and put us to flight with a volley of words, not all of which we had heard before.

A little further away was Knockmore Junction, where the railway lines to Antrim and to Banbridge branched off from the main Dublin line. The junction boasted a level–crossing and a large signal box. It was out in the country, a bike-ride from home, and a favourite spot for an outing in summer. The level-crossing meant you could stand within feet of the steam locomotives as they thundered past making the ground vibrate under your feet. We usually timed our visits to coincide with the passage of the mighty Dublin Express with its distinct light-blue engine.

If a friendly signalman was on duty we were allowed up into the box and could watch as he threw his weight onto the great levers that operated the points at the junction, and we could witness the handing over of the metal baton that controlled the entry of trains into the single-line branch routes. That was exciting, and we lived in hope that either the signalman or the engine driver would one day drop the baton, but they never did.

During the war, a camp of Nissan huts was built near the junction, surrounded by a high wire fence. It lay empty for some time, and then word leaked back to the Causeway End that German prisoners-of-war had arrived. This was really something, and we raced on our bikes to the camp, only to find that they were not Germans, but a detachment of Belgian soldiers, who were on our side, and of no interest at all.

The advent of the Americans livened things up in the run-up to D-Day. Lisburn, like most towns in Northern Ireland, was stuffed with troops, though we saw little enough of them in the Causeway End. Then, one day, we had the indescribable excitement of a *General Grant* tank rumbling round the corner close to our house. We knew it was a *General Grant* because we were well up in such military matters, and it had the US markings on its side. That same day the pavements on both sides of the Causeway End were black with soldiers taking a rest while their convoy paused on its way to some rendezvous point.

There were almost weekly parades in the centre of Lisburn, to raise morale and funds for *Spitfires* and for the war effort overall. General Eisenhower came to take the salute at one of them, and Montgomery also visited the town. We never missed a parade, even if some of them were on a Sunday, and we loved the military bands, particularly the pipe bands. Despite the black-out, rationing and something called austerity, growing up in the war was not dull.

D-Day and the Normandy landings absorbed us entirely. The *Daily Express* issued maps of Normandy and cut-out paper flags – British, American and German – which could be fixed to a pin and used to plot the fortunes of war. We talked daily of Beachheads and Breakouts, of Rommel and *Panzers*, and we agonised for weeks over a place called Caen which we could see on the map, but which, for some reason, the Allies could not capture.

At the urging of our mother we wrote regularly to our Uncle Hugh in the RAF. As he was a wireless operator, and therefore ground-staff, we knew he was not flying with bombers and was not fighting in Normandy. His short letters to our mother were heavily censored, with holes in the paper where passages had been cut out, and told us nothing of what he was doing. Our mother assumed he was somewhere in England.

On D-Day he was at an RAF base in the middle of England on a training course. He had been promoted to sergeant, and was being considered for a commission. As part of preparation for that he had been detached from his unit and sent on a special training course in radar. The first he knew of D-Day was the night before, when he stood outside his billet watching endless lines of infantry, fully kitted and with blackened faces, marching out to transport planes and gliders.

For hours into the night he stood and watched as what seemed thousands of planes roared overhead from other bases, all heading south. He had never seen anything like it, and he knew the invasion was on. The following day he was ordered to rejoin his unit. It took him several days to do so; all transport was being used in the movement of troops to support the invasion force; trains were crammed with soldiers. By the time he made it to his base, his unit had already left for Normandy. He was ordered to stand by, ready to board the first available flight.

It was D-Day plus a week or more before he made it to Normandy. When the call came, he was given minutes to get his kit together and board a US airforce *Dakota*, which would land him in Normandy close to where his unit was operating. The plane took off immediately, empty apart from the pilot, one crewman, a medical orderly, two wooden boxes marked 'Blood' and Sergeant Cuthbert. The blood was needed urgently, and was the purpose of the flight.

Hugh and the orderly were sitting in the gloom of the windowless plane when the pilot shouted back to them: "Come up here fellas, and see this. This is something you never saw before and will never see again."

They clambered forward and looked out from the cockpit. They were over land, flying very low, and beneath them a battle was raging. They could see hundreds of German tanks, with their black cross insignia, rumbling south in the same direction as their flight, and they were low enough to distinguish the infantry following behind. Some of the tanks were firing.

Minutes later they were flying over other tanks, American and British, moving northwards to stop the German attempt to strike south from Cherbourg and join the counter-offensive against the beachheads. It was a battle, the first one that Hugh had ever witnessed after almost four years of war, and he had a grandstand seat.

Almost immediately the plane was bumping and bouncing along a cornfield somewhere in Normandy. The crewman, Hugh and the orderly manhandled the crates of blood out the door, which was immediately closed and the plane taxied round to take off into the evening light. A Medical Corps jeep had been awaiting the flight, and the orderly and his cargo were whisked off, leaving Sergeant Cuthbert totally alone in a deserted field, with no map, no compass and no idea where his unit might be.

A high thorn hedge surrounded the cornfield and he headed towards it. Peering into it in search of a way through, he saw something that looked oddly familiar. It was a stretch of fine yellow and black cabling, just the sort his unit always used when setting up field telephones in training. The cable stretched away through the hedge in both directions.

Knowing whichever way he went, the cable would lead somewhere, he set off to follow it down the slope alongside the hedge, and then across a hollow into another field. This one was not deserted. Just behind the hedge a Canadian solider was systematically beating the life out of a young German. There was no one else around – no military units of either side, just the two individuals. The German, who looked no more than a boy was screaming in pain while the Canadian continued to hit him with his rifle butt. This was the second battle that Hugh had witnessed, and by far the uglier.

Two fields further on and the cable led him to a fox-hole containing two RAF corporals and a field telephone. Noting his brand new sergeant's stripes they jumped to their feet; yes, they knew where his unit had set up camp, and it was just a mile away near a village. The easiest way to find it was to keep following the cable. So he did, across fields, through an orchard and there it was, a large tent beside an old farm shed. His commanding office barely looked up from the box he was sitting on as he remarked, "Ah Cuthbert, so you made it".

The camp was about six miles inland from the beaches, and the unit stayed there for another week, and then began a long trek in the wake of the advancing allies through northern France into Belgium and then into Holland. Its task was to establish and maintain wireless and field telephone communications in the liberated areas, which meant that, while it was never far from the major battle arena, it was never actually involved in front-line fighting.

The nearest it came to that was just over the border into Belgium when its trucks swung into a small Belgian town and were greeted by cheering women and children celebrating their liberation and welcoming their liberators. When the unit commander discovered that the Germans were still entrenched on the outskirts of the town, and that no Allied forces had been seen in the area, he made his excuses and left, taking his unit back the road it had come.

By mid-September they were in Brussels, and Hugh was able to resume his main active combat role for the RAF – at left half for whatever football team was within reach. In Brussels he played for a Combined Services side in the national stadium, though he might have missed that, and any other football match, but for a bit of luck on his first night in Brussels.

After straggling through the Belgian capital, the unit was billeted in an army camp recently vacated by the Germans. Immediate town leave was granted and most of the men headed back into Brussels for their first chance to relax since landing in Normandy. Hugh, tee-total and tired, stayed in the almost deserted camp. Lying on a bunk in a room in the mess that had been designated a dormitory, he noticed some interesting water-colour sketches on the wall.

They were very competent paintings of local canal scenes, obviously the work of one of the previous German occupants of the room. Hugh decided they would make excellent souvenirs, and, forgetting entirely the warnings about booby traps, he took them down and stuffed them into his kit bag. Then he went on an exploration of camp's quarters to see what else he could find.

In one empty office, high above the mantelpiece, was a larger and better painting. He gazed at it, and looked around for something to climb on to reach it. There was nothing to hand, and too tired to go searching in other rooms, he made up his mind to return in the days ahead and take the picture. The next day another airman had a similar idea, but unfortunately for him he found a chair, reached the picture and was severely injured in the ensuing explosion.

After that it was on into Holland for the rest of the war. For us in Causeway End, the fruits of victory were a set of Belgian toy soldiers and endless souvenirs of Haarlem and many more unspellable and unpronounceable Dutch towns.

Of our Uncle Hugh's adventures we knew nothing at the time. Uncle Sam, for the moment, was everywhere. A US Airforce unit was based at Maghaberry, just a few miles out the Ballinderry Road. Everyone talked about the Yanks, about their inexhaustible supplies of chewing gum and silk stockings, about their wonderful *Sherman* and *Grant* tanks and about Ike their commander. But we never really warmed to them, and we could never forgive them for making Ike, not Montgomery, the Supreme Commander at D-Day.

Montgomery was our number one hero. He far outclassed Churchill, who went around dressed in a suit, smoking cigars, while Monty, who was an Ulsterman, wore a beret and ordinary soldier's uniform and was actually winning the war. Even the Mulhollands at this late stage accepted that Monty, rather than Uncle Andy, was the real victor at El Alemain. We cheered when Monty crossed the Rhine in March 1945.

But by then all eyes were on Uncle Joe Generalissimo Stalin, who was helping Monty win the war, or, more precisely, our eyes were on the formidable array of Marshals who commanded Uncle Joe's Red Army. We had long been familiar with these mighty men, and had seen their photographs in the newspapers, and as the Soviet armies were leading the assault across Europe towards Berlin in the first half of 1945, we each had to have our favourite marshal.

Mine had been Timoshenko, baldheaded and ruthless, but unfortunately he fell from favour and was not in the top three who were leading the charge. My brother had already picked Zhukov, so he was out. I preferred Rokossovsky to Koniev – much more Russian-sounding – and almost daily we plotted on our maps the progress of their respective armies. In the end I came third, while my brother celebrated Zhukov's triumph. Still, we both knew it was Montgomery who had really won the war.

On VE Day the Causeway End celebrated victory. We built a grand bonfire at the junction of the Causeway End and the Ballinderry Road, surmounted by a stuffed Hitler, complete with unmistakable moustache. He burned beautifully.

On VE Day plus one our mother took us up to Belfast on the train to see the celebrations. Outside the City Hall we were caught up in the biggest crowd I had ever seen. Outrageous things were happening; soldiers were kissing girls in the street, girls they did not even know. The war was over, at least in Europe. A whole new world lay in front of us.

It was on our way home that night that we heard Sergeant Colhoun declaring 'Put up that bunting'. Only one war was over.

We were children of the war, and had lived through one of the most appalling periods in human history. Millions had died in conflict and in air-raids on civilian targets and in the systematic extermination of the Holocaust. Cities across Europe had been destroyed, and in Japan the atom-bombs had taken devastation to a new level of awfulness.

Yet we remained almost untouched by it. We had seen one or two nights of blitz from our bedroom window, and had wandered round smouldering ruins in Belfast, but there were no bombs on Causeway End.

The war had started with our relatives being torpedoed on the *Athenia*, and we read about, and saw pictures of, the terrible carnage of warfare. We knew the statistics of those killed and wounded. Yet no one related to us was injured, the relatives we had who served in the armed services came through unscathed. The Mulhollands' Uncle Andy came home in working order and opened a newsagent shop in Bangor.

We had been deprived of sweets and chocolates, of ice-cream and bananas and oranges, of toys and lots of other things – and were to continue to be deprived of them for some years yet. We had no seaside holidays. We had had four years of black-out. Yet none of this blighted our childhood. Perhaps I was lucky; being only three years old when the war started I knew nothing else, and wartime was normal to me.

Petrol was severely rationed and private motor cars almost disappeared. But we had not owned a car before the war, nor had most of our neighbours, and we never did. My father died at almost seventy, having never owned a car in his life. Travel outside Northern Ireland was restricted, but trains and buses took us wherever we wanted to go inside the province.

The war taught us a lot. We knew all about Hitler and Mussolini, about Roosevelt and Stalin. We could show you Tripoli and Murmansk on the map, and Stalingrad and Caen, and Tokyo and Hiroshima.

We had met people very different from ourselves – first of all the Gibs, the Gibraltarians evacuated from the Rock at the height of the conflict and deposited in, of all places, Broughshane. Small swarthy people who spoke Spanish, and spoke it very loudly in the bus out from Ballymena – so loudly, in fact, that we assumed the word gibberish had been invented for them. They occasionally found themselves in dispute with the locals over the last seat in the bus, or in the Broughshane cars on a Saturday night. (The fact that they were Catholic did not make for a peaceful resolution of any dispute with the staunchly Protestant Braid men.)

We saw the Belgian soldiers, and we met some Danish officers at the Moller's one Christmas. The Americans invaded us, and then disappeared off to invade Normandy. Even if we had never been out of Ulster, we knew there was a bigger world out there, full of diversity.

Our first contact with the actual world outside Northern Ireland was via a small boat from Warrenpoint to Omeath, just after the war ended. We were on a Sunday School excursion to Warrenpoint, and the great attraction of Warrenpoint was the small boat across Carlingford Lough. We queued with our mother on the stony beach, and were helped into the boat with an outboard motor which took us across to the village of Omeath, about ten minutes away, in the neutral territory of the Irish Free State.

It was another world. The short street up from the slip at Omeath was lined with booths selling everything we did not have. We bought toffee without coupons. The street was crowded with jaunting-cars, offering rides to Calvary and Carlingford, and we opted for Calvary because it was closer and cheaper, and perhaps because our mother had heard of it, but not of Carlingford.

We clung to each other and to any part of the jaunting-car we could reach as we trundled along the narrow roads of the Carlingford Peninsula. Calvary turned out to be a garden shrine at the roadside, with stations of the cross and a tomb of some local saint or upright citizen. We stood in horror and amazement, grasping the iron railings that blocked the entrance to the tomb but gave us a satisfactorily frightening glimpse of the coffin within.

It was a great trip – the ride on the jaunting-car was exciting, and Calvary appealed to all our Protestant instincts; we saw with our own eyes just how superstitious and idolatrous Catholicism really was. Stuffed with Protestant self-righteousness and coupon-free Free State toffee we took the boat back to Warrenpoint.

The following year our mother took us on a holiday to Dublin. This was a major adventure for she herself had never been there, and we had no connections at all with the city. That meant we had no relatives to stay with. But she had an adventurous streak in her, and wanted us to see as much and learn as much as we could. She had been putting away small amounts of extra money earned from dressmaking and working with leather to produce handbags and purses which she sold to friends and neighbours. This reserve helped make possible an extravagance like a holiday in Dublin.

Through Mrs Gallagher next door she had arranged that we would stay in a house in Haddington Road, where her eldest son, Patsy, had had digs while a student at the College of Surgeons, and where Mrs Gallagher herself had stayed on visits south.

We set off at the beginning of July in the Dublin Express. For years we had watched in wonder as the pride of the GNR, pulled by its distinct blue engine, had roared under the Causeway End bridge. Now we were on it, seated in comfort close to the window, the occasion made all the more special by the last-minute arrival of a young honeymoon couple, still shaking the confetti from their hair, claiming the seats opposite.

The journey had everything; first there was the stop at Goraghwood for the British customs check, with uniformed men asking if we had anything to declare, and looking in people's bags. Then through the mountain pass and over the border – we could only guess where the border was – and another customs search at Dundalk. After that there was the thrill of the Boyne viaduct - the Boyne, the 1690 Boyne – and then, suddenly we were out at sea, as the train crossed the barrages at Lough Shinny and the really impressive one at Malahide.

By the time we reached Amiens Street we were thoroughly roasted by the sun beaming in through the windows, and exhausted by the excitement of it all. But we were not finished. Our mother had detailed instructions from Mrs Gallagher on how to get to Haddington Road via the Number 8 tram to Dalkey, which we could catch at Nelson's Pillar on O'Connell Street. First we had to find Nelson and his pillar.

Following the crowd, we streamed out of the station and down the long ramp that led down to street level, and pandemonium. The gates out of the station were crowded with people and the traffic on the road was halted. There were trams, lorries, carts, bicycles – lots of bicycles - and a great deal of shouting. The unwilling centre of attention was a lately deceased horse, lying still in its shafts in the middle of the road. One man was yelling at the horse to get up, and several more were yelling at the man that the horse was dead and would not be getting up.

Dublin, I decided, was fantastic. Our mother had to drag us away from the continuing drama at the station to go in search of Nelson. We found him, and the Number 8, and Haddington Road. The house was at the end of a tall terrace, just across from a very large church. We got a great welcome, and my mother chatted away about Patsy and about Mrs Gallagher, and about what we should do and see in Dubllin.

We were shown to a large upstairs room, with a double bed, and a holy water font beside the door. I didn't like the look of the holy water, but my mother told me not to be silly, it would do me no harm. The sun shone all week, we had breakfast every morning in a small conservatory built onto the rear of the house looking out onto a lovely garden.

The Dalkey tram took us to Dun Laoghaire as well as to Dalkey, and the train took us to Bray. Bray was even better than O'Connell Street for ice-cream, which I had never tasted, and we sampled Knickerbocker Glories and Banana Splits and other unheard of delights. We went out to the Phoenix Park, to the zoo – a real zoo, not like the cramped cages on the face of Cave Hill.

Back in O'Connell Street our mother paid our tickets and we went through the turnstile inside the base of Nelson's Pillar and climbed the stone spiral staircase up to the small viewing platform that ran round the top, just beneath the great admiral himself. We looked down on the GPO; we went into the GPO to buy stamps for our postcards. We stood at the kerbside waiting to cross the road at O'Connell Bridge and marvelled at the great army of cyclists pausing impatiently for the Guard to wave them forward. (The Guards, we had noted with some distain, had no revolvers in their belts, not like the RUC.) The sun was still shining when we boarded the Express in Amiens Street and headed back north. Dublin, I had decided, was great. I would be back there.

Our holidays after the war were usually to less exotic places – Carnlough and Portrush. To anyone like our mother who had grown up in Ballymena, these were the places to go. A holiday had to be at the seaside, and unless you had high social aspirations and could afford Portstewart, then it had to be Carnlough or Portrush. Our first holiday – the first holiday I remember that was not spent visiting relatives – was to Carnlough, for a few days in October. (It may even have been Hallowe'en. It was certainly cold enough, with gales and rain.) We stayed in a house on the outskirts of the village, just across the road from the stony beach, owned and occupied by an elderly lady. She gave us a room, and our mother, armed with our ration books, bought groceries and cooked for us.

It was my first experience of sea bathing. I inherited a one-piece yellow bathing suit from my brother - swimming trunks were still daring for grown men and out of the question for boys. The point of going on holiday to the seaside was to go into the sea; it was not an optional extra.

The beach at Carnlough had several drawbacks. First of all it had no sand, but consisted of small boulders. We were told it once had sand, but that a huge storm some years ago had deposited all these stones. The sand was still there, underneath them, and if you went into the sea you would, with some luck, reach the end of the stones and find the sand.

The second drawback was the sea itself; it was perishing cold. Walking on the stones fully clothed and wearing shoes or sandals was bad enough, walking over them in bare feet, cold, wet and shivering in a yellow bathing suit, was excruciatingly painful. It took me several holidays and a transfer to Portrush to overcome my initial horror of bathing in the sea.

But Carnlough had other compensations. There was dulse, always available for three pence a bag at several small shops near the harbour; dulse was that rarity, a treat that was good for you. There was the harbour itself, with its own small railway that brought limestone down from the giant quarries on the mountain above Carnlough, over the limestone ornamental bridge that crossed the main street just beside the Londonderry Arms right beside the harbour, and tipped the limestone into the hoppers that fed straight into the boat.

The boat – a ship we always called it – was the *Voorwarts,* from Holland, though we never knew where it took the limestone. To watch it manoeuvre into or out of the tiny harbour was half a day's entertainment in itself. We fished in the harbour, and we sat on the harbour wall staring across to Scotland. Very soon we could identify Ailsa Craig, the giant rock off the Ayreshire coast, and further north, the Paps of Jura. Once we found out what paps were, and what the two round hills were meant to resemble, we never tired of identifying them loudly to ourselves and anyone else within earshot.

We liked Carnlough so much that we went back for proper summer holidays and stayed in a proper hotel, the Seaview, right on the front and just along from the Londonderry Arms. We felt we were coming up in the world, though we could still only peer in wonder at the toffs coming in and out of the ivy-clad front of the Londonderry Arms.

But Carnlough was only a village, not a proper seaside resort, and was known only to people from Ballymena. So we graduated to Portrush, which was the genuine article, with three beaches – sand, not stones – a large harbour and Barry's Amusements. There was no question of affording a hotel in Portrush, so it was, at first, back to the boarding house, only now we gave our ration books to the landlady and she bought the food and cooked it. After that it was up-market to

Portstewart, and eventually to a caravan in MacIntyre's field, outside Portrush.

Holidays were part of a changing life, away from the closed world of the Causeway End, the gang, school and Elim. Shortly after the war, my brother left Central Public Elementary and went to the Lisburn Intermediate Schools, just re-christened Wallace High School. My parents had to pay for him, and it was evidence of my mother's determination that we would do well.

Evidence of the same drive showed itself in piano lessons. Despite the wilful wrong-headedness my brother and I had displayed by taking after our father and not having a note of music in our heads, we were enrolled for piano lessons with a young teacher in Ivan Street in the middle of Lisburn. Once a week I had to turn up at the small terrace house and face the displeasure of Miss Lewis for having failed to master any scale, let alone the *Snowdrop Waltz.*

I hated the music lessons and I hated having to practise. I did not understand music; I thought that all you had to do was learn the notes. That was simple, Every Good Boy Deserves Fruit, and FACE, and then play them. In geometry, once you saw how to do a theorem you could do it any time, with your eyes shut. The idea of going over something I already knew, time and time again, in order to be able to do it, had no place in my philosophy.

Those piano lessons were the first wedge between myself and my mother. She insisted I practise, and when I refused she would lock me in the parlour with the piano, and not let me out for an hour, whether I practised or not. She genuinely wanted us to play the piano and enjoy music as she did, but our inability, or worse still, refusal to do so was the final proof that we were taking after him, not her.

The piano lessons lasted less than six months. I left unable to play even the simplest tune. My brother mastered the *Snowdrop Waltz,* before he too became a lost cause.

By 1948, Wallace High School was beginning to loom large for me. There was a new examination, called the Qualifying, which, if you passed, meant you got a scholarship to the grammar school. Part of it was an Intelligence Test, so before the exam our teacher introduced us to this strange invention, handing out sample papers and inviting us to fill them in.

We thought it was a joke; it was like no exam we had ever seen, and every answer was blindingly obvious. So we had no fears of the real thing when it came round a couple of weeks later, and it turned out to be just as simple. That September I turned up with thirty or so new entrants into the rarefied world of the grammar school, the first unpolished wave of the educational revolution brought about by the 1947 Education Act, which implemented the Butler reforms in Northern Ireland.

A different school meant new friends, and though some of the Causeway End gang were also at Wallace, it was the beginning of the end of the gang. There were lots of new mountains to climb.

One in particular could not be avoided. We had to get saved. Every Sunday, at Sunday School and at the gospel meeting, and more frequently during missions, we were left in no doubt as to our parlous state, and what we had to do. Our mother's reproaches that Bobby-Alec-and-Hugh had all been saved at our age became more urgent.

I don't remember any serious problem about getting saved; it was not that I had any doubt as to the truth of the Gospel, or about the ghastly fate that awaited the unsaved. (I still remembered vividly *The Mark of the Beast*.) Nor did I lust after the flesh-pots of Egypt (in the form of Lisburn Picture House, or my father's Craven A). It was partly reluctance to do something others, particularly my mother, kept telling me I had to do, and partly shyness

That September the Elim Church had a mission. That meant a service every night for two weeks, and two on Sunday, with a visiting evangelist. That year he was Jack Sands, an Englishman, who, after the first week, was finding the Lisburn field somewhat less than ripe unto harvest. The success or failure of a mission depended on the number of hands raised during the appeal (God's blessing, like the height of a horse, was measured in hands) and there were no hands at all.

Towards the end of the mission our mother's hints became heavier. On the penultimate night my brother and I were sitting together near the back, while our mother was up at the front. After the sermon the evangelist called on the congregation to bow in prayer, and began the appeal. There was no response, so he persisted. Then, out of the corner of my eye, I saw my brother's hand go up, and before the preacher could say Hallelujah, I had shot up my own hand.

Then the preacher said Hallelujah, thanked God for the two souls won for the Lord, and closed the meeting. I was not sure what was going to happen. I knew I had just done the most important thing in my life, and half expected choirs of angels and seraphims with trumpets to emerge from behind the pulpit. Instead, the preacher asked the two young men who had raised their hands to wait behind and have a word with him.

As the small congregation streamed out my brother and I stayed behind. The preacher strode down the aisle pulling on his overcoat, shook both our hands, wished us every blessing and dashed off to catch his bus. When we got home we discovered our mother had not realised it had been her own brands that had been plucked from the burning. When we told her, all she could say was "'Well, about time".

POSTSCRIPT

POSTSCRIPT

The idea of visiting Slemish again had been in the back of his mind since he had come back to live in Belfast. The nearest he had come to it had been for May's funeral, May Currie that was, May of the Mountain, who had lived all her long married life in that lonely farmhouse right up against the face of Slemish. It was the house his mother and Minnie had inspected, and criticized, that day half a century ago when he had first climbed Slemish, just before May had married and moved to what was, by general consensus, the back of beyond.

Less than a year ago another family funeral had taken him back to Racavan graveyard, close to Slemish, and had reawakened all the fascination the mountain had so long held for him, all the enchantment it possessed for him. Then he had decided he would make the pilgrimage the very first chance he had.

It was early June before that happened. He had to go to Ballymena on business; it would be a good chance to see Slemish, close up, again, though actually climbing it would have to await another day. He could picnic at the foot of it, so he put a flask of coffee and a sandwich into a small back-pack. About mid-day he drove out through Broughshane towards Slemish. The loanin that led to the mountain had become a road, with a good surface and a name plate. It no longer meandered in and out of farmyards, but by-passed them on its way to a car-park, with a small visitors' centre, built in the rough field just above May's now deserted house.

A signpost now pointed to a footpath that led on up to the mountain. He thought he would walk a little way and have the picnic further up. He was not dressed for mountaineering, even of the modest degree demanded by Slemish, but it was a fine bright June day, the ground was baked dry, and, having started out, he simply kept going. His shoes slipped occasionally on the heather but he made good progress and in less than half an hour was almost at the top. So he decided to push ahead and have his sandwich with a view of Scotland.

He reached the broad broken ridge with a rush of excitement. It was as he had remembered it, apart from the graffiti painted on the rocks near the very top – now they were republican slogans, and green, white and orange tricolours. The last time he had been on top, almost 20 years earlier, he had been shocked by the crude Union Jacks and the 'No Surrenders' in red, white and blue. That had made him very angry. Now he reflected that neither side had a monopoly of vandalism. Maybe defacing a mountaintop with crude slogans was an appropriate enough way to express any belief as primitive and crude as nationalism, of whatever colours.

Scotland lay obscured in a distant heat-haze, so he turned westward and found a rock warmed by the sun; in its lee, sheltered from what wind there was, he sat in the sunshine and enjoyed his picnic. From where he sat he thought he could just make out the trees around the farmhouse at Kellstown, and, across from there, the farm at Racavan. He thought of Robert Hugh and Annie Currie and all the people now buried in Racavan graveyard, or in other graveyards as far away as New Zealand or New York.

He thought of his own parents in their separate graves in Lisburn, and allowed himself a smile. They had never been reconciled, but never separated, living out the bitter quarrel that had begun beyond the limits of his own memory. His father had died first, after a stroke and months in hospital. He himself had been living in Dublin, and had seen him only occasionally during that final year. His father had made a partial recovery, and asked to be taken home every time he visited him.

His mother, he was told, visited the hospital only to bring in clean pyjamas and take away the dirty ones. Once his father had begged her to take him home, only to be informed that he had made his bed and could lie on it. There was no softening on her side; the sense of betrayal that had been so bitterly felt when the marriage first began to go wrong had, if anything, increased with time.

His father had tried once or twice to make peace, a sort of armistice after exhausting years of battle, but his mother was not interested. The broken marriage had been the framework for her life; after 40 years there was no point trying to alter anything. When he died, she continued to live exactly as she had, eating her meals at the fireside or in the scullery, and refusing to have any of the defects in the house she had so often complained about attended to.

She had lived for another fourteen years, on her own in the house, until ill health and a weakening mind had meant a residential home and then hospital. Sitting in the sun on Slemish he recalled the bright and pretty young mother who had been so happy that first day they had all climbed the mountain, so far removed from the embittered and bewildered old woman she had become, and he reflected on what life could do to an individual, and what two individuals could do to each other.

As adults, he and his brother had long joked about how their mother had not allowed them to like herrings, or coffee, or pork, because they were their father's favourites. Seeing a funny side was, he reflected, the only way they could cope with their parents' permanent state of war – the reality was too awful to face.

He remembered how, towards the end of her life, she had started removing items from her china cabinet in the parlour. It had long held her treasures – some wedding presents, a memento of the 1939 New York World's Fair from Winnie, souvenirs brought home by Bobby, by Hugh from Hong Kong and Holland, and by himself when he had started travelling.

The cabinet, and the piano, were the only items in the house she cherished as exclusively hers, yet she now began to discard pieces from the collection. Some were given away, others just disappeared. They later discovered she had also begun removing photographs from the family albums she had kept from before her marriage. It was as if she was dismantling her own life.

Both he and his brother had been with her when she finally slipped away in her sleep. His brother had taken charge of all the arrangements, and had mentioned that he planned to bury her in the grave with their father. "She'll never forgive you," he had responded, meaning it as a wry comment. But his brother had taken it seriously, and immediately purchased a second grave at the other end of the cemetery.

The same month she died, the second of her stepbrothers also died, though she was beyond awareness of it. A few years later, word came from America that Winnie had died in her nineties. He thought too of Winnie, and of her beloved Slemish, as he sat on the summit in the sunshine. She had died in dementia, denouncing all those who had annoyed and infuriated her during her long life, still, no doubt, feeling she had been robbed of her inheritance. Still, he supposed, convinced that her father had been a wealthy educated man, when, as he had found out when he asked, all Kellstown knew it was a neighbouring farmer.

At her request he had actually gone to the Public Record Office and looked up her grandmother's will, which simply left the two farms and everything else to the two sons. But the fact that those two sons were also the witnesses to the will confirmed Winnie in her belief that she had been hard done by. Hard done by or not, she had died a wealthy woman of property, chairman of the motor business she had helped her sons develop.

He finished the sandwich and poured himself a second cup of coffee. Girls' voices interrupted his reverie and he was pleased with himself when he was able to answer their questions about where they would find St Patrick's Wishing chair. Then he was alone again in the sunshine.

He thought of other mountains he had climbed – Muckish and Errigle in Donegal, Lugnaquilla in Wicklow, and Brandon and Carrantouhill in Kerry. And still more in Scotland. He thought of another roasting June day when he and his then beloved had climbed Ireland's other Holy Mountain, Croagh Patrick, not on a pilgrimage, and with their thoughts on anything but self-denial.

Years later there had been mountains in America, and in Africa. It occurred to him that Slemish was, of all these, the smallest and the easiest to climb. Not that he had been a mountaineer; he had never gone in for proper rock-climbing, with ropes and pitons, but he had always enjoyed the challenge of finding a way up a mountain, of persevering until you reached the top, and then delighting in the view from the summit.

Maybe life was a bit like that. There were always mountains to climb. The biggest in his life, as he looked back, was religious belief. From his earliest days he had been pointed towards the mountain that had to be climbed. 'Climb, climb up Sunshine Mountain' they had chanted in the Sunday School in Wallace Avenue.

Getting saved had coincided with the start of his real education, and the beginning of a long struggle to make the two experiences compatible. Elim was big on the Bible as the infallible Word of God and on the right of the individual to interpret it for himself, as guided, of course, by the Holy Spirit. Elim was also very keen on miracles – on miracles of healing, and on the miracle of speaking in tongues.

It had no ritual, and, apart from communion, marriage and burial of the dead, its only real sacrament was adult baptism. There was no set age for that – everything was left to the individual to decide when he was ready, but once you were saved, there was no avoiding it. The only place it could be done was at the Ulster Temple, where a large tank with its painted backdrop of the banks of the River Jordan, concealed under the pulpit, would be revealed for special baptismal services.

He and his brother, in regulation white shirts and dark flannels, had been immersed at the same service one Easter. He had no doubts. He was a believer. But he had problems with most of the sermons he heard, and he still could not bear the hymns and their rhyming sentimentality. His old Sunday School teacher was still alive, in her nineties, and since his return to Northern Ireland he had started visiting her once or twice a year. She had always liked him and had taken a keen interest in his career. Now she enjoyed sparring with him over Elim and the past, and always ended by smiling at him and saying "You never believed a word of it. I can still see you sitting looking at me in Sunday School and I knew then you didn't believe a word I was saying".

When she first said that he had been surprised, and had argued that his problem was he believed every word of it. Now, as he sat looking at the clouds scudding across the sky, he wondered when he had first stopped believing.

As a history student he had taken to the 17th century; he liked the rigorous intellectual honesty of the Puritans, their rejection of ritual and formalism, their idea of the individual as supreme under God. He felt increasingly ill at ease with organised religion, bored by sermons, outraged by hymns, and more and more estranged from the language of evangelicalism, and its ritualised informality.

His first break, he remembered, had been with Elim. In it, paramount importance had been placed on the miraculous – the miracle of divine healing, and the miracle of the Baptism in the Holy Spirit, manifested in the speaking in tongues. He had heard of miracles of healing, but had never actually seen any. He had fervently 'sought the baptism' as Elim stalwarts put it, but the miracle never happened. For all his praying, and for all the laying on of hands, he never experienced any ecstatic visitation. If, as George Jeffreys had preached, miracles proved the truth of the Gospel, did the absence of miracles prove the contrary?

That was the trouble with being a Puritan; belief had to be intensely personal and total; it could not rely on the crutches of sublime ritual or tradition. It had to be logical, too. For a while he had tried not to believe, but that proved even more difficult. But he did leave Elim, and, years later, had quite suddenly abandoned his attempt to climb the mountain of religion. It had been a long journey and all sorts of factors had played a part. An early escape from Ulster by way of a year in America had helped; love of, and marriage to, a wife from anything but an Ulster evangelical background had been, perhaps, as much a sign of changing ideas as a cause of them.

For a long time an unlikely combination of St Paul and Mao Tse Tung kept him on the spiritual rails. Mao, or so the world was told, preached the transformation of man and society through permanent cultural revolution – the constant pursuit of an ideal, or an ideology, alongside equally constant rejection of the status quo. St Paul, centuries, earlier had written to the Roman Christians telling them never to be conformed to this present world, but to be "transformed through the renewing of your minds in Christ Jesus".

That was it: Christianity needed a new language, a psychological and philosophical presentation for the 20th century, not the combination of sentimentality and blood-sacrifice that had come down from the Victorians. He had put these ideas to the head of an international organization that had come to Belfast to offer him a job as a journalist in a Lutheran radio station in Ethiopia. Our ideas entirely, the earnest Norwegian had assured him. So he had signed up for three years in Africa.

It turned out the Lutherans were still a few hymns short of a cultural revolution, and many of the missionaries he worked with were more concerned with career patterns and fringe benefits than with revolutionary new ways of presenting old truths – bungalow dimensions were more important.

Ethiopia was marvellous for all sorts of reasons, but not great for blessed assurance. Back in Ireland, Dublin, this time, the Methodists took up where the Lutherans had left off, but fared little better. To be fair to the Methodists, his three growing children had helped; convincing oneself one still believed was child's play compared to the dilemma that arises when attempts to guide young feet onto the paths of righteousness are met with calls to 'Come off it Dad, you don't believe a word of it yourself'.

Ironically it was the return to Ulster that had facilitated the final break. He simply could not face the idea of attaching himself to any church. So he didn't. He still remembered the profound relief he had felt when he had abruptly terminated all connection with organised religion, and all intellectual attempts to work out his own salvation. It was not peace perfect peace, but it was much closer to it than anything up to then.

That memory cheered him up even more, and he wondered what spiritual agonies St Patrick might have gone through sitting on the same spot, or one near to it. That reminded him of the Wishing Chair, and he struggled to his feet, stretching his cramped legs, and set off towards the northern end of the ridge. It took him much longer than he had expected to find the distinct rock slab with the small seat in one corner formed by a fissure in the basalt, and when he sat in it, he could think of nothing to wish for.

Or to be more honest, he could think of lots of things he might wish for but none that he wanted so badly that he could summon up the energy you needed if you really wanted to make a wish. It was a bit like praying: there was a real commitment involved in formulating a wish; it was something you would have to follow up. So he wished for nothing, and headed down the mountain to the car.

On the way back, he detoured to Kellstown. The loanin was now a cemented road, no doubt paid for by a European grant. It still followed the same line, with the turn down to the right by the planting into the farm. The street had a cement surface now, and the madden was gone. There were no chickens scratching around, no Bruce chasing pigeons. Where the byre had been there was an open shed with a four-wheel drive car in it.

He knew the house and farm had been sold to one of the neighbours, but there was no one at home. He turned the car and was about to drive off, when he stopped, got out, and walked back around the corner of the house and up to the gate into the back field.

There was that magnificent view of Slemish again – sparkling in the sun and unmistakable in its outline. It was exactly as it always had been, just as it was when Patrick, if he ever existed, had first gazed on it, as it was when the first McMasters had settled beneath it, and as it was when he had first fallen under its spell more than sixty years earlier.

He gazed at it for a long, long time, and then drove home, smiling to himself, unaccountably cheerful and content.

Printed in the United Kingdom
by Lightning Source UK Ltd.
124619UK00002B/118-120/A